SEEKING
SANCTUARY

SEEKING
SANCTUARY

Stories of Sexuality, Faith and Migration

Written and compiled by
JOHN MARNELL

WITS UNIVERSITY PRESS

Published in South Africa by:
Wits University Press
1 Jan Smuts Avenue
Johannesburg 2001

www.witspress.co.za

First published 2021

http://dx.doi.org.10.18772/22021097106

978-1-77614-710-6 (Paperback)
978-1-77614-711-3 (Hardback)
978-1-77614-712-0 (Web PDF)
978-1-77614-713-7 (EPUB)

This book was published with the support of The Other Foundation, the Sigrid Rausing Trust, the GALA Queer Archive and the African Centre for Migration and Society.

Project manager: Simon Chislett
Copyeditor: Efemia Chela
Proofreader: Lisa Compton
Indexer: Sanet le Roux
Cover design: Hybrid Creative
Typeset in 10.5 point Sabon

Contents

Foreword

Africa, my mamaland, for how long will you ignore the cries of your own children? I am proud to be African; my heart will always belong to my mamaland. Belonging is an important aspect of ubuntu, a Bantu concept that refers to authentic humanity, realised through the recognition of shared bonds: *I am because we are*. For Vusi Mahlasela – known to most as 'The Voice' – the way our bodies 'say Africa' is an important aspect of what constitutes our Africanness. To paraphrase the great singer, we might walk the streets of Europe and America, but the dust on our boots and the rhythm of our feet will always 'say Africa'. Yet, sadly, Africa is not a sanctuary for all her children. The continent remains one of the most insulted, manipulated and interfered with places on the globe. Amidst the scourges of homo/transphobia and xenophobia, the insults of colonialism, neocolonialism and racism continue to rob Africa of its ancestral value of ubuntu.

Chinua Achebe's *Things Fall Apart*, Nelson Mandela's *Long Walk to Freedom* and many other influential texts point to what Wangari Maathai calls 'the challenge for Africa'. We certainly have much work to do if we are to realise what Desmond Tutu terms 'God's dream' for our beloved continent. This challenge is as urgent today as it was during the colonial, military and dictatorial governments that exploited, enslaved and killed our peoples. We continue to witness untold abuses of human rights in the name of politics and religion. And while state-sanctioned violence is condemned by many Africans, the relentless persecution of sexual and gender minorities – often referred to as the lesbian, gay, bisexual, transgender, queer and intersex (LGBTQI) community – attracts little opposition on the continent. In many cases, this persecution happens at the bidding of religious leaders, both Christian and Muslim.

Are LGBTQI persons not children of mama Africa? Are they not made in the sacred image of God? These are the questions that John Marnell's *Seeking Sanctuary: Stories of Sexuality, Faith and Migration* strives to answer. For many, African sexual and gender minorities simply do not exist; those who claim to be LGBTQI are the creation of evil forces of the West. This false narrative justifies the arrest, imprisonment and even killing of those perceived to violate socio-cultural norms. In many cases, it leads to the exile of LGBTQI persons – the unifying theme in Marnell's critical work. Rather than presenting logical abstract arguments, Marnell employs stories of how African sexual and gender minorities negotiate the identities, desires and hopes, both within their nations and in exile. It is important that Africa hears these living stories. We must all learn from those whose right to belong is being denied in the name of culture and religion.

Over the years, I have seen and heard how Africans defend or justify their mistreatment of sexual and gender minorities. One narrative emerges strongest of all: being LGBTQI is a 'lifestyle' imported onto African soil. But there are countless studies and stories, including those in this book, that disprove this popular misconception. The anthropologist Edward Evans-Pritchard records same-sex marriages among the Zande people of Central Africa and the Sudan,[1] while mission scholars Edwin Smith and Andrew Murray Dale document sexual and gender diversity among the Ila people of modern-day Zambia.[2] More recently, Marc Epprecht offers significant evidence of same-sex relations across Southern Africa,[3] and evangelical scholar Samuel Waje Kunhiyop testifies to sexual minorities (*yan daudu*) dancing openly in Nigeria as late as the 1970s.[4] Regrettably, the space for openness and acceptance is rapidly shrinking, as religious fundamentalists take hold in many parts of the continent.

The embrace of US-influenced Christianity and Roman Catholicism has intensified the denial of sexual and gender diversity in my mamaland. Even respected African Catholic bishops are quick to deny the truth to which their own catechism confesses: sexual diversity has existed for 'centuries and in different cultures' and the number of LGBTQI persons in the world 'is not negligible'.[5] Many local evangelical and Roman Catholic anti-LGBTQI movements take the easy route, spouting familiar US rhetoric as if it were irrefutable truth, despite science proving otherwise. In spite of US fundamentalist and Vatican claims, we are all sexual and gendered beings, and we each have the right to express our sexuality and gender openly without discrimination. Attempts to deny this diversity do not erase the lived experiences of LGBTQI Africans.

Seeking Sanctuary explores the intersection of sexual and gender identities with citizenship, religion, politics and human rights. To exist as an LGBTQI person in Africa is sacrifice one's rights citizenship, religion and belonging. The life stories of LGBTQI persons rarely make headlines on the continent, unless discussed in reference to arrest, rape and death, or linked to salacious gossip or sensationalised claims. As for those who want to defend the human rights of sexual and gender minorities, they are presented as enemies of African culture, destroyers of family values, or blasphemers distorting the teachings of Christianity and Islam.

'Stop copying foreign things!' is the accusation most commonly hurled at LGBTQI persons. As a rhetorical manoeuvre, this charge has two objectives: to deny the Africanness of those on the receiving end and to foreclose any discussion of human rights. A second accusation closely follows: 'If you want to be homosexual, then you must go to those places that allow for such things – South Africa, Europe or America!' However, as growing xenophobia on the continent attests, migration is far from easy. The stories in this book show that LGBTQI persons who move in search of safety come up against at least two phobias: as foreigners, they face insults, violence and discrimination; as sexual and gender minorities, they endure isolation from their fellow immigrants and local communities.

The marginalisation of sexual and gender minorities means they are not counted as citizens or religious adherents. Whereas LGBTQI persons remain invisible to states and faith communities, Marnell's work presents their lives through what I term the 'politics of being'. This refers to oppressed people's ability to contest dominant narratives through the telling of their own stories. In recounting their lives and experiences, LGBTQI persons reclaim their identities as Africans, both in their own nations and in exile. To tell one's story is to demand the right to belong. Just as Yvonne Chaka Chaka (aka the Princess of Africa) sang of her right to exist in her homeland during the struggle against apartheid, so too do LGBTQI persons refuse to be erased from their cultures and histories: 'My mamaland, who is that man calling me stranger . . . Who is that man telling me to go from my land . . . This is my heart, where I belong.' By refusing to stay silent, the storytellers in this book are staking a moral claim to belonging – not just as Africans, but also as proud LGBTQI persons.

In *Cry of the Oppressed: History and Hope of the Human Rights Revolution*, Robert Drinan speaks to the transcendence of human rights as regards national and international law. The very idea of human rights, Drinan argues, is an aspirational moral concept that pushes back against unjust and unequal systems. It has contributed to the fall of slavery, colonialism and, of course, apartheid, while also serving as a framework for critiquing racism and sexism. It is a concept smothered in stories of pain and death, stories that seek to shame oppressors by a wider global audience. While the moral claim of human rights is now primarily associated with secular principles, Drinan traces its origin to religious notions of universal connection: 'The deepest and firmest conviction of those who drafted the international human rights covenants was that there is a common and universal set of moral principles known or knowable to all human beings.'[6] In speaking to the universal, religion has the potential to provide the clearest vision of authentic humanity – as long as it is planted with the moral imperative for equality and justice. When this is done, Christians, for example, begin to associate the suffering of Jesus with the suffering of oppressed peoples. Thus, the fight for human rights becomes a religious issue.

The Christian story begins with the suffering of Jesus, a victim of religious and political bigotry. Long before that, the story of Israel speaks to God's unchanging concern and love for the oppressed – the theme behind African-American theologian James Cone's *God of the Oppressed*.[7] Cone strongly advocates Black stories or experiences (of both slaves and descendants) as the starting point of Black theology. The same can be said about African theology. Rather than speculating on what God is, African theologians problematise African myths, experiences and stories in their theological and moral reflections. The entire moral concept of ubuntu speaks to the story of being: we are made to listen and learn from each other; we only exist together. Listening to and learning from sexual and gender minorities demands acknowledging their humanity. Just as many white theologians are shamed by African stories of pain and dehumanisation, heterosexual theologians are likely to dismiss LGBTQI stories as demeaning to Christianity, Islam and African cultures. Yet these stories can aid new inclusive theologies built around ubuntu and divine justice by foregrounding that we are all Africans together.

Amartya Sen presents a similar argument in *The Idea of Justice*. He accepts the complexities of defining human rights as it relates to religion and citizenship. The idea of human right, he argues, invites ethical demands of what *should* be done, rather than what is enshrined in national laws. Ethical claims to human rights speak to the value of certain human freedoms and the social obligation 'to promote and safeguard these freedoms'.[8] Any legitimate claim to human rights, Sen contends, is an 'ethical assertion – not a proposition about what is already legally guaranteed'.[9] In this regard, demands for human rights are an invitation to initiate new laws, as opposed to merely protecting what is. Sen's observation is particularly pertinent when considering sexual and gender rights on the African continent. In refusing to stay silent and hidden, LGBTQI Africans invite us to respond morally to their plight. Their stories provoke 'public outrage against the violation of such rights'.[10] Denying this diversity doesn't erase the lived experiences of LGBTQI persons.

Human rights are not abstract ideals; we must never forget that they emerge in response to dehumanisation, suffering and pain. It is this connection that *Seeking Sanctuary* explores. Attempts to erase LGBTQI persons from the African continent are slowly resisted by ethical demands for belonging. Laws alone do not guarantee freedom. Even in South Africa, a country that boasts widespread protections, sexual and gender minorities exist in the shadow of death. Yet, through telling their stories – that is, by staking claim to the politics of being – LGBTQI Africans make visible their existence and demand our attention. For me, this potential evokes the power of the Gospels. Jesus' reaction to seeing another human being demeaned and destroyed by hate invites ethical rage. In encountering Jesus' life, whether directly from the Bible or through popular forms such as *The Passion of the Christ*, one grapples with serious questions about what it means to be and to belong. I am excited that the stories Marnell has gathered illustrate the battle that our fellow humans are fighting. Not all the stories featured here are about death and fear. Indeed, some are uplifting and reassuring. This is something I have personally experienced when engaging sexual and gender minorities on the continent and beyond. Such stories are often coloured with shame and guilt, but they nonetheless move both the speaker and the listener towards liberation.

Crucially, stories such as these show those who are struggling with their sexual orientation or gender identity that they are part of a wider community. They are not alone. We have seen a similar process with gender activism. While the specific dynamics of gender oppression may differ from one community to another, women's shared experiences of patriarchy and misogyny link their struggles, both on the African continent and across the globe. For LGBTQI Africans, encountering stories that resonate with their own lives can have an enormous impact on their sense of self and belonging.

I have grown to appreciate storytelling as an important tool in the struggle for justice. This is not to undermine the value of theoretical and empirical investigations. Theory informs how we look at and understand social issues, but stories allow us to visualise and empathise with victims of prejudice. Oppressors fear stories more than academic texts or arguments. That is because stories open our hearts; they bring into relief the humanity of those on the margins. In fact, stories are the most dangerous weapons in the fight for human liberation. Hearing living stories invites ubuntu in each one of us: we see ourselves in the demonised, the rejected, the exiled and the murdered. We become one with the marginalised. The lives of storytellers – in exile, in churches, in their homelands, in their graves – shame us all. It is not surprising that some African governments and US-backed anti-LGBTQI campaigners are demanding the criminalisation of advocacy as ferociously as they push for same-sex practices to remain outlawed. But, as former Catholic Archbishop of Durban Denis Hurley OMI asserted in his response to the 1972 student uprisings in apartheid South Africa, we cannot silence the pain of the oppressed: 'Pain,' he argued, 'is a sign of something that is wrong, a diminution of life, a threat to life. To reveal pain is to reveal the truth and the revelation of the truth is frequently a sacred duty.'[11] This is the goal of this book: it reveals the truth about sexual and gender minorities.

I have researched African sexual and gender minorities for over a decade and one thing I have come to realise is the transformative power of living stories. They are often what stays with me after a project wraps up: a daughter of a renowned pastor from Lesotho coming out as lesbian in the presence of her father and other Pentecostal pastors; a young intersex person in Kenya telling the Pentecostal and Roman Catholic bishops that his body is not a curse but something to be celebrated; two women in Malawi declaring their deep love for each other in public despite being married to men. I have also witnessed pastors change long-held positions after hearing the life stories of sexual and gender minorities. But other stories are lifeless: they speak to the arrests, rapes and murders to which sexual and gender minorities are daily subjected. Some of these experiences are simply too hard to tell.

African LGBTQI persons know better than anyone the cost of telling their stories. Thus, researchers must win the trust of those whose stories they wish to record. Marnell has clearly achieved this with his narrators, something that will make this book even more appealing to scholars, human rights defenders, governments and faith leaders across the globe. If we are looking to make an ethical case for the respect of sexual and gender minorities, this book has it all.

I pray that my fellow religious leaders will listen to these stories with humility. I also urge politicians, cultural leaders, faith communities and scholars of religion, politics, anthropology, sociology and sexuality to approach this book with an open heart. The demonised and killed may be your own son, daughter, niece, nephew, brother, sister, uncle or aunt, currently living in the shadows of pain. As for human rights advocates, the stories in this book will advance the cause of justice for all Children of the Soil.

I am humbled and excited to write this foreword. In honour of Marnell's work and the stories in this book, I sing an African song:

My life is pregnant with pain,
A desolate track I take,
A song of rage if joy,
Ungrazed buttocks of power,
My divine story to shame.
In the ocean of tears,
I bid farewell to my clan, kin and kith,
Only in name, I now belong,
For my new home is never my home.

Can the waves of solitary life stop me from dancing?
Can the alms of injustice welcome the song composed in hell?
It is my sacred story to tell,
In excruciating pain, I cry out, *eina*!
My place is here; I mean here!
The symphony of justice is my gift,
That kills the loud tunes of injustice,
And births the ghetto as my new home.

In this deadly ghetto, I dance,
Of joy unpolished by wealth,
With the tune that enrages the powerful
Africans, politicians, pastors and imams,
Yet my story God and ancestors celebrate,
My blood a sacrament,
My tears an ancestral libation to my mamaland!

REV. CANON DR KAPYA KAOMA,
BOSTON UNIVERSITY, JULY 2020

INTRODUCTION

REFRAMING SEXUALITY, FAITH AND MIGRATION

When Anold Mulaisho first arrived at Johannesburg's Park Station, he had little idea what his future would hold: 'I had no plan. I hardly had any money. Not even a place to stay.'

Anold tells me his story while we wander the streets of Braamfontein, slowly making our way back to my office at Wits University.

'That must have been very frightening,' I say, acutely aware of the inadequacy of my words.

'It really was,' he replies, 'but it was still better than staying in Zambia.'

Anticipating my next question, Anold inhales deeply and starts to describe a lifetime of homophobic abuse. I hear about schoolyard bullying, street harassment, multiple acts of violence and relentless pressure to be 'normal'. His voice is gentle and measured, but his sentences are punctuated by long pauses. There is no mistaking the emotional scars he is carrying.

'I was kicked out of home when I was still a teenager,' he explains. 'My family was very angry with me for being gay. There were even times when they told me to kill myself. Once my sister said I should pay for my funeral in advance because the family shouldn't have to waste money on burying a gay son.'

Taken in by the mother of a close friend, Anold managed to find part-time work and save enough for his school fees. Later, after graduation, he rented a place of his own and embarked on a long-term relationship. For a while it seemed that things would be okay.

'Then a friend with government connections tipped me off to an investigation. Somehow I had come to the attention of the authorities and now they were out to get me. It was time to leave.'

With few options available, Anold used his savings to buy a bus ticket for Johannesburg.

'I knew about the law in South Africa, that it is legal to be gay, and so coming here seemed like the best option. All I wanted was to be myself and to be happy. I was no longer free back home.'

Having worked with lesbian, gay, bisexual and transgender (LGBT) migrants, refugees and asylum seekers[1] for many years, I am unsurprised by the details of Anold's life; his experiences are disturbingly similar to most of the people I encounter professionally. It is only when I ask about his documentation status that I hear something unexpected.

'My [refugee status] interview didn't go well,' he tells me. 'The man said I can't be gay *and* a Christian. He accused me of lying.'

Anold rifles through his bag and hands me a document from the Department of Home Affairs (DHA). 'Look,' he says, gesturing at one of the pages.

It is the official ruling on Anold's refugee claim, and I see immediately that his application has been rejected. Written on the front page, in bold type, is the Refugee Status Determination Officer's (RSDO) decision: fraudulent. Such a finding isn't uncommon, especially in LGBT cases, but seeing the word still feels like a punch to the stomach.

Reading on, I become increasingly horrified by the RSDO's reasoning: 'Zambia is a Christian nation and as such the citizens of the country live by Christian values. The applicant would not have become gay if he was indeed a Christian. He would have adhered to those values.'

Aside from illustrating the absurdity of South Africa's refugee system, Anold's case provides a stark reminder that religion and homo/transphobia remain close bedfellows. The RSDO's Kafkaesque logic draws directly on anti-LGBT discourses popular with religious and cultural leaders, specifically the claim that homosexuality is foreign to African cultures, a Western import that threatens to subvert divine law and undermine traditional social structures.[2] By couching his rejection in such terms, the RSDO sought to not only invalidate Anold's constitutional rights but also reassert the moral superiority of heterosexuality. For many people on the continent – this RSDO included – the incompatibility of Christianity with sexual or gender diversity is irrefutable, as evidenced in well-known, oft-quoted biblical prohibitions. The same can be said for other religions on the continent, including Islam, Judaism and Hinduism.

Yet, while it is true that religion remains a driving force behind homo/transphobia, it is wrong to presume a causal link between the two. What often goes unsaid is the positive role that religion plays in the lives of many LGBT Africans. Despite being exposed to a wide range of harmful practices – everything from hate-filled sermons through to forced exorcisms and physical assaults – LGBT people continue to draw strength from faith, even when excluded from formal religious spaces. For these individuals, religion provides hope and solace during periods of suffering, and a sense of belonging and purpose during more hopeful times. Others still are redefining what faith can and should mean within a context of violently enforced heteronormativity. To reduce such complexities to a familiar refrain of African parochialism – as Western commentators are so quick to do – is to ignore the powerful ways in which LGBT people are contesting religious-based discrimination. More worrying is the tendency to equate strong religious beliefs with pathological conservatism, as if widespread faith correlates to some form of innate backwardness. Indeed, some Western journalists seem to gleefully cite homo/transphobic preaching as evidence of the continent's inescapable savagery, while affording little to no attention to religious groups that are championing diversity.

It was a desire to challenge this narrow reading of African religious practices that inspired this book. It brings together life stories from one specific religious group – the LGBT Ministry at Holy Trinity Catholic Church in Braamfontein, Johannesburg – to show that LGBT people of faith not only exist but also understand and express their beliefs in a wide range of ways. Although housed at a Catholic church, the LGBT Ministry is open to people of all faiths, including those with no specific religious affiliation, and is intended, in the words of co-founder Ricus Dullaert, to serve as 'a safe, inclusive space in which LGBT people can make peace with their identities while fulfilling their spiritual needs'. The LGBT Ministry is especially popular with migrants, many of whom regard the group as a proxy family, and thus it serves as an interesting case study for exploring intersections of faith, belonging, identity and mobility. Each member of the LGBT Ministry came to South Africa in search of something – safety, education, employment, all of the above – and has first-hand knowledge of religion's influence on attitudes towards gender and sexuality, both in their

3

country of origin and in their adopted home. And some, like Anold, have direct experience of religion's intrusion into the day-to-day operations of South Africa's border regime.

The LGBT Ministry members featured in this collection make no attempt to conceal the brutal mistreatment they have endured, but they also refuse to let these encounters define their lives or their beliefs. Each one recounts a personal battle to reconcile their faith with their identity, often in the face of direct persecution, and in doing so paints a disturbing portrait of contemporary homo/transphobia. But the stories are much more than a catalogue of miseries: as well as detailing painful struggles and uncertain futures, the narrators celebrate their own resilience, revealing the myriad ways in which LGBT Africans push back against unjust and unequal systems. Even after being bullied, denounced and assaulted, the narrators refuse to have their faith hijacked by those who value division and hate over inclusion and love.

***

It is not the intention of this book to make a case for or against religion. What I do hope to do is provoke a more nuanced conversation about the impacts of religion on the lives of LGBT Africans. That is why I have opted for a life-story format: unlike academic or journalistic texts, first-person narratives invite readers to see the world through another person's eyes. Each story in this collection shows how religion has shaped a particular individual's experiences, as well as how they have conceptualised their faith in different moments and spaces. By situating the narrators' reflections within the broader context of their lives, I hope to reveal the more insidious ways in which heteronormativity, patriarchy and other oppressive social systems operate. Life stories also produce a level of intimacy that is shared by few other literary forms; hearing a person's story in their own words helps us recognise our shared humanity, even if a narrator's experiences bear little resemblance to our own.[3] The generosity and enthusiasm with which these narrators have shared their experiences reminds us that LGBT Africans are real people facing real challenges.

The predominance of migrants within the LGBT Ministry was another motivator in adopting a life-story format. While there is an abundance of political rhetoric and media coverage devoted to South Africa's 'migration epidemic', very few migrant voices have the privilege of entering public discourse. Those migrants who do appear on our screens or in our newspapers tend to be reduced to stock characters: pitiful victims of violence, ruthless drug peddlers preying on impressionable youth, opportunistic scroungers draining state resources, and so forth. This situation is exacerbated for LGBT migrants, most of whom remain invisible to wider society. When an LGBT migrant's story does receive a public platform, especially in the Global North, it is usually for political ends – for example, to contrast the primitiveness of their home country with the progressiveness of their adopted one.[4] In the process, complex lives, identities and emotions are downgraded to convenient tropes of desperation and helplessness.[5] This isn't to say that LGBT migrants don't endure unimaginable levels of hostility and trauma, or that these aspects of their lives aren't worthy of urgent scholarly and media attention, but rather a warning about the 'dangers of the single story', to borrow Chimamanda Ngozi Adichie's ever-pertinent words.[6]

The stories collected here remind us that LGBT migrants make decisions and take action, even when faced with entrenched prejudice, institutional neglect and often savage violence. They touch on realities shared by most, if not all, LGBT migrants, but they certainly don't offer a definitive account of the LGBT migrant experience, for no such thing is possible. It is also important to reiterate that the narrators share a common experience, in that they are all somehow connected to the LGBT Ministry. Some have been long-term members, while others have attended only a handful of meetings, but all have voluntarily sought out the group's assistance.

Focusing on just one institution had many benefits, such as the opportunity to form strong bonds with group members, but it also limited the scope and number of narratives that could be collected, as is reflected in the nationalities, identities and faiths represented. In a way this is a product of the group's demographics – the LGBT Ministry is dominated by gay Zimbabwean men – but it also points to the relative security that certain migrants may experience (for example, due to their gender expression, English proficiency and/or documentation status) as well as their level of comfort with being featured in a book. While obviously a limitation, the over-representation of gay Zimbabwean experiences should not take away from the overall themes of this collection. Indeed, each story is unique, and each one tells us something important about faith, or identity, or prejudice, or belonging, or hope, or survival, or all of the above.

At times the stories can be difficult to digest, whether because of the violence that is described or simply because they do not align with preconceived notions about LGBT migrants. It is in these moments of disquiet that the stories are most powerful; it can be unsettling to realise that the narrators are regular people who, like all of us, make both good and bad decisions. Nor should we rush to condemn all those who feature in the stories: while we are right to be outraged by reactionary pastors and incompetent bureaucrats, we must acknowledge the supportive relatives and compassionate strangers who pop up along the way. We must also honour the more fluid and affirming interpretations of culture that some narrators encounter, occasionally from unexpected sources. In doing so we might move beyond the familiar scripts that dominate our thinking on religion, tradition, gender, sexuality, nationality, belonging and mobility.

The need to push back against stereotypes emerges as a strong theme in all the stories. For Thomars, a trans man from Zimbabwe, popular misconceptions lie at the heart of prejudice, including the xenophobia encountered by many of the narrators:

We need to find ways to shift people's negative perceptions of migrants. Most South Africans think we are out to steal their jobs and money. If only they could understand why we really left our homes. We are here because we have to be, and most of us want to contribute to South Africa.

Similar sentiments are expressed by Angel, a gay asylum seeker from Uganda. He believes that social change is only possible once there is empathy between communities. That is why he wants readers to focus on similarities, not differences:

The most important thing to remember is that all of us – locals and foreigners, heterosexuals and homosexuals – are facing the same challenges: poverty, violence, crime, unemployment. Turning on each other is not going to solve anything. Instead of blaming migrants, the government should fix these problems. We aren't here to make things hard for people. In fact, most of us would go home if we could.

It is in capturing both the quotidian and the exceptional – that is, the moments that make LGBT migrant lives both ordinary and distinctive – that these stories have the potential to bridge social divides. In sharing their personal experiences, the narrators invite recognition; they want to be seen, heard, understood and valued.

***

Near the end of my conversation with Anold, I ask how he feels about the RSDO's views on sexuality and faith. He responds without hesitation: 'I am proud of being gay and I am proud of being Christian. Why should I hide? I know that God would want us [LGBT people] to be protected.'

It is a sentiment I hear repeatedly while collecting the life stories; almost every narrator refers to the biblical commandment to love without judgement.[7] One of the most powerful articulations of this position comes from Zee, a young lesbian woman from South Africa who was forced out of her Pentecostal congregation:

> Church had always made me feel uplifted, but it ended up being a site of pain and abuse. It is hard to go from being loved and welcomed to being shamed and excluded . . . Again and again the Bible warns us against judging others, but still people treat us like we have done something unforgivable. When I read the Bible, I see a simple message of love. At the end of the day, we are all God's children.

When Zee says this, I am struck by the gentleness of her tone; she speaks without spite, her voice imbued with both pride and pain. I find myself wondering how she has managed to hold on to her faith given all that she has endured.

It is something I ponder with Anold too. 'What prompted you to bring up your faith?' I ask. 'Is it really that relevant?'

'I told him [the RSDO] the truth,' he replies. 'I have always believed in God, and I still do. My faith keeps me going. It is part of me, just like being gay is part of me.'

***

Anold's full story isn't featured in this collection – for a number of reasons, including ongoing legal proceedings against the DHA – but his voice is too important to be entirely absent. His experience reminds us that anti-LGBT sentiments aren't left behind when someone walks out of church, or mosque, or temple. Prejudice seeps into everyday life – it is in our households, our classrooms, our health facilities and our government agencies – and it can have far-reaching consequences.

Anold's case is also unique in that the discrimination he experienced was documented by the very people who perpetrated it. LGBT people encounter bigotry with alarming regularity, particularly when interacting with state agencies, but rarely do these encounters make it onto the public record. Anold's ruling, with its confounding logic and shocking claims, validates what LGBT migrants have been saying for years. It forces us to admit that the misinformation being spouted from our pulpits, or spoken in parliament, or reported in the media, affects people in very real ways. For LGBT people, coming up against conservative religious beliefs can mean the difference between safety and danger. For some, it can mean life or death. That is why we must change the narrative.

In presenting these stories, I hope to encourage others to speak out. *Seeking Sanctuary* is just the beginning – we need many more stories if we are to overcome religious-based prejudice. Stories like the ones featured here offer an antidote to the hateful rhetoric poisoning so many communities. They serve as a record of past events, one that helps us appreciate the conditions that compel LGBT migrants to leave their homes, as well as a rallying cry for a more just and equitable future. Each story ends with a vision for change: some narrators imagine African religious leaders who stand proudly alongside LGBT communities, while others long for more practical shifts, such as respectful treatment by state officials or better access to social services. All share a desire to be acknowledged.

D.C., a lesbian asylum seeker from Zimbabwe, concludes her story with a brief yet astute observation: 'As a society, we need to learn respect and acceptance.' It is a message that all of us – faith leaders included – must take seriously if the dream of equality is to become reality.

CHAPTER 1

BACKGROUND AND METHODOLOGY
On making and sharing stories

Seeking Sanctuary began life as a standard oral history project, one that sought to record the memories and experiences of those associated with the LGBT Ministry. It was not until the project was well under way that the idea of a book was first floated. By then it was clear that the stories would be of interest to a broader audience; what had begun to emerge were tales of family pressures, social policing, economic struggles, state neglect, institutional discrimination and interpersonal violence. The narrators spoke of multiple forms of prejudice, of long struggles to feel comfortable in their skins, and of difficult journeys – sometimes across multiple borders – in search of safety. Yet, within each story, no matter how bleak, was an unmistakeable will to survive, to connect, to grow and to love.

The project itself came about because of a long-standing relationship between the GALA Queer Archive and the LGBT Ministry. On top of providing financial and institutional support, GALA wanted to document the crucial work being undertaken at Holy Trinity, both to cement the LGBT Ministry's place within the historical record and to make sure that other religious institutions could learn from its experiences. What form this documentation process would take took longer to establish.

As a scholar of LGBT migration and a long-time GALA collaborator, I was approached to see if I would manage the project. It was an invitation I accepted without hesitation. Although I don't identify as a person of faith, I have long been interested in the nexus between religion and mobility. When these concepts are mentioned in my line of work, it is usually in reference to migration catalysts (for example, when people flee due to religious persecution), but I have long been intrigued by the possibility of faith communities being sites of belonging, especially for those on the margins of society.[1] Over the years, I have heard LGBT migrants of various backgrounds speak of traumatic experiences justified on faith grounds, yet seldom do these individuals frame religion in wholly negative terms. At first this would catch me off guard, shocking my humanist sensibilities, but with time I began to recognise the narrowness of my own position. I found myself wondering why religion features so sporadically in LGBT migration literature and, when it does, why it is depicted negatively, or at least ambivalently. Surely, I thought, there is more to the issue than reactionary zealots, brainwashed victims and hateful rhetoric.

I also had a more personal interest in the project. Nine years ago, when I first arrived in South Africa, I had the pleasure of viewing a body map by Azu Udogu, a Nigerian trans woman who was one of the first known people to claim asylum based on sexual orientation (this was a tactical manoeuvre as there was no legal precedent for transgender claims at the time).[2] In the lower right-hand corner of Azu's artwork was a small white cross, emblazoned with the words 'Holy Trinity'. Intrigued and somewhat confused, I asked the GALA archivist what this iconography meant and was fascinated to learn about the nearby church's efforts towards inclusion. A few years later, courtesy of my social activism, I had the pleasure of meeting Dumisani Dube, the LGBT Ministry's chairperson, and hearing more about the group's activities. All of this left me with a positive impression of the church. Yet, whenever I thought about Holy Trinity, I was left with niggling doubts about the place of faith communities in 'secular' matters such as human rights. While I could appreciate the good work being done, I struggled to grasp why LGBT migrants, especially those who had experienced religious-based persecution, would seek out a church group. My bewilderment increased when I heard about LGBT migrants running their own religious services inside Kenya's Kakuma Refugee Camp, an action that would no doubt intensify the violence to which these individuals are routinely subjected.[3] It was clear that I was missing something. What was it that brought LGBT migrants back to religion, whether in South Africa, Kenya or elsewhere? Had I been too quick to dismiss the positive impacts of faith?

It was a desire to answer these questions that pushed me towards life stories. While I was keen to document the practical side of the LGBT Ministry, I also wanted to engage with group members' emotions, memories and aspirations. A life-story approach, I reasoned, would allow me to view religion more holistically. I wanted to find out how faith fitted with other aspect of the narrators' experiences, not just here in Johannesburg but also in their countries of origin and any countries of transit. I also wanted to leave room for the contradictions and messiness that constitute people's lived realities. I had a hunch that group members' beliefs were more dynamic than one might assume and I wanted to ensure such variations were captured. In this way, I was motivated by a growing corpus of work that uses storytelling to explore the nuances of LGBT spiritual lives on the African continent.[4] I was also inspired by recent developments in religious studies, especially work looking at faith as negotiated and lived practices, rather than static institutions or dogmatic systems.[5]

Once the methodology was agreed upon, information about the project was shared at the LGBT Ministry's fortnightly meetings and then circulated to group members using social media. Those who volunteered to take part underwent an initial interview that mapped out key biographical events, significant interpersonal relationships and lived experiences within religious spaces. The interviews also sought to understand the role that faith plays in identity formation and to surface critical reflections on participants' hopes and dreams.

The interviews were somewhat formal, in that there were discussion prompts and an audio recorder, but they were designed to be as relaxed and conversational as possible. Participants were encouraged to share whatever memories came to mind and to talk for as long or as little as they liked. Some of the most interesting memories ended up being shared outside of the official interviews, such as when enjoying a cup of coffee or walking back to a taxi rank.

Like any conversation, a life-story interview can head in infinite directions; some never find their rhythm, while others flow quickly from anecdote to anecdote, each described in vivid colour. When this happens, a conversation can last for many hours, as happened repeatedly in this project.

While conducting the interviews, I had to remind myself that not everyone is comfortable sharing personal memories, especially with someone they have only known a short time. I myself am a gay migrant and in some ways I share a similar life trajectory to the narrators, but in reality we inhabit different social worlds, courtesy of my race, class, gender and nationality (I am a white, middle-class cisgender man with Australian citizenship). Such differences inevitably generate complex power dynamics, no matter how generous or well intentioned I may be.

The other major challenge was deciding which stories to feature in the book. Of the 30 interviews conducted, 14 were selected for inclusion, a number determined primarily by the space available. A key aim was to showcase diverse perspectives and experiences, and this guided editorial decisions as much as possible. Preference was given to stories of lesbian, bisexual and transgender narrators, although the group's demographics made it impossible to achieve equal representation (for example, there is currently only one trans group member). Other practical factors included the level of detail provided in the initial interviews and each individual narrator's willingness to have their story published.

The chosen interviews were transcribed and then shaped into chronological accounts. This was a daunting task: many of the transcripts exceeded 150 pages and decisions had to be made about which memories to leave in and which ones to exclude. Such choices weren't taken lightly; more than once they were preceded by crippling indecision and sleepless nights. I was also aware of my responsibility to maintain the tone and cadences of each narrator's speaking style, something that was easier said than done.

The solution to both challenges was to involve the narrators as much as possible. Follow-up meetings were held to clarify inconsistencies and ensure intended meanings weren't being misrepresented. Once complete drafts were produced, the narrators were invited to review their stories. As part of this process, they were encouraged to anonymise identifying details and amend wording that didn't feel right. Participants were also reminded of the potential negative impacts of being featured in a book and given an opportunity to withdraw their participation. Lastly, each narrator was asked to select a title and pseudonym. Although most narrators took up this option, some individuals, particularly those whose experiences are already on the public record, requested to use their real names.

Given that most participants had concerns about being identified, a decision was taken to avoid narrator portraits. However, a number of people indicated a desire to have their identities represented pictorially. A solution was found in the form of animal totems. Narrators were invited to select the animal that best symbolises their personality and to explain the significance of their choice. A drawing and quote reflecting these conversations can be found at the start of each story. These are, of course, inadequate proxies for the individuals they represent, yet they do evoke a sense of each narrator's character and the playfulness that was present at different moments in the interviews. The drawings and quotes are intended to connect readers with the narrators by offering another entry point into the storytellers' affective, sensorial and imaginative worlds.

The stories featured here are not verbatim transcripts, but they do remain faithful to the spirit and meaning of the original interviews. Indeed, many hours were spent crafting each story into an accurate representation of that narrator's life. This was a collective process: if a narrator wanted a memory added or removed, I adhered to the request without question. After all, the stories belong to them, not me.

It is important to remember that life stories are a particular form of meaning-making.[6] They are personal accounts presented from the perspective of those excluded from official histories. For me, the telling of a story is as important as, if not more important than, the details it may contain. This is not to suggest that the stories have been fabricated or exaggerated. It is merely an acknowledgement that storytelling is a complex process – memories are as much about the present as they are about the past; they are shaped by and interpreted through our identities, relationships, hopes and failures.[7]

In telling their histories, the narrators attempt to make sense of events that have largely been out of their control, while also seeking to legitimise their identities, motivations and social locations. To look back on the past is never easy, even more so when one's experiences are coloured by trauma, grief and violence. I am incredibly grateful to the narrators for their willingness to share such intimate accounts of their lives.

CHAPTER 2

THE POLITICISATION OF FAITH
Religious responses to sexual and gender diversity

It is difficult to appreciate the significance of the stories collected here without knowing something of how homo/transphobia operates on the African continent. In many countries, political and religious leaders fuel anti-LGBT sentiments with moralistic rants about impending social disintegration. Underpinning this rhetoric are religious justifications for a return to 'traditional' or 'family' values; influential figures point to sacred texts as incontrovertible proof that heterosexuality is the only natural, normal and acceptable expression of human desire.[1] While there isn't space to give a comprehensive account of religion's role in perpetuating homo/transphobia, the summary below should provide sufficient context for the narrators' experiences.[2]

Homo/transphobic attitudes tend to be shaped by four interlinked discourses: that LGBT people are abnormal, immoral, anti-family and un-African.[3] Circulating around these discourses is a broader claim that LGBT identities or expressions are expressly prohibited under Christianity, Islam or whichever faith dominates a region.[4] A popular refrain is that 'real' African values are under imminent threat[5] and therefore constant vigilance – usually in the form of criminalisation – is required to preserve society's moral fabric.[6] This is equally true for countries that have specific laws targeting LGBT people (such as Ghana, Sudan and Tanzania), countries that didn't inherit colonial anti-sodomy laws but still see high rates of homo/transphobic persecution (such as Benin, Mali and Rwanda) and countries that have undergone formal decriminalisation (such as Angola, Lesotho and Mozambique). Even in South Africa, the country with the most extensive LGBT rights, homo/transphobia remains pervasive and is often underpinned by conservative religious beliefs.[7]

In many contexts, the religious dimensions of homo/transphobia are plain to see. In Nigeria, for example, faith leaders of all denominations were quick to endorse former president Goodluck Jonathan's campaign to intensify penalties for same-sex intercourse and to criminalise support for LGBT individuals and organisations. In 2010, when debates about amending the law were well under way, former anglican Archbishop Nicholas Okoh claimed that Nigeria was at risk from an 'invading army of homosexuality, lesbianism and bisexual lifestyle [sic]', echoing comments he made at an earlier press conference: 'Same-sex marriage, paedophilia and all sexual perversions should be roundly condemned by all who accept the authority of scripture over human life.'[8]

In neighbouring Cameroon, Catholic authorities regularly denounce LGBT people as unnatural, sinful and a threat to God's model for human reproduction. A notable example is Archbishop Simon-Victor Tonyé Bakot, who in 2013 described homosexuality as a 'shameful, disrespectful criticism of God'.[9] The following year, the church released the *Declaration of the Bishops of Cameroon on Abortion, Homosexuality, Incest and Sexual Abuse of Minors*, in which the signatories call on 'all believers and people of good will to reject homosexuality', adding that 'homosexuality is not a human right but a disposition that seriously harms humanity because it is not based on any value intrinsic to human beings'.[10]

Comparable statements can be drawn from across the continent (noteworthy examples come from Côte d'Ivoire, DR Congo, Kenya, Morocco, Namibia, Senegal, South Sudan, Tanzania and Zambia) and are not limited to the Christian faith. In December 2014, Malam Shaibu, an Islamic cleric from Ghana, urged residents of Accra to capture and burn suspected gay men 'because Islam abhors homosexuality'.[11] More recently, influential clerics in Mali have mobilised thousands of people in protest against the 'moral depravity' of homosexuality. Mohamed Kebe, a member of Mali's High Islamic Council and one of the organisers of a 2019 anti-LGBT rally, has repeatedly demanded violent punishments for those 'who want homosexuality'.[12]

In other contexts, homo/transphobia serves as a useful bridge between religions, offering faith leaders a rare chance to express solidarity. In 2011, a Muslim mufti joined the heads of the Orthodox, Catholic and Protestant churches in Ethiopia in denouncing plans for an HIV conference that they claimed would promote homosexuality.[13] Further north in Egypt, LGBT rights have been condemned in similar terms by Grand Mufti Shawki Allam and Coptic Pope Tawadros II. Their framing of LGBT identities as inherently sinful in both faith traditions provides the moral justification for state repression,[14] the most recent example being the arrest and torture of LGBT persons after a 2017 concert by the Lebanese band Mashrou' Leila.[15] In the wake of this clampdown, leaders from both faiths spoke out against LGBT rights, implicitly endorsing the government's actions. Grand Imam of al-Azhar Sheikh Ahmed el-Tayeb said that 'no Muslim society could ever consider sexual liberty or homosexuality to be a personal right',[16] while the Coptic Church announced that it would be organising an 'anti-homosexuality' conference that would promote 'recovery' from sexual deviancy.[17]

Religious objections to LGBT rights also offer fertile ground for political point-scoring. In 2012, former Gambian president Yahya Jammeh used the swearing-in of a cabinet minister to assert his commitment to 'traditional' values:

[Homosexuality] is not in the Bible or the Qur'an. It is an abomination . . . Human beings of the same sex cannot marry or date. We are not from evolution but we are from creation and we know the beginning of creation – that was Adam and Eve.[18]

More recently, Paul Makonda, former regional commissioner for Dar es Salaam and a close ally of Tanzanian President John Magufuli, positioned his campaign to round up LGBT people as a religious crusade, noting that he would 'prefer to anger those countries [that object] than to anger God'.[19] In both of these examples, the line between secular affairs and moral regeneration was blurred, usually to the advantage of the politician involved.

South Africa hasn't been immune to such political manoeuvres. In 2005, Jacob Zuma, then ANC deputy president, infamously described same-sex marriage as 'a disgrace to the nation and to God', a statement that firmly positioned him as a protector of culture and tradition.[20] In the years since, local religious leaders have taken up the torch, publicly denouncing LGBT identities as sinful and abhorrent. One of the most well known is Oscar Bougardt, a Pentecostal pastor from Cape Town, who regularly conflates homosexuality with paedophilia and who has even called on ISIS to 'rid South Africa of the homosexual curse'.[21] More recently, Soweto's Grace Bible Church has faced scrutiny after a visiting pastor described homosexuality as 'sinful', 'unnatural' and 'disgusting'. Details of the sermon came to light after celebrity choreographer Somizi Mhlongo expressed outrage on Twitter, sparking a national debate and frenzied crisis management from the church's leadership.[22]

Despite what many people assume, homo/transphobia isn't restricted to evangelical or fundamentalist churches. Back in 2013, Cardinal Wilfrid Napier, Catholic archbishop of Durban, courted controversy when he described the legalisation of same-sex marriage as a 'new kind of slavery' in which African states were being forced to 'carry out someone else's agenda'.[23] In the wake of a public outcry, Cardinal Napier laughably asserted that he couldn't 'be accused of homophobia because [he didn't] know any homosexuals'.[24]

While it can be tempting to dismiss these cases as straightforward bigotry, they deserve closer attention. What do such statements tell us about the state of sexual and gender rights on the continent? Why are African religious and political leaders so quick to condemn LGBT people? How do we account for the spread and uptake of religious conservatism? There are no simple answers to these questions – the dynamics of homo/transphobia are distinct in each context – yet it is possible to observe broad trends, particularly in how anti-LGBT religious rhetoric is deployed for political gain.

First, religious objections to diversity allow state and cultural institutions to constrict the space available to those advocating for human rights.[25] They provide an effective means for propagating conservative notions of piety and for producing a new form of hetero-patriarchy embedded in distorted cultural norms.[26] Anti-LGBT religious rhetoric can thus be understood as a political tool, one that exploits anxieties around social change and foreign interference.[27] By linking LGBT identities to wider concerns about Western influences – that is, by suggesting that sexual and gender diversity is indicative of a new form of colonisation – political elites are able to counter efforts by activists to challenge oppressive structures.

Second, a religious framing allows political and cultural leaders to popularise a version of history that reinforces their status and authority.[28] In referencing sacred texts rather than social histories, influential figures are able to dismiss claims that sexual and gender diversity has a verifiable pre-colonial history.[29] By foreclosing any discussion of indigenous sexual and gender categories, and by obfuscating the fact that anti-LGBT laws are themselves a product of colonial occupation, African leaders are able to position themselves as protectors of the moral order. More often than not, anti-LGBT statements serve as a convenient distraction, focusing attention on a supposed external threat to the state rather than internal governance failures.[30]

Third, by tying heterosexuality to seemingly unrelated concepts – everything from religiosity, morality and pan-Africanism through to economic development, national security and foreign policy – political leaders can effectively determine the boundaries of sexual citizenship and therefore who is and isn't worthy of protection.[31] Anti-LGBT discourses relegate undesirable bodies to the margins of society and in doing so prescribe limits on understandings of and claims to individual rights. The performance of homo/transphobia within the public sphere shows that it is much more than an issue of faith.[32] Rather, it is a means through which political elites can resist processes of globalisation, assert a distinct national/cultural identity and push back against liberal notions like secularisation and gender equality.[33] Put another way, religious objections to sexual and gender rights serve as open signifiers that can be adapted and deployed to suit disparate audiences, contexts and objectives.

To fully appreciate the politicisation of anti-LGBT religious discourses, it is necessary to place homo/transphobic statements within a broader social, political and historical context.[34] Surges in fundamentalism tend to be shaped by both local and global forces and this has certainly been the case with Africa. Political and religious leaders will exploit religious anxieties in ways that suit their personal agendas. In Zimbabwe, for example, Robert Mugabe's anti-LGBT rhetoric noticeably intensified during election periods and served as a convenient way to provoke the ire of Western governments, cementing his reputation for being impervious to diplomatic pressures.[35] While ostensibly about the protection of Christian values, Mugabe's anti-LGBT pronouncements are better understood as a move to consolidate authority and position himself as the quintessential patriotic leader.[36]

Escalations in anti-LGBT rhetoric have also accompanied tensions within global church structures.[37] In the mid-2000s, African church leaders responded to the potential schism in the Anglican Communion by denouncing same-sex marriage and the ordination of LGBT clergy. One statement by the Anglican Church of Nigeria reasserted its 'commitment to the total rejection of the evil of homosexuality', labelling same-sex relationships 'a perversion of human dignity'.[38] Statements like this must be seen as a reaction to larger factional struggles as much as they may be a genuine assertion of scriptural interpretation.

In much the same way, a perceived intrusion into domestic affairs by a foreign power can stimulate local opposition to LGBT rights. Notable examples include Barack Obama's state visit to Kenya in 2015[39] and Ban Ki-moon's visit to Zambia in 2012,[40] both of which provided ammunition for political leaders keen to denounce the imposition of 'Western values'. Similarly, when David Cameron suggested that the United Kingdom withhold aid from countries that don't recognise LGBT rights, the head of Sierra Leone's Methodist Church, Bishop Arnold Temple, objected to what he perceived as an attack on local culture:

> We call on the government . . . to inform the British leader that such [homosexual] practices are unacceptable and we condemn it totally. Africa should not be seen as a continent in need to be influenced by the demonic threat, as our values are totally different.[41]

Although framed as a response to neocolonial interference, recent pushbacks against LGBT rights have been strongly influenced by Western churches, particularly evangelical and Pentecostal movements.[42] US-based organisations such as the American Center for Law and Justice, Family Watch International and Human Life International exert considerable influence across the continent, with churches, programmes and/or donor-receiving partners in countries as diverse as Cameroon, Eswatini, Kenya, Malawi, Mozambique, Nigeria, Tanzania, Zambia and Zimbabwe.

The fallout caused by US missionaries is perhaps best illustrated by Uganda, where notorious figures like Scott Lively and Lou Engle have provided the impetus for anti-LGBT crackdowns.[43] As has been widely documented, Lively's keynote presentation at a 2009 conference in Kampala, titled 'Exposing the Truth behind Homosexuality and the Homosexual Agenda' – an event that also featured inputs from US conversion groups like Exodus International – planted the seed for regressive legislative changes.[44] Lively met with Ugandan lawmakers both during and after the conference, and many of his talking points were included in the preamble to the 'Kill the Gays' Bill that was subsequently developed. The following year, Engle praised the Ugandan government's efforts to install the death penalty for homosexuality at a well-attended rally organised by his revivalist ministry, The Call.[45] Since then local pastors have continued to take their cue from US evangelicals, mimicking their frenzied and emotive rhetoric. This includes controversial figures like Pastor Martin Ssempa – known globally for his 'Eat the poo-poo!' sermon[46] – who continues to receive support from US churches.[47]

More recently, Steven Anderson, founder of Arizona's Faithful Word Baptist Church, attempted a regional preaching tour of Southern Africa.[48] Thanks to a vigorous campaign by local activists, Anderson's visa for South Africa was blocked and his speaking events cancelled. A week later he was deported from Botswana after calling for LGBT people to be stoned to death during a radio interview. Even the Malawian government announced that it would not accept Anderson's hate-filled preaching and refused him entry.

The pushback against Anderson, spearheaded by a number of local faith groups, points to the increase in progressive religious voices on the continent. The most notable example is probably Archbishop Emeritus Desmond Tutu, whose long-standing support of LGBT rights has drawn both praise and condemnation. Despite being labelled a puppet for the Western 'gay agenda', Tutu has remained steadfast in his endorsement of sexual and gender rights, as evidenced in famous quotes such as 'I would not worship a God who is homophobic'.[49]

While certainly the most well known, Tutu is by no means the only faith leader endorsing LGBT rights. In Uganda, former bishop Christopher Senyonjo has been an outspoken supporter of inclusion, winning multiple international accolades for his work.[50] At home, however, Senyonjo's advocacy efforts have been far less appreciated: his title and privileges were revoked by the Church of Uganda, and he continues to endure regular death threats. Similarly, Rev. John Makokha, leader of Nairobi's Riruta Hope Community Church, has openly advocated for LGBT people's right 'to express themselves without fear or victimisation', a stance that has drawn sharp criticism from political and faith leaders.[51]

Other religious figures have adopted a more measured approach, appealing for states to act with restraint and compassion. Only days after the introduction of the Same-Sex Marriage Prohibition Act in Nigeria, a strongly worded editorial appeared in *The Southern Cross*, a weekly newspaper supported by the bishops of South Africa, Botswana and Eswatini. As well as condemning the Nigerian government, the editorial called on African Catholics 'to stand with the powerless' and 'sound the alarm at the advance . . . of draconian legislation aimed at criminalising homosexuals'.[52] Significantly, the editorial acknowledged that the Catholic Church has too often remained 'silent, in some cases even quietly complicit', in the face of rising prejudice and called on its leaders to show greater 'respect, compassion and sensitivity'.

Competing positions on sexual and gender rights, such as those outlined above, tend to be reduced to a good-versus-bad dichotomy. In reality, the situation is far more complicated. In most contexts, conservative and progressive views exist side by side, even if the former tend to garner greater media attention. Caution is thus required when choosing examples to illustrate the role of religion in perpetuating homo/transphobia. In referencing Botswana, for example, I could easily quote Pastor Biki Butale, former national secretary of the Evangelical Fellowship of Botswana, who called on 'all Christians and morally upright persons . . . to reject, resist, denounce, expose, demolish and totally frustrate any effort by whoever to infiltrate such foreign cultures of moral decay and shame into our respectable, blessed and peaceful country'.[53] His words contrast sharply with those of the Botswana Council of Churches (BCC). In a media statement following the recent High Court judgment that effectively decriminalised homosexuality in Botswana, the BCC emphasised the value of being 'inclusive of all people regardless of social orientations' and 'appeals to the citizens of our country to co-exist in mutual respect'.[54] Had I included just one of these examples, I would have drawn a distorted map of Botswana's religious terrain.

Some of the most encouraging developments of recent years have come from pan-African religious movements. One example is the KwaZulu-Natal Declaration, signed in 2014 by more than 30 clergy, theologians and scholars from across the continent.[55] It begins with the following words: 'We . . . are highly concerned with the wellbeing of our beloved continent and with the demonisation and criminalisation of sexual minorities.' It goes on to denounce 'the misuse of religion to further marginalise and exclude sexual minorities' and calls on African churches 'to create safe spaces [for LGBT people]' and 'to break the vicious cycle of shame, secrecy, violence and silence that demeans, demonises and kills'.

Statements such as these inspire hope for future activism, as does the tireless work of faith-based organisations like the Interfaith Diversity Network of West Africa, the African Caucus of the Global Network of Rainbow Catholics, the Global Interfaith Network, the Inner Circle, Inclusive and Affirming Ministries, and INERELA+. At the same time, the courageous work of African religious scholars like Rev. Dr Kapya Kaoma, Dr Masiiwa Ragies Gunda, Rev. Prof. Allan Boesak, Prof. Ezra Chitando and Dr Nontando Hadebe is helping to promote inclusive, rights-based theologies on the continent. Finally, it is important to recognise the vital work being undertaken by LGBT churches such as the Good Hope Metropolitan Community Church (South Africa) and the Cosmopolitan Affirming Church (Kenya).

While too brief to adequately theorise the religious dimensions of homo/transphobia, the foregoing discussion should provide sufficient context for understanding the life stories. What I hope to have shown is the danger in presuming a causal link between faith and prejudice. Too many commentators fall into the trap of writing about 'African religion' or 'African homo/transphobia' as if these were homogeneous phenomena.[56] While there are certainly powerful anti-LGBT religious discourses at play on the continent, there are also growing counter-discourses, as well as concerted efforts to mobilise progressive faith communities.[57]

This is why it is so important to recognise the *politicisation* of anti-LGBT religious sentiments, rather than fixating on the supposedly inherent conservatism of African faith practices.[58] Many make the mistake of seeing religion as a site of static oppression when it is better understood as a nexus point for multiple beliefs, values, interpretations and contestations. Discourses around 'family values', 'traditional morals' and 'good citizenship' are undoubtedly being used to reinforce hetero-patriarchal authority and justify state intrusion into the private sphere, yet these discourses are also being subverted in powerful ways.[59] As the stories in this collection show, there is much more to African faith practices than the progressive-versus-conservative framing touted by the international press.

CHAPTER 3

A LIFE ON HOLD
LGBT migration and the (false) promise of freedom

As detailed in the previous chapter, homo/transphobia remains widespread on the African continent, prompting significant numbers of LGBT persons to flee their countries of origin. Some attempt to access states in the Global North via various migration pathways, such as study or work permits, national asylum systems, or the resettlement programme operated by the United Nations High Commissioner for Refugees (UNHCR). However, the deliberate erosion of international protection mechanisms, often enacted in parallel with the securitisation and externalisation of borders, places these options firmly out of reach for most people. The result is growing numbers of LGBT persons being forced to remain on the continent.[1] In turn, visible LGBT migrant populations are beginning to emerge, including recognised hubs in Ghana,[2] Kenya,[3] Morocco,[4] Senegal[5] and South Africa. While these countries may provide LGBT migrants with distance from hostile families, communities and/or governments, and in some cases even act as sites of belonging and connection, they rarely offer safety and stability. For example, in Kenya, which boasts one of the continent's largest LGBT migrant communities, those seeking protection are routinely mistreated and abused, even after the UNHCR enacted special measures to safeguard those deemed especially vulnerable.[6]

LGBT migrants encounter the same challenges as other groups on the move, but they also face unique obstacles that reveal the limitations of existing protection systems.[7] One of the most obvious difficulties that LGBT asylum seekers face is 'proving' their experiences in ways that sufficiently corroborate their claims.[8] Very few individuals are likely to have documentary evidence, such as photos or letters, as such items can intensify the risk of victimisation. LGBT asylum seekers can also struggle to articulate their histories and identities in ways that align with the Western ontological categories used to assess the veracity of their narratives.[9] This may be because they are unfamiliar with dominant terminology;[10] because they have spent years concealing their identities out of fear, shame or guilt;[11] or because they are suffering from trauma and related mental health issues.[12] All of these factors make it difficult for LGBT asylum claimants to verbalise their lived experiences to state bureaucrats and humanitarian workers, especially if these individuals are inadequately trained or exhibit the same prejudices as the wider community.[13] Even if an LGBT asylum claimant does satisfactorily establish their sexuality and/or gender, they may still struggle to prove persecution, given that homo/transphobia usually occurs within domestic or social settings, as opposed to the direct political oppression typically associated with refugees.[14]

Homo/transphobia may be only one of many factors compelling an LGBT person to migrate. When this is the case, state officials often invalidate the sexuality and/or gender component of the claim, dismissing it as a ruse to gain sympathy or to obfuscate the person's 'true' status as an economic migrant. As the stories in this collection attest, LGBT migrants move for myriad reasons, some of which can't be easily untangled or defined. They may all share a desire to reach a destination where they can safely explore their sexuality and/or gender, but each individual's ability to fulfil this dream will be constrained by various economic, social and political forces. What is important to remember is that sexuality and/or gender can be relevant to a person's migration even if they are also seeking educational or vocational opportunities, if they hold reservations about outwardly expressing their identity, or if they haven't directly experienced homo/transphobic violence.

Of all the LGBT migration hubs mentioned above, South Africa stands out due to its inclusive legal framework and its categorisation as a stable reception country (the others are classified as transit countries, even as the likelihood of third-country resettlement continues to dwindle).[15] Upon ratifying its post-apartheid Constitution, South Africa drew universal praise for its progressive and wide-ranging human rights protections, including an explicit prohibition against homo/transphobic discrimination. However, in the decades that have followed, many of the guarantees enshrined in the Bill of Rights have proven to be little more than a pipe dream. The reforms so eagerly welcomed in the first years of democracy have done little to address the country's staggering wealth disparity or deliver meaningful change to marginalised populations. LGBT people, in particular, continue to experience very high rates of violence, often in extreme forms, and remain marginalised in most aspects of public life.[16] The lack of political will to combat homo/transphobic persecution, compounded by widespread failures in the criminal justice system, has left many LGBT people – particularly those who are poor and black – with little optimism for the future.[17] This despair plays out in statistics showing that homo/transphobic attitudes remain pervasive. For example, a recent large-scale survey by the Other Foundation reported that 72 per cent of respondents consider same-sex sexual activity to be 'morally wrong',[18] while a national study by the Love Not Hate Campaign found that 44 per cent of LGBT persons had experienced direct discrimination in their everyday lives.[19]

Although South Africa's promise of equality remains illusory for most of its LGBT population, the country continues to be seen as a beacon of hope for those fleeing homo/transphobia elsewhere on the continent.[20] This is primarily because South Africa's Refugees Act recognises homo/transphobic persecution as legitimate grounds for refugee status, leading many LGBT Africans to believe they will be welcomed and protected within the country's borders. In practice, inconsistent and erroneous implementation of the Act means that most LGBT claimants become trapped in a state of limbo, forced to survive on temporary permits while their cases disappear into a bureaucratic black hole.[21] Those cases that do reach the determination stage are almost always denied, except in cases involving third-party intervention (for example, diplomatic pressure, extensive media coverage or appeals from human rights organisations).[22]

The South African state's failure to effectively implement its own legislation affects migrants across the board, but it reserves some of its most nefarious treatment for LGBT asylum seekers. As demonstrated in Anold's case, LGBT claimants regularly come up against conservative bureaucrats who are unwilling to even countenance the possibility of LGBT Africans, let alone those who identify as religious. Many claimants are subjected to intimate and humiliating lines of questioning, often about sexual practices or physical characteristics, only to have this information divulged to other departmental staff and sometimes even members of the public.[23] Those using interpretation services are forced to out themselves in front of individuals with strong ties to their ethnic community, thus placing them at increased risk of exploitation and violence.[24]

In addition to institutional incompetence and entrenched corruption, the Department of Home Affairs has demonstrated an astonishingly poor grasp of sexual and gender rights on the rest of the continent.[25] Rejections of refugee status are peppered with stereotypes, inaccuracies and seemingly arbitrary assessments of what constitutes 'evidence' of sexual and/or gender diversity. Popular misconceptions abound – that all gay men wear make-up, that lesbian women can't have children, that transgender individuals are 'hermaphrodites', or that LGBT people are suffering from a curable physiological or psychological disorder. When coupled with strong religious and cultural beliefs, such misconceptions are a recipe for egregious misapplications of law.[26]

Tales of mistreatment and violence at DHA offices spread quickly among LGBT asylum seekers, leading many to risk remaining undocumented, as is the case with some of the narrators in this collection. For these individuals, being caught without papers – an infringement usually resolved with a small bribe – is preferential to the secondary victimisation meted out by departmental officials.

In recounting their experiences with South African bureaucrats, the narrators featured here report bribery, apathy, disdain, ineptitude, mockery, intimidation and harassment, encounters that have left them feeling vulnerable and traumatised. Some were forced to apply for asylum on grounds other than their sexuality or gender, others circumvented the process by buying permits (a practice instigated and encouraged by corrupt officials)[27] and a few gave up on the system entirely. Those living without documentation tell of a struggle to secure housing, gain employment or access social services, as well as an increased susceptibility to police harassment.[28]

Those surviving on temporary permits fare little better. Forced to renew their asylum papers every three months at the issuing Refugee Reception Office – a process that is time-consuming, expensive and dangerous – these individuals find themselves unable to make long-term plans or build a life. The emotional toll of the procedure is palpable in D.C.'s story:

> I have been on a temporary asylum permit since 2005 and I still have no idea if I will be granted refugee status. Dealing with DHA has been a nightmare. My case file has been transferred between multiple branches and in the process important documents have been lost . . . When I first applied for asylum, I was met with shock and confusion. The DHA officer looked at me and said, 'I don't believe there are lesbians in Zimbabwe! Anyway, lesbians can't have children – you must be lying.' He told his colleagues about me and I became the joke of the centre . . . In all the years I have been going to DHA, I have never once had someone who knows about LGBT issues.

In many cases, the stress of forced precarity is compounded by an ever-present danger of violence, a reality intensified for those vulnerable to both xenophobic and homo/transphobic attacks.[29] For narrators such as Eeyban, a gay asylum seeker from Ethiopia, the risk of violence comes from all directions. He recounts multiple assaults – some perpetrated by other Ethiopians – as well as seemingly impenetrable barriers to support services. In the extract below, he describes the fear, isolation and helplessness that many LGBT migrants experience in South Africa:

> I went to the police station – bloodied, bruised, in shock – and reported the attack, but I was too frightened to say it was because of my sexuality. Police stations are dangerous places if you are gay and foreign. I also didn't want to cause more trouble in the community . . . After finishing at the police station, I went to the hospital. I sat in the waiting room all night, bleeding and bleeding, but no one did anything. Nurses don't like foreigners.

Most of the narrators have been lucky in avoiding serious harm, but studies suggest that this is not the norm for LGBT migrants.[30] What this may point to are the comparative advantages enjoyed by some individuals (for example, cisgender gay men with linguistic or cultural ties to South Africa) compared to those from elsewhere on the continent or those with a more outwardly 'transgressive' gender expression. This is not to say that cisgender gay men always enjoy a greater level of security, or that migrants from countries like Botswana or Zimbabwe are necessarily safer than those from further afield, but rather a reminder of the complex ways in which xenophobia and homo/transphobia intersect in South Africa.

The challenges referenced in these stories are by no means new. Researchers and activists have long critiqued the bureaucratic minefield that is South Africa's border regime.[31] Thus it is important to situate the anecdotes shared here within a broader context of structural xenophobia and a failed refugee apparatus. But the stories also point to the unique ways in which LGBT migrants are marginalised, both by state actors and society more generally. The degree of marginalisation may differ depending on the individual, but the overarching reality remains the same.

Yet, as some narrators point out, the difficulties faced in South Africa can still be preferable to the situation back home. For Mr D, life in South Africa couldn't be more different from life in Cameroon:

I wish my country could be more like South Africa, where LGBT people can live openly . . . The other day I saw footage of President Ramaphosa saying that LGBT people have a right to protection. What an amazing thing to see! Nowhere else on the continent would a politician say that. I hope more African leaders will follow his example.

Mr D's reflection challenges us to consider LGBT migrant lives in their totality. While South Africa may not be the progressive utopia that migrants seek, it can still bring a level of safety and security. Nonetheless, these positive experiences shouldn't distract us from the South African state's failure to meet its domestic and international obligations, nor overshadow the social challenges that LGBT migrants endure on a daily basis.

CHAPTER 4

PREACHING LOVE
A history of the LGBT Ministry

Dwarfed by the towering blocks of Wits University, the Holy Trinity Catholic Church goes unnoticed by most passers-by. Yet, for large numbers of Johannesburg's inner-city residents, particularly the homeless and destitute, the church is a lifeline: its daily soup kitchen feeds an average of 150 people, its weekly clinic supplies vital health services and its outreach projects provide much-needed livelihood opportunities. For those familiar with the church, its social apostolate is personified in an unassuming artwork by its main gate. Titled *Homeless Jesus*, the bronze sculpture depicts a figure sleeping on a bench, his body shrouded in a thick blanket, the only hint of his identity being two pierced feet exposed to the elements. Those hurrying past could easily mistake it for a real person, one of the many faceless figures haunting Braamfontein's streets, but those who stop and look are invited to contemplate Jesus' directive to care for the meek and needy. What does charity and compassion mean, the artwork asks, in a society riven by multiple inequalities?

It was the church's commitment to rethinking social justice that led to the formation of the LGBT Ministry in 2009. The years preceding its establishment had been tumultuous: Thabo Mbeki's AIDS denialism had widely exacerbated the country's HIV epidemic;[1] simmering xenophobic tensions had led to periodic eruptions of violence, culminating in the death of 67 people in 2008;[2] and brutal physical and sexual attacks against LGBT people, particularly black lesbian women, had become rampant.[3]

While a few prominent South Africans chose to condemn this surge in homo/transphobic violence, the majority remained silent. Some even used the opportunity to lament recently won legislative rights for LGBT people, often embedding their objections within doomsday prophecies and moral panics. In 2008, Jon Qwelane – later appointed South African ambassador to Uganda – published an opinion piece entitled 'Call me names, but gay is NOT okay', in which he equated same-sex marriage with bestiality, condemned progressive voices within the Anglican Church for 'the rapid degradation of traditions and values' and referenced a covert campaign by LGBT people to destroy 'the natural order of things'.[4] A short while later, arts and culture minister Lulu Xingwana walked out of an exhibition by renowned photographer Zanele Muholi, whose images of lesbian women Xingwana described as 'immoral', 'offensive' and 'against nation-building'.[5]

These cases were far from isolated. In the mid-2000s, religious and cultural groups actively campaigned against LGBT reforms, particularly the push for equal marriage rights. In 2006, for example, the Catholic Bishops' Conference of Southern Africa described same-sex marriage as an attempt to 'flout the traditional customs, religious beliefs and moral sensitivities of people'.[6] Around the same time, the Congress of Traditional Leaders referred to LGBT people as 'oddities' and a 'problem' that needed to be solved, and later moved to block ANC members from voting in support of the Civil Unions Bill.[7] Similarly, political figures like Rev. Kenneth Meshoe, leader of the African Christian Democratic Party, dismissed same-sex marriage as an attempt to 'legally perpetuate a sinful lifestyle that is not only unhealthy and unnatural but that is frowned upon by all traditional, cultural, religious and tribal groups in Africa'.[8]

Concerned by this rise in religious conservatism, Holy Trinity's parish priest, Fr Russell Pollitt, began to denounce homo/transphobia in his sermons. 'I decided [the church] couldn't keep quiet,' he tells me. 'I began to speak out about the scourge of hate crimes and the need to accept, support and love LGBT people.'

There were several factors motivating Fr Russell: first, as a Jesuit, he felt compelled to help those on the margins of society; second, he had observed high-profile religious leaders condemning LGBT people 'in the most appalling of ways'; third, as chaplain for Wits University, he had encountered students who openly questioned the church's stance on LGBT rights and who challenged him to do the same; and fourth, he had recognised that LGBT individuals were attending his parish and wanted to make sure they felt comfortable and accepted.

'All of this made me convinced that we needed to rethink the church's position on homosexuality,' he says. 'I knew nothing would change if people like me remained silent.'

But there was one incident in particular that galvanised Fr Russell into action:

> One evening, I received a call from Milpark Hospital requesting a priest attend to a patient. When I arrived, I was shown into a room with a young coloured man. He couldn't have been more than 16 years old. He was in a terrible way – bloodied, bruised, unconscious. His head was so swollen that I assumed he had been in a motorcycle accident. It turns out he had been beaten by his father after coming out as gay . . . It was unimaginable to me that a parent could harm his child in this way.

It was an experience that would have a profound effect on both Fr Russell and his congregation: 'I retold the story during Mass. I wanted to show that homophobia is an urgent justice issue.' He recalls a handful of parishioners coming up to him afterwards, eager to share their own concerns about homo/transphobia. One of these people was Ricus Dullaert, a Trinity congregant from the Netherlands who was in South Africa managing an HIV programme.

Ricus, too, was worried about the growing pushback against LGBT rights, particularly its impacts on those excluded from traditional support networks. Like Fr Russell, he traces his concern to a pivotal personal interaction.

'I was contacted by a young gay man named Takunda,' Ricus recalls. 'He had recently converted from Pentecostalism to Catholicism and was now attending Mass at Trinity.'[9]

The two met at a nearby café, where Takunda told Ricus about his life:

> He had moved from Zimbabwe and was surviving through sex work. It was clear he wasn't in a good place. He had joined Trinity because he was looking for spiritual nourishment, but what he needed was a platform from which to explore his faith as a gay man.

Over time the two became close. Ricus remembers visiting Takunda's home and being appalled by his living conditions: 'He was sharing a room with four other gay migrants. They had very few belongings and were always on the verge of being evicted.'

What they needed, Ricus reasoned, was a place that was safe and supportive, somewhere they could gather without fear:

> These guys had been totally uprooted; they had lost the stability of their families and communities because of the stigma in their home countries. Now they were drifting through life – they had no security, no stability, no direction.

Ricus considers his friendship with Takunda as the primary impetus behind the LGBT Ministry, noting how it opened his eyes to the myriad struggles facing LGBT migrants:

> I thought to myself, 'How many others like him are hiding in the pews of churches?' I knew South Africa was a popular destination for LGBT people fleeing conservative societies. I wanted Trinity to be a space where these individuals felt welcomed.

AN IDEA IS BORN

Spurred on by what he had seen, Ricus reached out to Fr Russell, convinced that the church could play a more active and accommodating role. They agreed that a practical intervention was needed: 'Referencing LGBT rights during Mass was important,' Fr Russell recalls, 'but it wasn't enough.'

After a number of chats, the pair decided that a dedicated ministry was the best way forward. But before such a group could be launched, permission was needed from the archbishop and the Parish Council. There was also the hurdle of getting the congregation on side.

'If you want to create change as a religious leader,' Fr Russell says, 'you have to bring people with you. You have to help them think through the issues.' This was something that he and his colleagues approached incrementally:

> The team at Trinity – it wasn't just me – consciously tried to open up spaces through the way we said things in church. For six or seven months, every now and then, especially when it came to justice issues,

we deliberately pushed the conversation beyond feeding the poor. We wanted to highlight that there are lots of other issues that we, as Christians, need to consider.

A similar tactic was adopted with the Parish Council, as Fr Russell explains: 'Once again we approached the topic cautiously; we didn't just drop our plan on them. It was important for people to understand why we wanted to do this.'

The Parish Council's endorsement didn't come as a surprise to Ricus, although he acknowledges that approval wasn't immediate:

We needed [the Parish Council] to recognise that the ministry would nicely fit with the church's social apostolate, in the sense that it would be open to and benefit both parishioners and the wider community. The social apostolate has always been very strong at Trinity – there were already programmes for the poor, for migrants, for people living with HIV, even for women who had undergone abortions – and we needed to show that this group would align with the church's stated objectives.

In making his case for the LGBT Ministry, Fr Russell wanted to emphasise a scriptural rationale as much as a desire to promote social cohesion. This meant spending considerable time engaging with theological debates around diversity.

'The church is holding on to a vision of gender and sexuality that is frozen in the past,' Fr Russell explains. 'There is a desperate need to rethink how these things are spoken about within theology.' Part of that includes being open to shifts in science:

Developments in many disciplines – genetics, biology, neurology, psychology, etc. – are challenging traditional notions about gender and sexuality. And if science has something to say on these topics, then the church needs to listen.

For Fr Russell, the church's position will only change once the issue itself is reframed:

We must bring the focus back to sexuality, rather than specific sexual acts, which is what these conversations are so often reduced to. There is too much energy wasted on prohibitions – who you can do it with, how you can do it, when you can do it, and so on. We speak about human beings being made in the image of God and recognise the need to see people in their totality, yet we reduce or deny this important aspect of our humanity. Sexuality is a broad and ever-discoverable part of human beings and it deserves closer theological attention.

Supporting Fr Russell in developing Trinity's position was his assistant priest, Fr Bruce Botha. Having just returned from theological studies in the US, Fr Bruce was able to draw on global shifts towards inclusive faith practices.

'I had the privilege of doing a course on pastoral care for the LGBT community while at Berkeley,' he says. 'That opened my eyes to the amazing range of ways in which people love and relate. I became very much aware that the church's treatment of LGBT people was something that needed to evolve.'

Fr Bruce's approach was to shift the focus from reproduction and regulation to the biblical imperative to love healthily and respectfully:

Our starting point was the idea that the church calls on all of us to use our sexuality responsibly . . . We framed the LGBT Ministry as something that would help people love better, regardless of their gender, sexuality or personal circumstances. It was envisaged as a space that would help people find a way of being in the world that was good and healthy.

This framing was also useful in getting buy-in from the Parish Council, although Fr Bruce is quick to emphasise that any reticence wasn't theological:

It wasn't as if the Parish Council believed that LGBT people aren't worthy of care. Their hesitation was due to a lack of familiarity with the needs of the LGBT community and a concern over the practicalities.

A DREAM BECOMES REALITY

Once approval for the LGBT Ministry had been granted, Fr Russell and Ricus set about organising the first meeting. 'I stood up one Sunday and made an announcement,' Fr Russell recalls. 'I said: "LGBT people are an affected part of this community and we are doing something to help."'

Language and framing was something they considered from the outset, as Fr Russell explains: 'I consciously avoided terms like "support group" or "gay group". I didn't want to give the impression that LGBT people need help getting better, in the sense that alcoholics might need a support group.'

While reasonably well attended, the first meeting wasn't what Ricus had envisaged: 'There were a couple of older white men who came along. They were looking for a space to connect and chat, which was perfectly fine, but it wasn't the demographic I had anticipated.'

Yet it didn't take long for things to change: 'First a couple of Zimbabweans showed up,' Ricus says. 'These guys brought along a friend, and the next week that friend brought along another new person.'

Both Fr Russell and Ricus look back on those early meetings fondly, happy that their gamble paid off: 'We didn't have much of a plan,' admits Fr Russell. 'We decided to throw open the doors and see who showed up.' In his mind, the LGBT Ministry had to develop on its own terms:

> I didn't feel it was up to us to set the agenda or tell people what they needed. Our job was to accompany people . . . Those who came along just wanted a space where they could tell their stories. That is all that happened for the first few months. Most of the stories were what you would expect – being rejected by families, by churches, by communities.

For some founding members, especially the white men, having the opportunity to be heard was enough, and many moved on once they had articulated their trauma. But for others, especially those coming from other parts of the continent, the group began to take on a more significant role. These new members were battling poverty, unemployment and precarious living conditions, all the while struggling to reconcile their identities with their faith.

The significance of the space was immediately apparent: 'I can so clearly remember those first meetings,' says Fr Bruce. 'It was devastating to watch people turn up on a Sunday afternoon and try to sneak into the basement [meeting room] without raising suspicion. People were terrified of being recognised.'

Ricus, too, remembers the crippling anxiety that some members battled. He shares a story about a young man who was almost paralysed by fear:

> He would spend 10 to 15 minutes peering through a tiny glass panel in the door, checking to see if other Cameroonians were in the room. He was petrified one of his countrymen would expose his sexuality and that he would lose his family, his home, his job.

BUILDING VISIBILITY AND NAVIGATING TENSIONS

Despite Fr Russell's best efforts to prepare the congregation, he still faced pushback, especially in the early years. Some parishioners shared their concerns directly, telling him that they felt ashamed and embarrassed by what he was doing. Others took the matter further, either by raising the issue within the Catholic hierarchy or by expressing their dissatisfaction online.

'There was one woman who sent a letter to the archbishop,' Fr Russell remembers. 'She wrote pages and pages about the "homo heresy" taking place at Trinity. I invited her to discuss her concerns, but in the end she left the parish. The reason she gave was not wanting to be tainted by my "gay agenda".'

While not everyone was vocal in their opposition, it was clear that an undercurrent of dissatisfaction persisted. Surprisingly, much of the initial resistance came from other migrants, as Ricus notes:

> Nationality, rather than age, seemed to be the biggest factor. A lot of opposition came from the Young Adult Family Ministry. That group has members from all over Africa and many were upset by what we were doing. It wasn't because they were bad people. It was a lack of education, a lack of exposure, that was driving the fear.

Both Fr Russell and Ricus felt that these tensions needed to be addressed head-on: 'I have never seen the LGBT Ministry as separate from the rest of the church,' Ricus explains. 'It is there to challenge prejudice inside of Trinity as much as prejudice in the community.'

One of the earliest attempts to achieve this was a public screening of *For the Bible Tells Me So*, a documentary about the dangers of literal interpretations of scripture. When introducing the film, Fr Russell asked the audience to watch with generosity, hoping this would lead to a frank and open conversation. Even he was surprised by the reaction:

> For some people it was a real turning point. After the screening, one woman stood up and said, 'Father, I came here today to say that you are wrong, but now I am going home to think about what I have seen.' It was heartening that some people were open to hearing other perspectives.

Another strategy was to openly include the LGBT Ministry in major church activities, such as the Stations of the Cross, one of the most important devotions on the liturgical calendar. 'I encouraged the LGBT Ministry to lead the Stations,' explains Fr Russell. 'I wanted them to feel valued and to know that they were making a contribution.'

He also incorporated the LGBT Ministry into important Easter celebrations, such as the Mass of the Lord's Supper, which commemorates Jesus' washing of the Apostles' feet. Traditionally, a priest re-enacts this deed with 12 male parishioners, but Fr Russell chose to use representatives – both male and female – from the church's various ministries (an increasingly accepted practice since Pope Francis adopted a similar approach in 2016).

For Fr Russell, visible demonstrations such as this were critical to changing attitudes: 'The congregation was able to see that we were actually doing something. We weren't just giving lip service to social justice, but actively including diverse people in church structures.'

Inspired by these expressions of solidarity, the LGBT Ministry decided to participate in the 2012 Jo'burg Pride Parade. 'We had just had T-shirts made,' recalls Ricus. 'People wanted to wear them during the march. It was important for them to identify as LGBT Christians.' In preparation, group members built a large processional cross onto which the names of hate-crime victims were nailed. To signal his support, Fr Russell organised an ecumenical service for the morning of the march. As he explains, the service was intended to serve two purposes:

First, I wanted to pray a blessing for those taking part, to show that they had our love and support. Second, I wanted to make it clear that we, as a church, were proud of what the group was doing. There were quite a few religious leaders speaking out against us and I wanted it known publicly that Trinity fully supported the LGBT Ministry.

A VERY PUBLIC DISPUTE

Despite having the tacit approval of his immediate superiors, Fr Russell continued to face censure from some quarters, with the most vociferous criticism coming from a senior Catholic cleric. 'Somehow he got the idea that I was running a gay dating service,' Fr Russell says. 'The next thing I knew he was denouncing me on Twitter, claiming that I was violating church teachings.'

The criticism was something Fr Russell felt he needed to address, but with hindsight he admits to acting hastily: 'Responding [on Twitter] put me in a difficult position . . . I wanted him to understand what was really happening at Trinity, but in confronting him I gave my detractors the ammunition they needed.'

The situation was further aggravated when the *Mail & Guardian* published interviews with both Fr Russell and the cleric. Neither party knew the other was being interviewed, or that the pieces would be run side by side. Such a public breaking of ranks was not welcomed by the Catholic hierarchy, as Fr Russell explains: 'We were saying quite different things. The episode brought me into conflict with him and many others. It wasn't helpful for any of us.'

These tensions soon spilled over into other spaces, with conservatives criticising Fr Russell in the Catholic press and expressing dissatisfaction at diocesan meetings. 'There were people who were steadfastly against our work,' he says. 'I remember one meeting when objections to the LGBT Ministry were raised. There were, thankfully, people who defended us. Representatives from the Parish Council stood up and expressed their pride in this aspect of Trinity's work.'

What Fr Russell and Ricus weren't expecting was for these incidents to reignite tensions within the congregation. It had become rare for parishioners to openly express dissatisfaction, yet suddenly homo/transphobic prejudices began to resurface.

One incident that stands out for Ricus involved Yannick, a gay man from Cameroon who was a member of both the LGBT Ministry and the Young Adult Family Ministry. His dual participation didn't sit well with members of the second group. Things came to a head when Yannick died and both ministries were asked to contribute to his funeral. 'The other group was determined to gloss over Yannick's sexuality,' Ricus remembers, 'and that obviously upset our members.'

While Ricus acknowledges the harm caused by such incidents, he is anxious about misrepresenting the intentions of those involved:

> It is important to remember that you often run into enormous differences in cultural backgrounds. This is very in true in a parish like Trinity, where you have people from all over the continent, all walks of life, many of whom have never been exposed to progressive views on sexuality. The only way you can deal with these prejudices is to tread lightly. You must recognise the feelings of other people, especially when there is a lot of cultural baggage involved, but you must also be firm in addressing any misconceptions and maintaining visibility.

AN EXPANDED FOCUS

Recent years have seen changes in how the LGBT Ministry operates. Discussion and prayer remain the core activities, but other focus areas, including psychosocial support, vocational training and life skills, now play a larger role. While this shift was primarily due to external factors, specifically the South African state's growing animosity towards migrants, it was also driven by changes in the group's operations. Fr Russell and Ricus were initially hesitant to formalise the LGBT Ministry, but soon realised that a proper structure was vital if it was going to meet members' needs. Ricus, who up until then had both co-ordinated the group and served as its representative on the Parish Council, approached Dumisani Dube – whose story is featured in this collection – and invited him to take on the role of chairperson.

'The group is what it is today because Dumisani became involved,' Ricus says. 'He had experience in LGBT activism in Zimbabwe and was well connected within the LGBT migrant community. He brought with him strong ideas for how the group could develop.'

Central to his vision was for the group to become more than a discussion space. 'People had to be taking something positive away,' Dumisani tells me. 'It wasn't enough to sit around and talk . . . LGBT migrants are often excluded from education and struggle to find jobs. I wanted the group to help people become more settled, more connected, more driven, more hopeful.'

This aspiration was shared by Ricus, who set about finding additional funds. Resourcing has always been a stumbling block for the LGBT Ministry, not only limiting opportunities for expansion but also making it difficult to offer meaningful assistance in moments of crisis.

As Ricus notes, the ability to offer emergency support is particularly urgent considering the constituency served by the group:

Helping members find a level of stability is essential. A group like ours works best with committed and focused members, but that isn't possible when people can't afford food or rent. To get to the point where we could have the conversations we wanted to have, we first had to find ways to help members become secure. It isn't possible to address someone's spiritual needs when they are hungry.

Aware that members were facing common challenges, Ricus and Dumisani began to identify and respond to key issues. Some proved easier to address than others: Dumisani was able to organise on-site HIV testing, invite guest speakers specialising in LGBT rights and facilitate sessions on coming out. But when it came to matters of faith, it was clear that a more nuanced approach was required. Where possible, visiting theologians were invited to address the group on topics of diversity and inclusion, and the Trinity team was always on hand to address scriptural concerns. However, Fr Russell, Fr Bruce and later clergy made a conscious decision to attend meetings only when invited.

'I said from the outset that I didn't want the group to be controlled by me,' Fr Russell says. 'It was important that the group had the freedom to evolve in line with members' needs.'

While the overarching focus on spiritual care was welcomed by members, it did little to address the economic and social insecurities that these individuals faced. One solution was to incorporate a skills training programme for regular members, as Ricus explains:

> There isn't a lot of cash available, but we can usually cover a certificate-level course. About 20 members have undergone training in all sorts of areas: hospitality, gardening, domestic work, disability care, even photography. It has to be something that can open up job opportunities.

Ricus tells me first about Panashe, a gay man from Zimbabwe who qualified as a carer and now has full-time work in Pretoria, and then about Sulman, a gay man from Pakistan who now lives and works in Durban. He considers Sulman one of the group's biggest successes:

> He came to the LGBT Ministry in a terrible state – depressed, always crying, deeply conflicted about his Muslim faith. We sent him for a retreat with the Inner Circle [in Cape Town] where he learnt about progressive interpretations of the Qur'an. He came back reborn; he had found his voice and could speak comfortably about his identity. Then we sent him to be trained on domestic work and healthcare. This led to a job with on-site accommodation, which was important because he had been kicked out by his family.

For Ricus, Sulman's transformation epitomises the potential of the LGBT Ministry:

> Sulman is as a nice example of how we want the group to operate. He wasn't Catholic – not even Christian – but he was still able to come along and participate. He ended up taking a lot away from the experience. This is what the social apostolate means: it is for everyone who needs help, no matter their religion, history, health or documentation status. People must be able to come as they are and find there is an open ear and a welcoming heart.

Ricus smiles as he recounts other positive outcomes, an unmistakeable glint of pride in his eyes, and yet he refuses to ignore the grim reality. I hear about Rutendo, a gay man struggling with psychosis due to crystal meth addiction, whom the LGBT Ministry supported through rehab and who is now rebuilding his life.

Then there is Simphiwe, whose HIV had deteriorated to the point that he was close to death. 'Simphiwe struggled with homelessness, just like so many of our members,' Ricus explains.

> One day we found out he was in the makeshift infirmary at Central Methodist.[10] His CD4 count was extremely low. I managed to get him a bed at Nazareth House. He stayed there for almost a year, supported by the group, and in the end he came out alive and kicking, aware of how to use ARVs to stay healthy . . . There are many stories like Rutendo's and Simphiwe's. The LGBT Ministry can become a safe haven for those who don't have a community backing them. We are a surrogate family, stepping in when there is no one else willing or able to help.

While this emphasis on health and wellbeing continues, a more recent focus has been documentation, as Dumisani describes:

> Before, most of our members didn't have papers. Some were unable to raise the money to get to Marabastad [Refugee Reception Office], others had permits that had expired and were scared to renew them, and a few were unsure of how the system even worked . . . We brought in experts to demystify the process and helped members with transport money. Now more than 60 per cent of the group is documented.

In addition to material and emotional support, the group strives to create spaces in which members can relax and have fun. 'When someone's life is defined by uncertainty, their mental and emotional health suffers,' says Dumisani. 'It is important for people to have social outlets, even if only once or twice a year.'

The group's social programme has included a wide range of activities, everything from workshops and retreats to parties and Pride events. The highlight of the social calendar is undoubtedly the annual spring party, as Ricus notes:

> The parties are more than a bit of fun. Our members rarely have a chance to access LGBT spaces. They certainly don't have money for commercial clubs. It is great to see people letting their hair down.

It is moments like these that keep Dumisani involved. He describes his greatest joy as seeing members excel: 'Over the years I have seen members go on to do great things – some have studied, some have found jobs, some have built stable relationships.'

Evidence of these successes comes in many forms, but for Dumisani the most compelling examples involve members advocating for their rights:

> We have had members attend meetings with international human rights organisations. We have had members get interviewed about their experiences on TV. We have had members go on to start organisations. Seeing people find their voice keeps me inspired.

But while Dumisani and Ricus take great pleasure in listing these accomplishments, they are quick to point out that this isn't the whole picture. Ricus concedes that not every challenge is overcome:

> There are plenty of former members who continue to struggle, be it with unemployment, homelessness or substance abuse . . . Obviously we are pleased when someone is doing well, but we also want to be there for those who are still struggling. We will never turn our back on someone in need.

Dumisani also refuses to gloss over the harsh realities of members' lives. He tells of going to hospitals and watching friends pass away, abandoned by families and forgotten by society: 'We have members who can't afford to look after their health, who have been beaten up, who are struggling emotionally. It breaks my heart when we can't do more.'

EBBS AND FLOWS

As with any organisation that has been active for over a decade, the LGBT Ministry has faced periods of adversity as well as triumph.

'Migrants are by nature transient,' Ricus says. 'We often have members who disappear as suddenly as they appear.' But by far the biggest difficulty is trying to cope with the overwhelming challenges facing LGBT migrants:

> Our resources are next to nothing, and some people come with unreasonable expectations of what we can do. We help as best we can, but we aren't able to find people jobs or pay their rent. Often people will come for one or two meetings, but then leave once they realise we can't magically fix their problems. That makes it hard for the group to grow.

While the group's ever-changing composition has been a long-term challenge, recent years have seen greater stability. 'We now have a committed core,' says Ricus. 'There are about 15 members who are strongly invested in seeing the group continue and who put in a lot of time and energy.'

Internal changes at Trinity have also brought their own challenges. When Fr Russell was transferred in 2013, the LGBT Ministry was faced with clergy who were far less enthusiastic, although ongoing support from the Parish Council ensured the group's survival.

'When I first arrived at Trinity, there was a clear faction that wanted the LGBT Ministry to end,' says Fr Graham Pugin, who took over as parish priest in 2015, two years after Fr Russell's departure. But he also observed unwavering support from key congregants:

> There were a few dissenting voices on the Parish Council, as well as noticeable pushback from inside the Young Adult Family Ministry. But there were also very reliable supporters. People like Dawn Linder would always speak in defence of the LGBT Ministry. She would say her piece very articulately and forthrightly.

A long-time supporter of the disenfranchised, Fr Graham made his position on the LGBT Ministry abundantly clear, much to the relief of group members: 'I signalled quite clearly that I wasn't buying into any kind of homophobia.'

During Fr Graham's tenure, the LGBT Ministry again became visible in the parish, taking part in activities like the annual Christmas feast, in which the congregation provides food and gifts to the poor and homeless. For Fr Graham, it was unthinkable that the LGBT Ministry would be excluded from such an important event:

> I wanted members to be recognised as a resource we could draw on, just like other groups in the parish. Including the LGBT Ministry [in the Christmas feast] was a way to play with negative stereotypes. The group's table, which was decorated with a rainbow flag, was one of the outstanding ones, and the members were extraordinarily good hosts. It was tremendously important for the group to feel that they were, without a shadow of a doubt, making a contribution to the life of the parish.

THE FIGHT CONTINUES

Although stable for the time being, the LGBT Ministry faces an uncertain future. 'Our funding is limited, and the needs of LGBT people, especially refugees and migrants, are so great,' says Ricus.

Yet these ever-present challenges have done little to dampen the leadership's commitment or enthusiasm. Funding is important, Dumisani admits, but it isn't everything:

> It would be a shame if we can't help members with practical things, but whatever happens we will continue to provide spiritual and emotional care. LGBT people deserve a place where they can openly explore their faith, and that is something we can always offer.

CHAPTER 5

THE STORIES

A NOTE ON THE STORIES

This book has been in development for a number of years. In the period since the interviews were conducted, the narrators have undergone significant shifts in their personal lives. Some have formed or ended romantic partnerships, some have experienced positive or negative shifts in familial relationships, and some have embarked on new business ventures or study pathways. An oral history project is always a time capsule, in that it records people's experiences, memories and perspectives at a particular moment in time. While the narrators featured here are still happy to have their stories published, they expressed a desire for me to emphasise that their lives have since moved in many different directions.

1

WE MUST PREACH LOVE, NOT HATE

Narrated by Dumisani (Zimbabwe)

Most of my friends call me Dumi. I am 45 years old and have been living in South Africa since 2009. I joined the LGBT Ministry not long after arriving in Johannesburg. A few months later, I took over as co-ordinator. The LGBT Ministry has been a very important part of my life; it is a space in which I can practise my faith while also fighting for social justice. I am very proud of everything the group has achieved. Even with all the obstacles we face, we continue to fight for our rights. We are a family.

CHILDHOOD AND FAMILY

I grew up in Bulawayo, Zimbabwe's second city. I am the third of five children: I have an older brother and an older sister, as well as a younger brother and a younger sister. My parents divorced when I was still young, leaving my mother to raise her children as a single parent. She was a talented seamstress and would provide for us by sewing and selling clothes. She worked very long hours, diligently saving for our food, rent and school fees.

My grandmother looked after us children while our mother worked. She was loving and kind, but also very strict. Each evening the front gate would be closed at 6 pm sharp. By then we had to be inside, bathed and seated at the table for supper. I hated this routine at the time, but now I see that it brought stability to our lives.

Faith was an important feature of my childhood. My mother was raised Catholic, but converted to Methodism later in life, meaning I too changed churches. I was a devout child and loved going to worship. As I grew older, I became heavily involved in church activities, such as the Boys Christian Union and the Scripture Union. It was through these church structures that I

'The animal that best represents me is the zebra. It is always sought out by other animals. Yes, it looks beautiful, it decorates everywhere it goes, but mostly it is prey. I know I add value and character wherever I am, but sometimes people take advantage of my generosity.'

developed the leadership skills that I still use today. Church also taught me a sense of responsibility, specifically the belief that one has to step up in order to create change.

NEW FEELINGS

I was not a very social child and would often spend time alone. It is a characteristic I inherited from my grandmother. Even today I tend to keep to myself. Still, I enjoyed school, despite my introverted tendencies. My grades were good, and I got on well with my teachers and peers. The other learners knew I was different, but no one had the language to explain how or why. One time, when we were all mucking about, some other boys pretended to propose to me like they would a girl. They were only teasing, but there must have been something to it. I guess they could see a quality in me that I had not yet recognised in myself.

It was only in high school that I came to recognise my attraction to men. There was one guy in particular, Ishmael, whom I had a big crush on. There was something about the way he smelt that I found intoxicating. I started noticing other boys too. We all used to wear short shorts when playing sports and I would be mesmerised by my classmates' thighs as they ran around. I gave one of them a nice gold chain, hoping he would like me, although I was still too young to grasp the full nature of my feelings. Sometimes I would even sit next to men on the bus and imagine we were a couple going on a trip. It wasn't so much a sexual thing as a fascination with romance.

These feelings were confusing, but they weren't scary or upsetting. While I knew I couldn't tell anyone, I didn't feel immoral or dirty. I just knew I was different.

BIG CHANGES

I had my first gay encounter when I was 19. I had just finished high school and was working part-time while awaiting my matric results. The guy was a friend from church. We used to go back to his place after service, just to talk and hang out, and soon enough I developed a crush. One day, when we were sitting in his room, I couldn't take it any longer: I leant forward and kissed him. He reciprocated the kiss, much to my relief. After that we would fool around regularly. I remember him sending a Christmas card in which he had written 'I love you'. I was giddy with happiness – it was just what I had always dreamed of. Our fling continued for a couple of months, right up until I left for teachers' college.

Once I had my qualification, I was posted to a school in Hwange. I soon joined a local church and it was there that I met a guy who seemed flirtatious. We eventually kissed, but then he started panicking. He said the Bible was against homosexuality and accused me of tempting him into sin. Back then blackmailing gay men wasn't common and so it didn't turn into a huge drama. I am still thankful he didn't tell anyone else in the congregation.

In 1995, I quit my teaching job and moved back to Bulawayo. My mother had taken ill and I wanted to be close to her. She died soon after; I was only 22 years old. My mother and I had always been close, and her passing affected me greatly. For the next decade, I was a lost soul. Unable to accept her death, I started to behave irresponsibly.

Short of money, I accepted a job at an office supplies company. It was through this job that I made my first gay friend, Lionel. I could tell he was like me as soon as he walked into the shop. Lionel was not only at ease with his sexuality – something that impressed me greatly – but also well connected to the LGBT community. We quickly became friends, and through him I was introduced to a new world.

Lionel and I were always painting the town red. In those days there was a gay house party on the last Friday of each month. It was hosted by Raymond, a white man who lived in an upmarket part of town. I clearly remember going to Raymond's place for the first time. I walked in and saw men openly kissing other men – an amazing sight to behold! It was also my first time seeing people in drag. Everyone there seemed totally carefree. I remember thinking, 'Wow, all these people are just like me!' It was exactly what I had been searching for.

Raymond was linked to Gays and Lesbians of Zimbabwe (GALZ), even though the organisation didn't have a strong presence in Bulawayo back then. It was at one of his parties that I received my first invitation to a GALZ event. I had already heard about the organisation thanks to the controversy earlier that year. GALZ had applied to host a table at the Zimbabwean International Book Fair, but had been rejected after the government put pressure on the event organisers. It was this fiasco that inspired Robert Mugabe's infamous comment about gay people being 'worse than dogs and pigs'. That speech was reported in all of the newspapers and created a big stir. Ordinary people who didn't know anything about LGBT things were suddenly outraged.

The first GALZ event I attended was a safe-sex workshop, followed by a raucous party. It was in Harare and so I had to catch the train up. I had asked an uncle to collect me at the station and drive me to the venue. For some stupid reason, I gave him the phone number for the GALZ office. Later that evening, my uncle called to see how I was getting on. A queen picked up and said, 'Gays and Lesbians of Zimbabwe. Helloooooooo!' My uncle was dumbstruck. When he finally asked for me, the queen yelled out very loudly: 'Dumi, sissy, you have a phone call.' My uncle confronted me, asking if I was at GALZ. I stayed silent, unsure of what to say. After a few minutes, he hung up. My uncle never came back to collect me. Thankfully, GALZ was able to provide accommodation and transport. I didn't really care that my uncle knew – I was too busy drinking and partying – but it did teach me a valuable lesson in discretion. My uncle didn't raise the subject again or tell the family, much to my relief.

SEARCHING FOR SOMETHING

In 1996, I moved to Harare. I had been going there regularly for about six months, seeing a guy I had met at the GALZ workshop. Relocating seemed like the sensible thing to do. After all, there was nothing keeping me in Bulawayo.

Harare didn't bring the stability I craved. Quite the opposite, in fact! My life was messy; I didn't have control over my emotions or behaviours. I was careless with my relationships, careless with my health, careless with my finances. My mother had been my anchor and without her I struggled to stay moored. I did many things of which I am ashamed: lying, stealing, betraying people who cared for me.

Things improved once I started volunteering at GALZ. I mainly helped out with publications and resources, a job that I loved and was good at. In 2003, I was taken on as a proper employee. That was the first time my skills and potential were properly recognised. I was overjoyed.

GALZ was a positive and supportive environment, but like any workplace it had its challenges. It is difficult to work for a community organisation when you are part of that very same community. Things can get murky quickly. At times I found it difficult to maintain boundaries between my professional life and my personal life.

My time at GALZ is something I treasure. I am still close with my former colleagues, and I am grateful for all that they taught me. On reflection, I can see how much my involvement with GALZ has shaped my life. It undoubtedly planted the seed for my future activism, as well as giving me confidence in my abilities.

It certainly wasn't an easy job. The government was vocal in its opposition to our work and put us under a lot of pressure. Over the years there have been numerous raids and arrests, especially at election times. My most vivid memory from that period is the 2003 International Book Fair, the first one GALZ participated in since the 1995 controversy. As the person in charge of publications, I was tasked with managing the stall. When Mugabe arrived, the police surrounded the table, trying to block us from the president's line of sight. It didn't work, and I clearly remember Mugabe looking me in the eye as he walked slowly by.

A VERY PAINFUL TIME

It was around this time that I was publicly outed. The *ZimDaily* published an article about my involvement with GALZ, including information about my private life. They had included a photo and so there was no hiding. There was a huge reaction: people would stare, point and gossip. I remember greeting a friend on the street only to have his sister yell abuse at me: 'My brother isn't gay! Stop trying to seduce him.' That was only the tip of the iceberg.

People in Bulawayo soon found out and didn't react well. Very few of my old friends would even acknowledge me. It wasn't long before my family heard the news. I decided to send my brother a letter explaining the situation. I wanted to tell him about my sexuality in my own words. He was surprisingly encouraging, saying it is my life and I should be free to live it how I want.

Most people in my family have reluctantly accepted my sexuality, although it is still rarely mentioned. Some of my siblings don't agree with homosexuality, but they refrain from making negative comments. They have even visited me when I have lived with boyfriends. My grandmother doesn't approve, but she still loves me. Looking back, I think my mother always knew. She would tease me when a male friend dropped over, saying it was my boyfriend, but she did so in jest rather than spite. I know she would be supportive if she were still alive.

Being outed was one of the most painful periods in my life. The only way I survived was by blocking everything out. People were saying the most vicious things. If I had let their words get to me, I would probably have done something terrible. All I could do was carry on, day by day.

In May 2009, I moved back to my family home. Things had got out of control in Harare and I needed to escape. My brother quickly realised how much I was suffering. He knew I would be better off in South Africa, that it was my only real shot at happiness, and offered to fund my journey. It all happened very quickly: I bought a bus ticket, told my boyfriend I was leaving and later that evening I was on my way. Leaving wasn't easy, but I knew it was the right thing to do.

A NEW BEGINNING

I arrived in Johannesburg in July 2009. A cousin collected me at Park Station and took me back to his place in Hillbrow. He and his family welcomed me into their home, but I still felt like an imposition. I didn't have a job and was only surviving through the generosity of friends and family. My cousin and his wife didn't know about my sexuality, though I suspect my cousin had an inkling. His wife wanted to set me up with her younger sister and things became awkward when I said I wasn't interested. My cousin stood up for me, telling his wife that I would never propose to her sister. That is why I think he knew about me. Even so, I didn't feel comfortable talking openly about my sexuality. Being forced back into the closet made me miserable.

With very little to fill my days, I would head to Park Station and cruise for guys. Back then it was a popular gay pick-up spot. If you were lucky enough to meet someone, you could go back to his place, or just have a quickie in the toilet. We didn't do it for money. This was before Grindr and other gay dating apps, back when cruising was the easiest way to hook up with someone.

It was at Park Station that I met my next boyfriend, Rhu. In 2010, we moved in together in Mofolo, Soweto. Rhu helped me get a job at a call centre, where I worked for almost three years. Being in a committed relationship and having a steady income allowed me to get my life in order. This was the first time in a long while that I felt stable and happy. I began to attend church again, and even joined the Christian Life Community.

A SPACE OF HEALING

My faith has been the backbone of my life. There were times when I wasn't attending church, but I never lost my faith. No matter how out of control my life was, I would still pray for guidance, confident that God had not abandoned me. That being said, I think my distance from the church contributed to my problems; instead of using my faith to heal after my mother's passing, I ran away from my pain. Not being part of a spiritual community left me feeling lost and alone.

When I got to Johannesburg, I realised I needed to reconnect with my faith and started looking around for a church. By then I had returned to the denomination into which I had been born. I now believe it was God's plan all along for me to return to Catholicism.

I was still living in Hillbrow when I found Holy Trinity. I was impressed from the very first Mass I attended. Fr Russell delivered the sermon, and I remember liking his tone and approach. I became even more impressed once I learnt about the church's social apostolate. Back then Holy Trinity even ran a support group for women who had undergone abortions! It was the church's progressive outlook and commitment to social justice that appealed to me. I knew straightaway it was the church for me.

One Sunday, I noticed an advertisement for what was then called the Gay and Lesbian Group. My first thought was that it was a pray-the-gay-away type of situation, but my curiosity was stronger than my apprehension. I sent an email to Ricus, the group's co-ordinator, and he gave me all the details.

Walking into my first meeting, I was both nervous and excited. I wanted to meet other gay Christians, especially those with similar life experiences to mine, but I had no idea if those were the type of people I would find. But my nerves didn't last long: I immediately recognised some friendly faces from back home in Zimbabwe. That first meeting was small, just a few guys sitting around and talking, but I remember being grateful to be part of the conversation.

After three months, Ricus asked me to take over as group co-ordinator. He said he had discussed it with the other members and that they were keen for me take on a leadership role. I am not sure why Ricus approached me – perhaps it was because of my work with GALZ, or perhaps he could see something in my personality. Whatever the reason, I am glad he asked.

It was in late 2010 that I took over as chairperson. The group has faced many hurdles in the intervening years, but I am as committed to it as ever. In a way, the LGBT Ministry is my baby; I even have sleepless nights if there are tensions between members. Some people don't realise I do the job voluntarily. They assume there are endless funds and that I get paid for being the co-ordinator. In reality, I do it because I believe in LGBT rights.

I do my job as best I can. I spend a lot of time preparing for the fortnightly meetings, and I think long and hard about how I can help people grow. It isn't always easy: our members come from diverse backgrounds and often have differing needs. Some have outlandish expectations of what I can do for them.

There are benefits to the job, of course. I often get to participate in different forums and trainings, including some international conferences. I see these opportunities as blessings and try to use them to help my community. I just wish more people knew that the LGBT Ministry is a passion project. None of us in leadership roles get paid, and the group itself runs on a skeleton budget. We only survive thanks to the generosity of the church and our partner organisations.

AN EVOLVING MANDATE

There have been many changes to the group over the years. However, our mission remains the same: to provide a safe haven for people of all sexualities and genders, especially those who have been kicked out of churches, families or communities. We offer spiritual care, something that LGBT people are often denied. In recent years, we have placed more emphasis on psychosocial wellbeing. This shift came about because of needs within the group, rather than a deliberate decision by the leadership team. More and more people were asking for help with accommodation, food and medication. We responded as best we could, but it was always ad hoc, basically whatever we could arrange at short notice. Over time this part of our work has become more structured.

Another recent focus has been helping with documentation. Many of our members wanted to get their asylum status formalised, but were scared about engaging with the Department of Home Affairs (DHA). This is because DHA officials are often intolerant and corrupt. I ran a few sessions on the asylum process, explaining how it all works, and also invited lawyers and activists to answer members' questions.

The other way we help is through skills development. This part of our work also emerged organically. A few people approached the leadership team and requested money for this or that course. More and more members began asking for this type of assistance and we realised that a formal approach was necessary. We reached out to some donors and fortunately received support from the International Christian AIDS Network. We don't have a big pot of money and so have had to limit the training programme to short vocational courses, such as computer literacy, home-based care or hospitality skills. The main thing is that a course helps someone find work.

Perhaps we made a mistake in branching out like this. There are just so many people in need, and we are often overwhelmed with requests for help. Sometimes it feels like we have bitten off more than we can chew. But I also don't think it is possible to provide pastoral care without addressing a person's material needs. You can't grow spiritually when you are struggling to eat. That is why we do our best to help members in crisis, or at the very least refer them to an appropriate service.

Like everyone in the group, I have had to ask for help. When my job at the call centre ended, I received financial support from the other members. Another time I was very sick and needed help paying for a doctor's appointment. Having been on both sides of the coin – that is, having both sought and given help – puts me in a unique position. I understand what our members go through and that makes it easier for them to approach me. I am grateful for the trust placed in me and do my best to honour this responsibility.

Yet sometimes the burden weighs heavily on me. Over the years I have seen members really struggle. Some people have become seriously ill, and a few have even passed away. I will never forget the times when I have comforted dying members in hospital. Some had no relatives willing to care for them and so it fell on the group to provide them with love in their final days. There have even been times when the group had to raise funds for bodies to be repatriated.

For some members, the stress of being an LGBT migrant becomes too much. I have watched people turn to drugs and alcohol to numb their pain. Others have ended up on the street. It is hard to watch, but I will never turn my back on a member. I know from my own past what it is like to be out of control.

CHALLENGES AND OPPORTUNITIES

The LGBT Ministry is far from perfect. Over the years we have faced many hurdles, including financial pressures, personality clashes and distrust from the broader parish. It hasn't been easy dealing with these issues, and I am thankful for the support we have received from Fr Russell and Fr Graham.

Like Holy Trinity itself, the LGBT Ministry is a transitory space. Some people only come along when they want something, disappearing as soon as that need is fulfilled. I am not criticising anyone who makes that decision – each person has their own reasons for joining and leaving – but it does make it hard to build up the group.

I hope the LGBT Ministry continues to grow. We have achieved a lot over the years, but we still have more to do. I honestly believe we provide a vital service: we are one of only a handful of places offering spiritual care to LGBT people, especially migrants. Other faith communities can learn a lot from Holy Trinity. Religion plays such an important role in our society, yet LGBT people are being forced out of churches and mosques.

As a person of faith, I know just how important it is to have inclusive religious institutions. Churches should be places of safety, not fear. The LGBT community is sick of being told that we need exorcisms. We are not possessed. We are just looking for somewhere to practise our faith. Religious leaders need to look to Jesus and follow His example. The Bible shows us that Jesus loved and cared for all people; religious leaders must do the same. There is one question they should ask themselves: what would Jesus do? I know He would care for those in need, not turn them away.

The LGBT Ministry can serve as a model for other churches. Starting a support group is an easy way to provide care for those who are suffering. It can also be a way to build skills and confidence among those who are on the margins of society. I have had the pleasure of seeing our members excel – in their studies, in their relationships, in their careers. These successes show what is possible if religious communities adopt an inclusive attitude.

We can't shy away from tough conversations; we must strive to bring everything out into the open. This goes beyond religion and sexuality. There are still people being raped, and we aren't talking about it. There are still people who aren't getting proper medical treatment, and we aren't talking about it. There is still too much silence around HIV, abortion, gender-based violence and other issues. This must change.

I also want to help South Africans develop empathy and compassion. They need to realise that people migrate for many reasons and that one day it could be them seeking sanctuary. People should treat migrants the way they would want to be treated if the situation were reversed. People across the continent need to know that LGBT people don't choose their gender or sexuality. It is a natural part of who we are – none of us want to be mistreated or shamed. Our straight brothers and sisters can play a role in ending hate. Our governments don't seem interested in stopping homophobia and transphobia. It is up to everyday people to take a stand. Together we can win the fight against ignorance and intolerance.

2

WE DESERVE FREEDOM

Narrated by Mr D (Cameroon)

I am a 33-year-old bisexual man from Cameroon. My country is very conservative and so I didn't have many opportunities to explore my sexuality while growing up. That made it hard for me to come to terms with who I am. It was only after moving to South Africa that I felt free to express my desires. But even here it can be hard, sometimes dangerous, to identify as anything but straight. The Cameroonian migrant community can be very homophobic; I have to be cautious whenever I am around my countrymen. Joining the LGBT Ministry was an important step in my journey towards self-acceptance. Religion has always been an important part of my life, but for a long time I struggled to reconcile my identity with my beliefs. Now I feel comfortable in who I am.

CHILDHOOD AND FAMILY

I was born in Douala, Cameroon's biggest city. I was raised in a stable household, with loving and supportive parents. I was close to both my mother and my father, and I still have a special bond with my mother. Sadly, my father passed away in 2000, when I was 15 years old. His death was a blow to our whole family. My mother suddenly became the primary breadwinner and had to work harder than ever. We all had to make sacrifices: my sisters and I transferred to public schools, and I found a part-time job.

I have very fond memories of my father. He was a policeman and was well respected in our community. What I remember most of all is his caring nature. He loved to play games, no matter how exhausted he was, and would take every opportunity to spoil my siblings and me. Whenever

'I identify with a lion because I can be wild and hard to control. I am a hyper person, but that doesn't mean I am crazy. I just have a lot of energy, a lot of drive, a lot of excitement. If that energy isn't contained, I go wild – but not in a destructive way.'

he came home from work, he would bring us a treat. It was only ever something small, usually a lolly, but it meant the world to us.

My mother and I had an awesome relationship; I treasured her with my whole heart. She was a seamstress, and when I was young she would sit me on her sewing table so I could watch her work. I would be mesmerised by how quickly she worked the fabric, guiding it carefully under the needle. Sometimes she would put my feet on the pedal and let me 'drive' her machine. It is impossible for me think about those times without smiling.

I have three siblings – an older brother, an older sister and a younger sister – with a three-year gap between each of us. My brother lived with our grandparents in the village and so we didn't see much of him growing up. It was only after my dad passed, when I was already in boarding school, that he came back to live with the family.

Growing up, my sisters and I were very close. We went to the same school and would always walk there and back together. In our free time we would occupy ourselves with games: hopscotch, dodgeball, skipping. These were all considered girlie games – definitely not something for boys – but I still loved them. I guess it shows that I have always been different.

SEXUAL AWAKENING

At 13 I started boarding school in Bamenda, a city in the English-speaking region of Cameroon. That is one of the reasons I was sent there: my mother wanted me to be fluent in English.

It was a co-ed institution and many of my friends were girls, just like in primary school. This seemed perfectly natural to all of us; the girls weren't fazed by my presence and treated me like one of them. The other thing that marked me out as different was my talent for certain subjects. I excelled at literature, history and languages, all of which were considered more suitable for girls. This led to teasing from some boys. They found my behaviour suspicious and would call me a *pédé*, the French word for 'faggot'. The word would hit me like a punch to the stomach, because being a *pédé* was considered shameful and disgusting.

When I was 15, I began to feel sexually attracted to other boys in my dorm, something that made me frightened. I hoped it was a phase, that the feelings would pass, but they never did.

Things are bound to happen when you live in a single-sex dorm. We all had to share beds and during the night our bodies would touch. One thing would lead to another, which wasn't that surprising considering we were hormonal teenagers. Most boys experimented in some way, but it was different for me. I know this because I have spoken to one of the boys as an adult. When I mentioned the things we did in the dorm, he became angry. He was clearly ashamed, and he warned me against ever bringing it up again.

LIFE AS AN ADULT

After I finished secondary school, I began teaching at a business college. I wasn't able to pursue my dream of becoming a journalist because my family didn't have the funds. I didn't mind too much because I enjoyed teaching. I was good at it, too! I ran computer courses and took pleasure in watching my students develop new skills. Most importantly, the job paid enough for me to support my family. By then I was the family's main wage earner.

My job also gave me independence, something I greatly valued. It was in Bamenda, the same city where I had studied, and so I wasn't able to see my family often. I didn't have anyone controlling my movements or checking up on me. It wasn't that I hated my family; I just needed space from them.

It was during this period that I had my first relationships, both of which were with women. My first relationship was when I was 19 and lasted for just under two years; the second one started when I was 21 and lasted for four years. While I had strong attachments to both women, I am not sure I would have started the relationships if it weren't for peer pressure. All of the boys my age were dating women and I felt compelled to do the same. To not have a girlfriend would have raised suspicion, and the last thing I needed was to be a topic of gossip.

This was also the time when I first encountered other gay and bisexual men. There was one guy in particular, Samuel, with whom I became very close. We met through a mutual friend, and I knew instantly that he wasn't straight. He must have thought the same about me because he quickly opened up about his sexuality. It was exciting to have someone I could talk to about this stuff. For a long time, Samuel was the only person I could confide in. We spent many hours together, listening to music, chatting about our lives, dreaming of the future. It was the closeness of our friendship that made my second girlfriend suspicious, leading her to break things off with me.

Over time I met other gay and bisexual men, although we were never a big group. I don't think I ever knew more than five others. There were no LGBT organisations back then and so it wasn't easy to find like-minded people. Occasionally I would bump into someone who seemed gay or bisexual, but I would have to be careful in how I broached the subject, just in case I was wrong.

My friends and I would hang out as often as we could. Amongst ourselves we could talk openly about gay things, something that wasn't possible with other people. When we felt like a party, we would go to a tavern or club, but mostly we just chilled at home. If we did go out, we would be careful not to draw attention. We had to party at straight places – there are no LGBT bars in Cameroon – and that can mean danger if you act flamboyantly or show affection.

HOMOPHOBIA IN CAMEROON

My friends and I were mostly left alone, but occasionally we would face discrimination. Usually it was verbal harassment: someone would see us talking in the street and call us *pédés*. If any of us gestured or walked in a feminine way, we would be mocked and maybe threatened.

If you are suspected of being gay in Cameroon, you will be shunned and attacked. One time, after I fooled around with a guy, he told my neighbours that I had assaulted him. People in the community stopped greeting me, some stared and whispered, and others avoided me entirely. I dismissed the rumour as nonsense and, thankfully, people forgot about it. Other LGBT people aren't so lucky. Gossip can be dangerous – you never know what will happen if a story gets back to your family.

The other big danger was police violence. This didn't happen all the time, but when there was an incident, it would trigger panic. Sometimes there would be raids on venues suspected of being LGBT friendly, and every now and then you would hear about someone being sent to jail. All it takes is a hint of suspicion and the authorities can take someone away. Whenever my friends and I heard about someone being beaten or arrested, we would do everything to avoid attracting attention. We would dress more conservatively and stop hanging out together in public.

My friend Pierre had a very serious incident. He was attacked by an angry mob after he was outed. It got so bad that the police came and took him away. They said it was for his own protection, but then they also beat him. I consider myself lucky because I never found myself in that situation. I am also thankful for having left Cameroon before the situation got really bad.

Homophobia in Cameroon is driven by misinformation. People don't understand about different genders and sexualities. They think a man sleeping with another man is a form of witchcraft, a satanic ritual for gaining wealth and influence. The tabloids spread all sorts of lies. They especially like stories about politicians raping young boys to increase their power. A rumour like that is a great way to discredit a rival, but an ordinary person won't understand that it is a political trick.

Tabloid journalists play a big role in fuelling hate. These days it is not uncommon to see sensationalised reports about LGBT people. They include ridiculous claims – for example, that men who have had anal sex must wear nappies because they can't control their bowel movements. The editors print this nonsense because they know it sells papers. They want readers to feel disgust. The stories are always about sex, never love, because scandalous content gets people talking. Priests and politicians spread similar lies. They tell people that we are sick because we have 'unnatural' sex – that is, sex that doesn't make a baby. They don't care that straight people commit all sorts of sins, such as adultery and sex before marriage.

EXPRESSING MY DESIRES

The homophobia in Cameroon made it difficult for me to explore my sexuality. I was too cautious to have a full-on relationship with another man, yet I still experimented in different ways. Just like at boarding school, I would fool around with guys looking for a quick release. There was one time when a colleague stayed at my place after a work event. He slept in my bed and during the night we touched each other, but it wasn't the same for him as it was for me. The next morning he said he would only do it again if I paid him.

When I was 24, I had a sexual encounter with a family friend. We played around for a bit, but it was nothing serious. The next morning he panicked and told my mother I had tried to seduce him. My mother confronted me, demanding I tell her the truth. My heart was pounding, but somehow I managed to keep my cool. I brushed off her questions, saying it was up to her if she chose to believe silly rumours. She looked confused and disappointed, and I was terrified of losing her forever. That is what happens to LGBT people in Cameroon: they are rejected by their families. It is the fear of abandonment that forces us to lead double lives. I was lucky that particular day because my mother dropped the topic. She had too much love for me to push any harder. Deep down, she must know who I am, but that is not the same as acceptance. It is more wilful denial – we both go about our lives, pretending there is nothing different about me.

DREAMING OF A NEW LIFE

I was 25 when I started to seriously consider leaving Cameroon. I was motivated by two factors: first, I knew my sexuality would never be accepted; second, I imagined there would be better job prospects in South Africa. I was desperate to be a good son and provide for my family.

South Africa was on my radar from the beginning. I had seen footage of it during the World Cup and thought it looked beautiful. Johannesburg is also well known in Cameroon as a place of opportunity and prosperity. Those who have emigrated share pictures on social media, presenting their lives as easy and carefree, a portrayal I now know to be untruthful. But the most compelling factor was the country's Constitution, which I had learnt about by chatting with South African guys on the GayRomeo website.

There was a lengthy gap between my decision to migrate and actually leaving. The first step was letting people know. I told my gay friends the full story, explaining that I wanted to be free and happy, and they encouraged me to go for it. Samuel wanted to come with me but wasn't in a financial position to make it happen. I felt bad that I couldn't help him, but now I know it was for the best. A few years after I left, he was able to migrate to the UK.

When I raised the topic with my relatives, I emphasised the economic side of my plan, explaining that I wanted our family to be better off. My mother knew I would do right by the family and gave me all of her savings to put towards the airfare. Yet, even with my mother's contribution, I had to save for a whole year to make my dream a reality.

In Cameroon, we use migration agents to organise visas. The first time my agent applied, my permit was denied, but on the second attempt I was granted a three-month visitor's visa. I spent over a million Central African francs on the two applications – a huge sum for my family. Having used all of my mother's savings in the process, I felt a strong obligation to succeed. I promised myself I would do everything in my power to make her investment worthwhile.

MOVE TO SOUTH AFRICA

By 2011, I had saved enough for a ticket on Kenya Airways. I flew from Douala to Nairobi and then on to Johannesburg. It was my first time on a plane; everything was new and confusing, but also thrilling. I was eager to start my new life and that helped ease my nerves. 'Whatever happens, happens!' I thought as the plane took off.

Before I left Douala, I tracked down the phone number for someone living in Johannesburg. Victor was part of my extended family – a nephew of a distant aunt – so I consider him a cousin-brother. I called Victor when I was in transit in Nairobi: 'I am coming to South Africa,' I said. 'And I am already on the way!' Victor had few options: it would have been frowned upon in our culture if he didn't show me hospitality. He took down my flight details and told me he would meet me at the airport.

Because I was coming from Cameroon, I was treated with suspicion by the immigration officials at O.R. Tambo International Airport. I had a legitimate visa, but they still wanted to check everything. I was taken into a small room and asked a lot of questions. It was a full interrogation, but thankfully they let me go.

Victor was waiting to collect me as promised. As we drove through Johannesburg's suburbs, I was amazed by how different it was to Cameroon: the roads were smooth, the traffic lights were working, the houses were large and modern. It was like being on another planet. I smiled to myself, confident I had made the right decision.

I stayed with Victor for about six months. He was very welcoming and generous; I still use the bed that Victor first bought for me. He would drop me in Braamfontein each day on his way to work. The area has a large Cameroonian community and he said I could find work there. Eventually I landed a job at an internet café. It wasn't the best pay, but at least I could put my computer skills to use. The job turned out to be a godsend because it helped me understand South Africa: how things work, how people interact, what phrases to say, and so on.

Victor also helped me formalise my stay in South Africa. He suggested I get married as soon as possible so I could apply for a spousal visa. He found a woman who was willing and made all the arrangements. I was uncomfortable with the plan, but I didn't have another option.

NEW FRIENDS, NEW OPPORTUNITIES

It was through the internet café that I made my first real friend, a Nigerian guy called Patrick. I could tell he was gay from the moment I saw him. I asked him in Pidgin and he openly admitted his sexuality. We soon became friends, and Patrick introduced me to more and more LGBT people. It was through one of these new friends – a Nigerian who we lovingly call Sister Emmanuelle – that I got my current job. I started out as a regular customer service agent, but after a year I was made a supervisor, a role I have now held for seven years. Once I had a steady job, I was able to dissolve my fake marriage and transfer to a work permit. Back then it wasn't difficult to change visa types, but it certainly wasn't cheap. I ended up spending over R30 000!

STILL STRUGGLING

Although I haven't faced as many obstacles as some LGBT migrants, I have still had to overcome challenges. One difficulty has been housing. Not long after I started at the internet café, I moved into a flat in Braamfontein with four other Cameroonian guys; the place was so small that I had to sleep on the balcony. It didn't take long for my flatmates to become suspicious of my sexuality. I wasn't bringing any women home, and I struggled to join in with their conversations about sex. If any of them saw me on the street with Patrick, they would mention it in front of the others, the disapproval evident in their tone. The comments soon turned nasty: 'Ah, this one is a dirty *pédé*,' they would say. 'We can't trust him. He will try to rape us.' I felt increasingly unsafe and moved out as soon as I could.

Since then I have lived in many locations: Hillbrow, CBD, the southern suburbs, the northern suburbs. Sometimes I have moved of my own accord, but other times it was because a place became dangerous, either because of my sexuality or my nationality. Since February 2018, I have lived with two gay asylum seekers. I am the only one with a job and so I pay for everything: rent, groceries, utilities. It puts a lot of financial pressure on me, but I feel a responsibility to help those who are less fortunate.

The other difficulty is my mother's constant requests for money. I know things are tough for her and I wish I could do more to help, but I already send home every spare cent. I am not angry with my mother because I know how tough her life is, but her relentless demands stress me out. There have even been times when I have ignored her calls, and that breaks my heart.

LIVING OUT AND PROUD

It was only when I came to South Africa that I was able to embrace my sexuality. In countries like Cameroon, people who are attracted to the same sex must hide themselves. This adds to the feeling that you are sick and dirty. Even though I had gay friends back home, I never felt like I was normal. That changed when I arrived in Johannesburg: I started seeing people like me, talking to people like me, and that made me feel more confident. Knowing there are laws protecting LGBT people also helped me accept myself. I realise there are still problems in South Africa, but the government's recognition of LGBT rights makes a huge difference.

My gay life in Johannesburg really started when I met Patrick. He took me along to the LGBT Ministry at Holy Trinity and also introduced me to his friends. These guys would take me along to popular gay spots, like Factory and Buffalo Bills, where we always had a great time.

I am thankful for the freedoms I have in South Africa. Living here has allowed me to do things I could only dream of in Cameroon, such as going to gay clubs and having a steady relationship. I was with my South African boyfriend for four years – from 2014 to 2018 – and we had so much fun together. He was originally from KwaZulu-Natal, and he and I used to go on trips to his village. I am sad that our relationship ended, but I guess these things happen.

Even though I have accepted my bisexuality, I still can't come out to my family. I wish I could tell my sisters – especially my younger one – but it is too risky. I don't want to lose the people I love. It is sad that I can't be open and honest, but that is the reality of Cameroon.

A PERSON OF FAITH

I believe in God with my whole heart. My faith has always been an important part of who I am, and that hasn't changed since I moved to South Africa.

When I was young, I was part of a Baptist congregation. I have beautiful memories of my family singing in church, praising God with our voices. I continued attending services at my Baptist boarding school, but often felt conflicted because of my sexuality. I prayed many times to be straight, not understanding back then that this was God's plan for me.

Cameroon is a very religious country (most people identify as Catholic) and that shapes people's attitudes. If homosexuality is ever mentioned, it will be a comment like 'God created Adam and Eve, not Adam and Steve'. The general belief is that the Bible only condones sex between a man and a woman, within marriage.

After I moved to Johannesburg, I converted to Pentecostalism. I was still staying with Victor and he invited me along to his church. I was impressed from the beginning. I loved the atmosphere, the singing, the preaching – everything about it felt great. What struck me was how different it was to a Baptist church. You definitely can't fall asleep during a Pentecostal service! I don't think one is necessarily better than the other, but right now I prefer the energy of a Pentecostal service.

I still attend Victor's church, even though I now live in a different part of the city. It is a space where I feel comfortable and safe; I am a valued member of the congregation. I choose not to disclose my sexuality, but not because I have been exposed to prejudice. Unlike some other Pentecostal preachers, mine has never mentioned homosexuality. I am thankful that my church is a tolerant space.

FINDING A NEW FAMILY

It was in 2013 that I first learnt about the LGBT Ministry. Patrick had been pushing for me to come along to Holy Trinity, saying the church had a special group for LGBT people. I couldn't believe such a thing existed. The fact that it was at a Catholic church made it even more unbelievable.

I met up with Patrick before my first meeting. I wanted us to go together because I was scared. My biggest fear was meeting another Cameroonian and being outed. Gossip travels fast in migrant communities; I was petrified my family would find out about my sexuality. Looking back, I realise this is a silly thing to have been worried about: any other Cameroonians would have been there for the exact same reason. It is easy to be paranoid when you are in the closet.

It turns out I had nothing to fear: that first meeting was a lovely experience. It took a while for me to feel comfortable, but once I started talking I realised how important it is to be honest and open. It was reassuring to know there were people who could understand my inner turmoil. I remember feeling like a weight had been lifted off me.

Over time the group became my second family. Being part of a safe space allowed me to work through issues with which I had long struggled. This emotional support is the group's best feature. Many LGBT migrants are isolated and scared; they might not have friends who understand about their lives. Even though I no longer attend meetings, I am still in contact with people I met through the LGBT Ministry, and I still lean on them if I need help. I am very thankful for these friendships.

The group's biggest impact was in helping me rethink my faith. When I was young, I thought that being gay was a bad thing, an abomination before God, a spiritual sickness. The LGBT Ministry allowed me to confront these negative feelings. I learnt that it is possible to be an LGBT person *and* a Christian. Hearing a priest say that LGBT people are God's children and are loved by Him had a huge impact on me.

THE POWER OF ACCEPTANCE

Holy Trinity showed me exactly why we need inclusive religious spaces. I have seen first-hand how the LGBT Ministry has helped people make peace with their sexuality. Religion is important for many LGBT people, yet we are forced to hide who we are in order to attend church. We are facing real discrimination, real hostility, and this makes it hard for us to grow. If a person comes to a church wanting to know God, then they should be welcomed, no matter how they identify.

I am lucky because my pastor doesn't preach homophobia, but I have friends who have had very different experiences. They have had to sit through sermons in which they are called all sorts of names. It is very upsetting to be told that you are possessed and going to hell. These messages drive LGBT people away from God.

My message to faith leaders is to be more accommodating. We have all been made according to God's plan, and each of us is deserving of His love. Faith leaders must take responsibility for promoting diversity. They have the power to challenge lies, such as this myth that we are demonic and diseased. There are too many people out there who want to harm us. They excuse their prejudice with Bible quotes, but these verses are often taken out of context. Pastors should be confronting such intolerance head-on. They must preach love, not hate. We didn't choose to be this way: it is how God made us. We must honour His creation.

DREAMS FOR THE FUTURE

I pray for Cameroon to change. People back home are stuck in a negative mindset. They need to be educated on LGBT rights so that they can look beyond the myths. Right now LGBT Cameroonians have to hide. That is not fair: we deserve our freedom. It is unhealthy for people to live in fear. If you are known to be gay in Cameroon, you will be an outcast and an object of ridicule. There is a chance you will be beaten and left for dead. It has happened before: LGBT activists have been tortured and killed, just for who they are. I wish my country could be more like South Africa, where LGBT people can live openly.

I think South Africa is a good country, but there is still too much violence. Locals need to realise that LGBT migrants are human beings and that we deserve respect. I hope the South African government will continue helping LGBT people. The other day I saw footage of President Ramaphosa saying that LGBT people have a right to protection. What an amazing thing to see! Nowhere else on the continent would a politician say that. I hope more African leaders will follow his example.

3

ONLY LOVE CAN BRING UNITY

Narrated by D.C. (Zimbabwe)

I am a 38-year-old lesbian woman from Bulawayo. I moved to Johannesburg in 2003, thinking life would be much easier here. Whenever people back home spoke of South Africa, they described it as a land of milk and honey. During my journey to Johannesburg, I dreamed about all the things I wanted to achieve, like finding a job so I could support my children. Things haven't turned out quite like that. It is very hard to get by without a South African ID book. I have been on a temporary asylum permit for 14 years and still have no idea when or if a decision on my refugee status will be made.

FAMILY AND EDUCATION

I had a happy childhood, even though my family struggled. Things got much worse when my father died in 1993. I was only 13 at the time. My father was self-employed and the family's sole breadwinner. Things were tough after he passed. My mother hardly had time to mourn him. She knew it was up to her to look after us and so decided to start growing and selling vegetables. She was adamant that her children would continue at school, no matter how hard it was to raise the fees. Life wasn't easy, especially for my mother, but through the grace of God we survived.

My mother has always been the rock of our family. After she became the head of the household, she worked tirelessly to give us a decent life. No matter how bad things got, we always had food on the table. Occasionally we would argue, especially when I was a teenager, but she was always there for me in the end. Her defining features were her strength and determination, and for that I have always admired her.

'It might seem strange, but I think I am most like a sheep. It is their softness I relate to. I am a mother and am very nurturing. I have a big heart and am gentle by nature.'

I have two brothers – one is older and one is younger. We used to fight when we were kids, just like all siblings, but most of the time we had a good relationship. I was never a girlie girl so that made it easier for us to get along. In fact, I hung out with boys much more than I ever did with girls. It is still the same today.

In 1996, I fell pregnant with my first child. I wasn't even in a relationship with the guy. I was just acting out, being a silly teenager, and I gave in to peer pressure. Being pregnant was tough: the other learners teased me, making me feel ashamed and humiliated. I managed to hide the pregnancy from my family for the first few months, but eventually my mother noticed. She was more embarrassed than angry; her biggest concern was what other people might say. Yet my mother still acted with love and compassion, helping me prepare for the baby's arrival. The one thing she insisted on was that I return to school as soon as possible.

I finished high school in 1997. I didn't graduate with the highest marks – I was more interested in sports than academic pursuits – but it was still an achievement, especially as a young mother. I immediately started looking for work, but couldn't find anything. Zimbabwe's economic troubles were only just starting then, but it was already difficult to make a living.

In 2000, after being unemployed for two years, I relocated to Harare, thinking I would have a better chance of finding work. I moved in with my aunt, but she treated me like a slave, forcing me to do all her domestic work. She then sent me to look after my great-grandmother in the rural areas. This made no sense: what I needed was a job so that I could support my daughter. I returned to Harare after a few months, determined to find work, but again my aunt mistreated me. Her abuse forced me to seek comfort in the hands of a man, and I fell pregnant for the second time. I was so frightened: how was I going to provide for two children? I knew I had to make a plan. I decided to move back in with my mum so I could help with her business. In the end I took over the food stall. The small income I made from selling vegetables had to support five of us: my mother, my younger brother, my two children and me.

A DANGEROUS JOURNEY

By 2005, the economic situation in Zimbabwe was terrible, with most of the population struggling to survive. The political climate was also getting more and more restrictive. I always had a strong interest in politics, but it was too dangerous to speak openly or to get involved in social activism. These were the two main reasons why I decided to leave: first, I wanted to make money so that I could support my family; second, I wanted to be free to express my political views. My sexuality wasn't a major motivation because back then I was still denying my true feelings. I knew I was attracted to women, but I hadn't allowed myself to explore those desires.

I didn't tell anyone about my decision to migrate. I was worried my mother would try to stop me, and I couldn't face telling my children directly. I organised to leave on a Sunday since I knew my mother would be catching up with friends from church. When I could see that she was distracted, I threw a plastic bag with some clothes out the window. I wanted to avoid passing through the kitchen with my bag since I knew it would raise suspicion. The only thing I was carrying when I waved goodbye was my favourite novel. I told my mother I was going to my friend's house to swap it for another book, and then I left.

The transport I had organised was waiting at a nearby bus stop. My heart was beating so fast, both from fear and excitement. As I climbed into the back of the van, I saw that it was already full of people. I smiled nervously as I squeezed into a spot. The drive to the border was very uncomfortable as we were squashed tightly and the road was bumpy. It was about six in the evening when we finally arrived at Beitbridge.

Around midnight, we had a briefing with the *amagumagumas*. I didn't have a passport and so wasn't able to cross the border legally. It was only then that our journey really began. We were using the old train bridge, rather than the river, and had to pull ourselves up the pylons using ropes. Once we were all on the underside of the bridge, we walked slowly across, one behind the other, in complete silence. It was pitch-black, and I remember hearing baboons barking in the distance. I don't think I have ever been so scared: one wrong move and I would fall into the crocodile-infested river.

Disembarking was no easier than getting up. Again, a rope was used, but this time the *amagumaguma* helped to lower us. There were two levels to get down before reaching the ground. I could feel the *amagumaguma* rubbing himself up against me, but there was nothing I could do. Once we were at the lowest level, he told me to jump down and roll onto the ground. I had bruises on my hands and my head was aching, almost as if I had been struck with a rock.

After everyone was on the ground, we were given further instructions. We were told to move in a quiet line, just like schoolkids going to assembly. We couldn't make a sound, not even a whisper, in case the border guards heard. I am not sure how far we walked – it felt like time had frozen. The final obstacle was crossing the fence, but the *amagumaguma* knew where we could get through. From there we walked to the van waiting to collect us.

When we got to Musina, we encountered a nasty surprise. We had paid to be transported all the way to Johannesburg, but the driver didn't have enough money for fuel, let alone food and other supplies. After scrounging money from a few of us, the driver filled the tank and we were on our way. I was excited, but also exhausted. I soon nodded off. When I finally woke up, I could see the lights of eGoli – the City of Gold.

ALWAYS ON THE MOVE

I had arranged to stay in Yeoville with a former neighbour from Bulawayo, but it turned out she was having problems with her husband – lots and lots of fights – and after a few days I had to leave. I managed to contact a friend's brother and explain my predicament. He was at work and couldn't pick me up in Yeoville, but said I could stay with him if I made it to Mzimhlophe in Soweto.

I remember sitting quietly in the taxi, listening to other passengers, unable to follow the conversation. I was confused and scared. We passed signs with lots of arrows and place names; I had no idea where to get off. I handed the driver a piece of paper with the street name. He said something in Sesotho, a language I didn't yet understand. All I could do was smile and nod.

When I found the property, I was shocked. It was a small house surrounded by shacks. I assumed I would be staying in the house, but an old man directed me to one of the shacks. It was my first time inside such a dwelling. There was one bed, one hotplate and a broken cupboard. I wondered where I would sleep since I was sharing with my friend and his two brothers.

That night I was given a blanket and some cardboard to put on the ground. I shed a tear as I lay down on the cold floor. In the morning, I was given a bucket to use as a bath. We had to take turns using it to wash ourselves. I was sad, but I took comfort in the fact that I had shelter.

The other people in the area were friendly. I became especially close with some of the women, who generously shared clothes and supplies. It was a challenging time as I didn't yet have an income. I didn't even have enough money for sanitary towels! I set about finding a job and was eventually hired as a cleaner in Sophiatown.

In 2005, I moved to Joubert Park with two friends, but after only a few weeks our flat was burgled. The only belongings I had left were the clothes on my back. I reached out to another contact in Yeoville and she was kind enough to let me stay for two months while I got back on my feet. I used the time to start an informal business selling clothes and accessories, and after a while I had saved enough to rent a small flat in town. Since then I have moved around a lot: first to Braamfontein, where I stayed for two years, then to Marshalltown, Doornfontein, Yeoville and Pimville. Moving is a part of life when you don't have a steady income. The good thing is that I haven't had to face this alone: since 2014, when I rented the flat in Doornfontein, I have lived with my girlfriend, Zee.

In December 2016, Zee's sister offered us a place in Vosloorus. She owned the property and said we could stay for free. I was a little uncomfortable with the idea, but Zee and I agreed because neither of us had a regular job. We needed to save whatever we could scrape together. I had to send money home to my family and couldn't waste a cent. But this arrangement didn't last long. We had a big fight with Zee's sister and ended up moving out. We still live in Vosloorus, but now we have a place of our own and a kind landlord.

TRYING TO GET BY

Life is a mix of ups and downs. That is exactly how Johannesburg has been for me: I have faced many trials, but I have also found love and learnt new skills. Money, or the lack thereof, has been my biggest challenge. I have mainly survived through informal jobs, such as domestic work and street hawking, but occasionally I have had semi-regular jobs. Back in 2011, I found work at a catering company that was contracted by Nedbank. I worked there for a couple of months and was good at the job, but then I was fired because I didn't have proper paperwork.

In 2013, I decided to expand my skills by attending a photography course at Market Photo Workshop in Newtown. I graduated from the one-year course and saved up to buy my own camera. I have now had a few gigs taking photos at different events. I really enjoy photography and would love to pursue it as a full-time career.

Not having a regular income makes life difficult. There have been times when I haven't had enough money for rent, food, bills or transport. These are frightening moments. Things were okay for a while because the Jesuit Refugee Service was helping out with rent, but that programme has now finished. I don't know what Zee and I will do from here. I have applied for so many jobs, but employers don't like to hire foreigners.

Part of the reason I have struggled to find work is my documentation status. I have been on a temporary asylum permit since 2005 and I still have no idea if I will be granted refugee status. Dealing with the Department of Home Affairs (DHA) has been a nightmare. My case file has been transferred between multiple branches and in the process important documents have been lost. I first lodged my application at Rosettenville in 2005 and since then my file has been transferred to Crown Mines, Pretoria Showgrounds and now Marabastad.

When I first applied for asylum, I was met with shock and confusion. The DHA officer looked at me and said, 'I don't believe there are lesbians in Zimbabwe! Anyway, lesbians can't have children – you must be lying.' He told his colleagues about me and I became the joke of the centre. In the end I was forced to provide a different reason for my asylum claim. I was eventually granted one of the old black-and-white papers. Since then I have had to renew my permit, in person, every few months.

In 2009, when I was renewing my permit at Crown Mines, I had to sleep outside for three nights. I had to pay R5 for a piece of cardboard to sleep on, with nothing to protect me from the rain. There were lots of criminals around and so I barely slept a wink. This is not the only time I have faced danger when renewing my permit. There are always tsotsis hanging around, ready to rob or take bribes. Standing in that queue for hours at a time, I always feel exposed and scared.

In all the years I have been going to DHA, I have never once had someone who knows about LGBT issues. Not all of the officials are intentionally prejudicial, but even the nice ones don't know what to do with my case. They don't believe Africans can be lesbian or gay or trans. They have no interest in protecting our rights.

I have also faced various types of discrimination. Some service providers are openly homophobic, while others are just ignorant or incompetent. Once, when I was having a health check-up, I mentioned that I was in a lesbian relationship. The nurse was shocked and ended up telling the other clinic staff. One by one they came into the consultation room and stared at me. I could hear them sniggering and whispering. Dealing with such people makes you feel worthless.

It is also scary when there are outbreaks of xenophobic violence. I was living in Joubert Park when things got really bad in 2008. Back then it was frightening to even step outside, especially around people who knew I was Shona. Luckily things aren't too bad in Vosloorus. People here let you get on with life.

MAKING PEACE WITH MYSELF

When I left Zimbabwe, I hadn't yet accepted my attraction to women. I am not sure if it was because homosexuality is taboo back home, if I was too frightened or ashamed to admit it, or if I just hadn't worked it out. Probably a mixture of all three! Growing up, I wasn't exposed to LGBT people. That made it difficult to understand my feelings. But once I was settled in Johannesburg, I started exploring this side of myself. Some of my neighbours in Braamfontein were gay, and over time I met more and more LGBT people. I had a few relationships, but none of them lasted. Then, in 2014, I was introduced to Zee, my partner, and we have been together ever since.

Most of my family now know about my sexuality. The only people who don't know are my mother and my son. My mother couldn't handle it and so I have decided to never tell her. I don't want to jeopardise our relationship. My son is still too young to understand, but I will tell him when the time is right.

My daughter was the first family member to find out about my sexuality. By then she had also moved to South Africa. Her friends at school would tease her about me, saying I was like a man. At first she didn't believe it, but then she found out about my relationship with Zee. She didn't take it well. Angry and upset, she went to tell my brothers, both of whom now live in Johannesburg. They reacted better than I could have ever hoped. They chastised my daughter for interfering in my personal affairs, telling her to have more respect. It took time for her to adjust, but now she is fine with my sexuality.

A RELIGIOUS LIFE

My Anglican faith has always been important to me. My mother is a devout Christian, and back in Zimbabwe our whole family was expected to attend services. I loved being part of our faith community and eagerly participated in church activities.

My faith remains an important part of my identity. I express my spirituality through my thoughts and deeds, and I try my best to live a loving Christian life. I don't think my sexuality is a problem in that regard. I have a strong personal communion with God. He alone knows the strength of my faith; He is the only one who can judge me.

Homosexuality was never mentioned at our church in Bulawayo. In fact, the topic was barely spoken about in Zimbabwe. It is only when I attended a church in Yeoville that I encountered negative comments, both from the clergy and congregation. One incident that comes to mind happened just after Archbishop Tutu spoke out in support of his daughter's same-sex relationship. This caused outrage at my church, with people calling it a sin and saying all sorts of nasty things. I ended up confronting one minister, asking him to show me the Bible verse condemning love between two women. Homophobes waste so much energy quoting this or that scripture and in the process overlook the Bible's central message of love.

There is so much hypocrisy in society. Religious people pretend to be righteous, but their comments and actions tell a different story. I know from my own experience just how much prejudice and judgement remains in churches. I am a stubborn person and try not to let such things affect me, but it is not easy. I remind myself that I go to church to worship God, not to get caught up in other people's nonsense.

A CHOSEN FAMILY

I have known about the LGBT Ministry since its formation. My neighbours in Braamfontein were actually involved in establishing the group. Back then I wasn't interested in going along, mainly because I was busy with other things. It was only two years ago that I decided to check it out.

I was nervous before my first meeting. I was worried I would be asked personal questions that I wouldn't want to answer. But my nerves didn't last long: once I walked into the room, I was immediately put at ease by the friendly atmosphere. Everyone smiled, making sure that Zee and I felt welcomed. That warmth and friendliness has never gone away: we are, and always will be, part of the Holy Trinity family.

The LGBT Ministry has allowed me to grow as a person. I am more confident, open and self-assured. I know who I am, and I better understand my rights. There are also practical ways that the LGBT Ministry has helped me. When times are tough, I know I can reach out to the group. Once, when Zee and I were short on rent, we were able to borrow money from other members. More recently, when I had to travel to Pretoria to renew my asylum permit, I had to ask for financial support. Helping each other out is something we all try to do. Zee and I are not always in a position to provide money, but we always open our hearts and our home.

DREAMS FOR THE FUTURE

One of my biggest hopes is that the LGBT Ministry expands. I would like to see more lesbian women and trans people join. Having more diversity will only make us stronger.

I also wish people would be more committed. I have noticed that some people stop coming once they have received whatever help they wanted. I understand that some members won't want to be involved forever, but it would be nice if more people stuck around. We each have a role to play in building up the group and taking our message of love into the wider community.

I would also like to see other religious institutions start LGBT groups. These could serve as a channel for spreading accurate information. It is only through exposure to LGBT people that society will change for the better. The more that people interact with us, the more they will see that we are just like them. Churches should be open to all of us; we should be allowed to practise our faith without fear or judgement.

Church leaders can also do more to help. They need to stop using the Bible to attack LGBT people. I don't know why they insist on calling us demonic. Where are they getting this from? The Bible should be used to promote love, not spread fear and hate. Ordinary people need to hear positive messages from the pulpits. As a society, we need to learn respect and acceptance.

Most of all I pray for unity, both here in South Africa and across the globe. People in Africa still see homophobia and transphobia as acceptable. We have to work hard to challenge this misperception. South Africans also need to confront their xenophobia. People like me are coming here for protection, but that is not what we receive. First, the laws of this country need to be better applied. Then we need to educate the population by sharing our stories. If locals knew the hardships that asylum seekers endure, they would treat us better.

4

STILL SEARCHING FOR SAFETY

Narrated by Eeyban (Ethiopia)

I am a gay man from the Oromia Region of Ethiopia. I am now 32 years old. As a child, I was teased for being feminine, the worst thing a boy can be. Once I reached adulthood, it became too unsafe for me to stay in Ethiopia. I left my country in 2008, when I was 22 years old. Since then I have been on the move, trying to find a place where I can be free and happy. I had hoped South Africa would provide protection, but that hasn't been the case. I still fear for my life; I still experience violence. Every day is a struggle for survival. I wonder if I will ever be able to live without fear. I hope things will get better now that I have discovered the LGBT Ministry. It means a lot to be around people who have similar problems.

PUNISHED FOR BEING DIFFERENT

Ethiopian families are large and mine is no exception: I have six brothers and three sisters. I was always very close to my sisters, but I had a difficult relationship with my brothers. The most important person in my life was my mother. We loved each other very much; she always tried to protect me. My heart hurts when I think about my mother because I don't know if she is alive or dead. Even though we haven't spoken since I left home, I know she is with me in spirit.

The other significant person in my life was my grandmother. She could see that I was different, that I was soft and gentle, but she loved me regardless. We shared a special bond; I was always her favourite. She would punish my brothers if they bullied me. I miss her so much.

I was very happy as a young boy. All of the children in our area would play games together. Back then people didn't treat me badly. That changed

'I feel like an impala that is being hunted. I must be careful or I will be attacked. It is no safer in Johannesburg than back home. I am afraid. There is no protection for me here. No peace, only suffering.'

when I got to school. The other boys teased me for behaving like a girl. Even some adults would express concern, encouraging my mother to be stricter so that I would learn to be a 'proper' boy.

Like many Ethiopians at that time, I wasn't able to complete my secondary education. My family didn't have the money. I wasn't sad about leaving school because I thought I would be free of my tormentors.

Even though my formal schooling had finished, I was still expected to attend the local madrasa. The teachers there would punish me for being feminine. At first they would just use words to make me feel bad, but over time they began to beat me. They would say that Islam doesn't tolerate boys like me.

My effeminacy was also becoming a problem in my family. Male relatives would make fun of how I walked and talked. They would yell at me or hit me so that I would toughen up. When I was 14, an uncle hurt me very badly. He burnt me and used pliers to pull off some of my toenails. The pain was unbearable. 'I will not have someone like you in our family,' he said. 'Next time will be worse. You better start behaving like a man.' He threatened me with more torture if I ever told my mother what had happened.

After that I became sick. I was broken, physically and emotionally. I couldn't stand or walk because of the pain, and I would get terrible headaches because I was afraid. My mother kept asking me what was wrong, but I kept quiet out of fear. But then she threatened to discipline me if I didn't tell her the truth. I loved her very much and couldn't keep lying. I explained that my uncle had hurt me and that I was scared.

My mother convinced my father to send me to her sister – my aunt – who lived in another province. I stayed with her for almost two years. At first life was easier because no one there knew me. I kept to myself as much as possible, but over time people became suspicious of my sexuality. Some men would call me names and threaten to hurt me. I became too frightened to leave the house. Being trapped inside made me feel isolated and afraid; I would dream of being reunited with my mother and sisters. My homesickness grew more and more intense. Eventually I decided to return to my family, despite the risk.

A HOME OR A PRISON?

Although my mother was overjoyed at my return, she was worried about my safety. She knew there were people in the community who might hurt me. She became very protective of me. I will never know what she actually thought about my mannerisms, or if she understood about my sexuality, because it was not something we could talk about. But I do know that she cared for me very much. I felt sorry for her, and I still do, because the constant gossiping and bullying caused her much anguish. There were times when she would become sick with worry.

At this point in my life, I had only one friend. His name was Beekan and he was a few years older than me. People also teased Beekan for being different, but he wasn't ashamed like me. I am not sure where his courage came from. We didn't see much of each other because I was too scared to walk the streets. I only went out if my mother needed something urgently. Most days I helped my mother and sisters with domestic chores, like cooking and cleaning, something that angered my brothers.

It was nice knowing another gay man, even if Beekan and I didn't see each other regularly. My mother liked that I had a friend, but she was nervous when we visited each other. She knew it would raise suspicions – and she was right to be afraid.

I was harassed every time I went out alone. I would walk as fast as possible, hoping to get to my destination without incident, but inevitably I would be noticed. Men would call me a woman and threaten to hurt me. Sometimes the situation would turn violent. One time, when I was about 16, a group of men threw stones, forcing me to run for my life. After that my mother was reluctant to let me leave the house. She was exhausted from trying to protect me, and I was sick of being under attack.

Beekan, too, was sick of the abuse. One day he announced that he was leaving. He encouraged me to go with him, but I was apprehensive about leaving my mother. Instead, I stopped going outside; I spent every single day in our house. With Beekan gone, I was even more isolated.

It was a couple of months until I saw Beekan again. When he came home, he announced that he was leaving Ethiopia. He told me that he could never be happy in our country. His plan was to move to Kenya and he encouraged me to do the same. 'What kind of life is this?' he asked. 'You stay home every day. These people don't like us. There is too much danger.' He was right: I was suffering every day, getting sicker and sicker, the fear eating away at me. Even though I wanted to escape, I didn't have the strength to leave. I had fallen into a deep depression and could barely look after myself.

My depression got very bad when Beekan left for the second time. The situation with my brothers had worsened, and I didn't have a single friend. My mother made sure my brothers didn't hit me, but that didn't stop them from expressing their disgust. Every day they would yell at me: 'Are you a women or a man? Stop acting like that!' They would say that I brought shame on our family. If they got very angry, they might push me around, but never in front of my mother. The only person who got angry in front of her was my father. It wasn't all the time, but every now and then he would curse me for being a girl child. It was a bad life.

GETTING OUT

In 2008, when was 21 years old, I reached breaking point. I told my mother that I could no longer be a prisoner. She was upset, but she understood my decision. She gave me our family savings so that I could make the journey to Kenya. She didn't tell my father or brothers because she knew they would be angry. My family isn't rich and so it was a big deal for her to give me that money. That is why we had to keep our plan a secret. We both knew I would be in danger if anyone found out.

It wasn't difficult to get to the border because I had money for transport. It was only when I arrived that I faced my first hurdle: crossing without a passport. I was stuck at the border for a couple of days, asking truck drivers if they could help me. They all wanted more money than I could afford, but eventually I found someone willing to take me. The driver and his friend used most of my money to bribe the guards and kept the rest for themselves. They turned out to be very bad men. They put me in the back of the truck, without food, water or fresh air, and during the night they took turns raping me. All I could do was cry and cry; I thought I was going to die. We were still a few hours' drive from Nairobi and they left me locked in the back, alone and afraid.

Once we arrived in Nairobi, the driver gave me a couple of scraps of food and some Kenyan shillings. 'You are on your own now,' he said. At first I panicked: I was exhausted, afraid and unsure of what to do. Luckily, the driver had dropped me in Eastleigh, a suburb where many Oromo people live. Some kind strangers helped me contact Beekan and looked after me until he arrived. I told Beekan everything that had happened to me. He was very angry and said we must report the driver, but I was scared to go to the police because I was undocumented. In the end he took me to a clinic, but there was little the sisters could do.

Life in Kenya wasn't much better than in Ethiopia. Beekan and I were staying in an impoverished area and our neighbours didn't like us. Some people would yell nasty things or threaten to hurt us. Our only friends were some gay Kenyans and Ugandans that Beekan had met.

The other problem was money. Beekan survived by hawking things on the street. He would sell whatever he could get his hands on: T-shirts, gadgets, toiletries. He didn't earn much and tried to save whatever he could. I tried to contribute, but found it difficult to do anything. I was in a very dark place since my rape.

After a few months, I found myself in a bad situation. Some men in the area had started making my life very difficult. They would yell rude things and sometimes throw stuff at me. I was very scared. Beekan suggested I move on, perhaps heading south. He said that LGBT people are free here in South Africa. I wanted him to come with me, but he had a boyfriend whom he loved. Beekan was very generous and gave me as much money as he could spare.

A LONG JOURNEY

I asked around for advice and was finally put in touch with a smuggler. I was driven with a group of people to Mombasa, where we were put on a boat. I didn't realise I would be travelling by sea and was very scared. I didn't know how to swim, and the boat was crowded with people. By the grace of Allah, we made it safely to Bagamoyo. From there we travelled by road to Dar es Salaam.

On my own in Dar es Salaam, I fell victim to criminals. Three guys surrounded me and demanded everything I had, including my remaining money. 'What am I going to do?' I thought to myself, my eyes filling with tears. A kind mama took pity on me. 'What is wrong, my son?' she asked. 'Why are you crying?' She gave me some food and offered words of comfort.

I didn't know how I could possibly continue to South Africa and decided to head back towards Nairobi. At least then I could be with Beekan. This time, however, I wasn't so lucky. I was caught by the police and taken to jail. It was a very bad place – dirty, crowded, dangerous. I was attacked many times by the other prisoners.

After a while, I couldn't stand it any longer. I started refusing my food. It was the only way I could protest my treatment. The guards knew I was being raped, but they didn't care. In fact, the guards were just as bad – more than once they held me down and assaulted me. I lost all hope in that cell.

The guards became angry with me for not eating. They would throw food at me and demand I eat, but still I refused. Not even the porridge they give you for breakfast. Eventually one of the wardens came to ask why I wouldn't eat. I told him I wanted to die because it was the only way I could escape this hell. I soon became very sick. I didn't even have the energy to stand or walk. A doctor was called and he gave me water and medicine. He begged me to eat, but I told him I was ready to die.

The next day I was taken to see a magistrate. I am not sure if it was the doctor's doing or if it was just my turn. It was decided that I would be deported, but the immigration officers were corrupt and dumped me by the side of the road. Perhaps they hoped I would die out there, alone and abandoned.

Once again I was saved by a kind stranger. His name was Abdullahi and he could see I was in a bad way. He ran a food stand near the border and gave me food to eat. It felt like a lifetime since I had tasted something so delicious. My plan was to continue heading for Nairobi, but Abdullahi thought this was silly. 'Brother, you must not give up on your plan,' he said encouragingly. He told me there were always people travelling south and that he could help me. Suddenly my dream of making it to South Africa, of being free and happy, didn't seem impossible.

I stayed with Abdullahi for quite a while, helping with his business and saving whatever I could. When I had enough money, I was put in touch with a smuggler who could take me to Malawi. Abdullahi assured me that his contact could get me across the border with no problem.

We were not long in Malawi before the truck was stopped and searched. Thankfully, the Malawian police were much nicer than the Tanzanian ones. They treated me with respect, even when they found out I didn't have a passport. I thought I was going to prison again, but instead I was taken to a reception centre in Karonga. The people there gave me cassava to eat and water to drink. They even let me eat outside in the fresh air.

I was then transferred to Dzaleka Refugee Camp, not far from Lilongwe. Things in the camp weren't great – lots of people, bad facilities, little food, no hope. It was mainly people from DR Congo and Mozambique. I found it hard to communicate because I didn't speak French or Portuguese. 'Guys, what is there to eat?' I asked, trying to work out how things worked.

Even though the camp conditions were bad, it wasn't anything like jail. People from the camp could farm the surrounding areas, and occasionally locals would hire them for short-term jobs. I managed to find work as a labourer. It was very exhausting: I had to push a wheelbarrow stacked high with bricks in the burning sun. I was sweating constantly and only had one set of clothes. Some days I thought I would die from exhaustion.

The camp was a hotspot for brokers. They knew people were desperate to get to South Africa and would promise to assist. They claimed they could arrange safe transport across the border . . . for a price! Getting away from the camp isn't difficult because the brokers bribe the authorities. Money is king in these situations.

It took a while for me to raise the cash, but eventually I had enough to leave. I travelled with many people in the back of a truck. It was dark and crowded, with little oxygen. When we got near the border, the driver made us get out and walk through the bush. Even with a guide, the journey was terrifying. We could hear animals making all sorts of sounds, but we had no idea how close they actually were.

In Mozambique, we had to be careful about not being caught. We spent many days hiding in a house, waiting for someone to collect us. A guy eventually came and took us to a hole in the fence with South Africa. We had to be quiet at all times so as to avoid detection from border patrols.

Smugglers aren't good people. They offer so much, but in reality they are thieves. They don't provide food or water, even though you are paying. They get very angry if you ask for the smallest thing. Once I had made it across the border, I was searched and anything of value was taken. By the time I was put on the transport to Johannesburg, I was beyond exhausted. I didn't even have the energy to celebrate making it so far.

ARRIVAL IN SOUTH AFRICA

In Johannesburg, I was directed towards Jeppe Street. I knew immediately when I had arrived because there were Ethiopians everywhere. I must have looked confused, standing in the street alone, because a man came up and spoke to me in Amharic. 'I am new here and don't know what to do,' I explained. He gave me food and helped me catch a taxi, telling the driver to drop me in Mayfair. 'There are people there who will assist you,' he promised.

After I arrived, I went into a shop and asked for help. By then I was sick of travelling; all I wanted was to wash and sleep. My emotions became too strong and I burst into tears. The shopkeeper called for some men from the mosque. 'You must stop crying,' they said when they arrived. 'We will help you.' I wanted to believe them, but deep down I knew I was still unsafe.

One of the men, Abdii, proved to be very kind. He was also Oromo and said that I could rest at his house. He fed me, gave me clothes, made sure I was okay. He could see that I was desperate and offered me work in his shop. But it didn't take long for the rumours to start. 'What is wrong with this guy?' the customers would ask. 'He acts like a woman!' Abdii ignored the comments at first, but soon they affected his business.

By then I had managed to sort out my asylum permit. Abdii had insisted I go to Marabastad Refugee Reception Office as soon as possible. It was a frightening and confusing experience. The transport costs a lot, and you have to go a few times before you make it inside. Even waiting in the line is dangerous, especially if you look and sound gay. People say nasty things, and sometimes they are violent. I remember one man pointing at me and saying, 'Look at this dog! Look at this gay!' He said it loud enough so that the other men could hear. Someone else said, 'If you act like a woman, then we will kill you.' These threats made me very scared.

When I finally made it inside, I discovered that an interpreter would be present during my interview. I wanted to tell the Home Affairs official all the horrible things that had happened to me, but I was frightened to say the truth. I was scared of three things: first, that I would be disbelieved and deported; second, that the interpreter would tell everybody in the community about me; third, that my whereabouts and personal information would get back to my family. I don't trust my fellow Ethiopians, even if they are professionals like a translator. People from my country hate gay people. I would be in danger if my sexuality became public knowledge.

Luckily, Abdii had coached me on what to say. I did exactly as he suggested. I told the official – through the interpreter – that I had fled Ethiopia because of political persecution. This was not hard to believe because there had been lots of fighting between Oromo people and the government. I wish I could have said the real reason, but I couldn't risk it. I was scared of being killed. If I reveal my sexuality in front of another Ethiopian, I am putting myself in danger.

STILL NOT SAFE

People in Mayfair were starting to talk; I realised it was time to leave the area, if not the whole of Johannesburg. Abdii suggested I go and live with a friend of his in Secunda. This guy ran a spaza shop and, according to Abdii, was kind and trustworthy. 'He will be grateful for the help,' Abdii said. 'I will tell him how good a worker you are.'

It was in Secunda that I met my first boyfriend, Hendrik. I tried to see him as often as possible, but it was hard because I worked long hours. The other problem was that being with Hendrik attracted unwanted attention. Ethiopians can be suspicious of outsiders, and people started noticing that I was meeting up with a strange man. I would brush off their questions, but couldn't shake the feeling I was under surveillance. People would look at me funny and make offhand comments. After a while, I could no longer take the attention and decided to move back to Johannesburg.

A CONSTANT STRUGGLE

The money I had saved in Secunda allowed me to get a room in Randfontein. I hoped I would finally be free, but again the rumours started. Randfontein has a lot of migrants, including people from Ethiopia and Somalia, and people quickly noticed me. 'Oh, this one wants to be a woman,' they would say. 'He must be a dirty gay!' There was a lot of xenophobic violence happening at that time and it was important for migrants to protect each another, but no one was looking out for me. Instead of helping, the community wanted to harm me. People would say rude things, sometimes even follow me, and that made me feel unsafe.

In 2013, I had to renew my permit. I was nervous about going back to Marabastad and put it off for as long as possible. However, this time something wonderful happened: I met the love of my life, Absra. We were both standing in the line, and I could hear him speaking on the phone. I could tell immediately that he was gay. I was excited to know there was another gay Ethiopian. I introduced myself and asked, very discreetly, if he was gay. I could see him sizing me up, trying to work out if I could be trusted. I recognised the fear and suspicion in his eyes. The only way I could think to reassure him was by showing him some adult pictures on my phone. 'See,' I said. 'I am like that too. You don't need to worry.' That moment was very special. At last, I had someone I could trust and confide in.

Absra and I have lived together ever since. We have stayed in many places: Mayfair, Germiston, Berea and now Bertrams. We have faced many problems during that time. There is too much homophobia in our community. We stay in one place for as long as possible, but in the end we are always forced out.

Mayfair was meant to be a safe place, but it wasn't like that for us. I remember one time when I was attacked by a group of guys. I was standing on the street, minding my own business, when I was suddenly hit from behind. As I fell to the ground, I covered my head, trying to shield myself from kicks. My assailants said lots of hurtful things: 'If you act like a lady, we will treat you like a bitch. We are going to kill you.'

I went to the police station – bloodied, bruised, in shock – and reported the attack, but I was too frightened to say it was because of my sexuality. Police stations are dangerous places if you are gay and foreign. I also didn't want to cause more trouble in the community. In the end I said I was robbed. I wanted the police to know that bad things were happening on our street, but deep down I knew that nothing would change.

After finishing at the police station, I went to the hospital. I sat in the waiting room all night, bleeding and bleeding, but no one did anything.

Nurses don't like foreigners. Sometimes they say bad things, but most of the time they force you to wait until you give up hope and go home.

Bertrams, where we stay now, is like hell. We moved there in 2017 and have had problems ever since. We both fear for our lives, but it is especially bad for Absra since he is even more feminine than me. The people in the community hate us for being gay. We have been followed; we have had things thrown at us; we have been assaulted. It is hard to know when a situation will escalate from words to violence.

Men are the worst offenders, especially when they have been drinking. One time, when Absra and I tried to go out, some guys threw bottles and stones at us. We started running, glass smashing around us, one bottle narrowly missing Absra's head. We ran as fast as we could, scared that they would kill us. Since then, Absra locks himself in our room, only going out when it is absolutely necessary.

Some of the women in the community feel sorry for us. After the bottle incident, one woman said, 'Those men are dangerous. You must stay away from them. They will hurt you.' But even she no longer talks to us. She knows it is bad to be seen with gays. There might be others who don't want to harm us, but they are probably wary of being associated with us.

I have tried to get help a few times. The police say it is a community matter and there is nothing they can do. 'Do you want us to arrest everyone?' they ask mockingly.

Like Absra, I stay indoors as much as possible, but I have to go out so that we can get food. When I step outside, no one greets me. I just keep my head down and walk fast.

I earn money by hawking. Whenever I have cash, I go to Small Street Mall and buy cheap T-shirts, which I then sell for a slightly higher price. It is not an easy way to make a living. It can be dangerous too. One time I was selling goods near the train station and some tsotsis stole everything – my money, my phone, my T-shirts. The police also make life difficult for street traders by demanding bribes.

I have tried looking for a proper job, but people don't want to hire gays, especially in the Ethiopian community. It isn't easy surviving by street hawking. Absra and I regularly go without food. On those nights, we drink water and lie down, trying to ignore the pain in our stomachs.

AN UNEXPECTED SUPPORT NETWORK

I first heard about Holy Trinity through a South African guy. I was on the street near Ellis Park, getting ready to sell T-shirts, when he started talking to me. He must have guessed I was gay. He asked me all about my life. He told me about the LGBT Ministry at Holy Trinity, but I didn't understand what he meant. At first I thought he was trying to convert me, but now I realise he was just trying to look out for me.

A few months later, when I was hustling in town, I started talking to a Zimbabwean. He shared details of his own life: how he had left home because of his sexuality, how it isn't safe in Zimbabwe for LGBT people, how he has struggled here in South Africa. I knew instantly that I could trust him and opened up about my own situation. I explained that Absra and I were desperate, that we were alone and scared. The guy gave me his number and urged me to stay in touch. He also told me about the LGBT Ministry, saying I could get help there.

Absra and I have only been to a couple of meetings. That first meeting made me so happy. It was great being around other LGBT migrants, especially as they were all laughing and having fun. I hadn't felt that relaxed in a long time. For once I was safe and at peace. When you are around happy people, you can forget your troubles, even if only for a short while.

Even though Absra and I feel comfortable with the group, it still isn't easy for us to say our stories out loud. I get upset when I think about the bad things that have happened to me. That first day I just said we are from Ethiopia and we are having a hard time. The best part was that everyone understood our situation. Hearing other people's experiences made us feel less alone. There were finally people who could relate to us.

At first I worried that I wouldn't be welcome because I am Muslim, but that isn't the case. The group members are very kind and accepting. Dumi shared his number and said we can call any time. That made us feel supported. I haven't reached out for assistance yet, but it is nice to know there is someone who will help. I am looking forward to attending more meetings. I am most excited about making friends and having fun.

HOPES AND DREAMS

All I want is a nice life, a normal life, a safe life. I am sick and tired. Every day I am under attack. Things were meant to be better when I left Ethiopia, but life is still hard. We have nothing. Our lives are nothing. I wish people could understand that we are just like them: normal people. All we dream about is being free and happy. We need protection here in South Africa. Without it, the Ethiopian community will keep hurting us, maybe even kill us. I hope that one day we will be treated nicely. I also dream about seeing my mother and sisters, but I know it will never happen. My heart hurts when I think about the people I have lost.

5

A CAGED ANIMAL SET FREE

Narrated by Thomars (Zimbabwe)

I am a 31-year-old trans man. I was raised in Harare, but have been living in Johannesburg since 2011. I consider myself luckier than most: I have a steady job, a nice home and a strong support network. That doesn't mean life is easy, though I realise I am better off than most migrants. I have seen first-hand how LGBT migrants are struggling. Some members of the LGBT Ministry are barely able to buy food, let alone save for emergencies. For me, the biggest challenge is my relationship with my family. Things have improved in recent years, but I still have a rocky relationship with my mother. It is my dream to help other trans and gender-nonconforming migrants. We need more than financial handouts: we need help getting permits, accessing healthcare, gaining qualifications and starting businesses.

A COMPLICATED FAMILY LIFE

I am the baby of my family and have always been treated differently. Even today, as someone in their 30s, I am taken less seriously than my siblings.

As a child, I thought my family was normal, but looking back I can see how dysfunctional we were. My parents had a very tense relationship and eventually divorced. While their separation was hard to cope with at the time, it was definitely for the best.

My mother is a faithful Catholic, but my father isn't religious at all. I have no idea when he last set foot inside a church. My father takes his Shona heritage very seriously and that has shaped his relationship with his children. He always had a specific notion of how African men are supposed to behave and this translated into him being distant and

'I like to think of myself as a lion. It is the king of the jungle. A lion is fierce. I am not sure if I am scary, but I am definitely fierce. Not in a bad or aggressive way – I just try to be brave and protective. I don't keep quiet if someone disrespects me or my girlfriend. I always stand up for our rights.'

domineering. Everyone in our household was afraid of him, including my mother. He would arrive home each day just before the 8 o'clock news. As soon as we heard his car pulling in to the driveway, we would all get out of sight. He had a soft spot for me as the youngest child, but even I had to act with caution. My mother took advantage of his fondness for me. If she needed money for cooking oil or other essential items, she would send me to ask, knowing it was the only way my father would comply.

My mother was my hero when I was young. She was warm and loving, and she worked hard to make sure her children were well taken care of. My father was the opposite: he really didn't know how to relate to children. He wasn't the sort of parent to play games, or help with homework, or attend school events. Most of the time he was stern and unapproachable, which used to frighten my friends.

I have three sisters and a brother. I was very close to my brother growing up. There are only two years separating us, and as children we were constantly getting up to mischief. The next two siblings above us are close for the same reason. Our other sister is quite a bit older and was never interested in our childish games. We all loved her, but we didn't have the same sort of bond.

My sister Vimbai is very protective of me. She lives in the UK, but we are in regular contact. She fully accepts who I am. I think it is because she has lived overseas for so many years. Being in the UK has exposed her to different people and ways of thinking; nothing about my gender or relationships fazes her.

The rest of my family struggle with my identity; they still think it is a phase. My mum and I have fought about it often, but most of the time she pretends it isn't real. All she wants is for me to give her a grandchild – even though she has eight already! She begged me to have a child before I transitioned. That was her biggest concern when I started hormone therapy.

I am not sure how much my father knows about my transition. I have only had irregular contact with him since my parents separated. But I am Facebook friends with his side of the family and I am very honest and open on social media. I assume someone has told him by now.

My parents' separation had a significant impact on me. In 2000, just after they split, my mother moved to the UK. Things were starting to get tough in Zimbabwe and lots of people were emigrating for work. Back then Zimbabweans didn't need visas for the UK and so it was much easier to travel. My mother found a job in a nursing home and would send back as much money as possible. I was only 14 when she left. I realise now that she had our best interests at heart, but at the time I felt abandoned.

Not long after my mother left, my father moved in with one of his other families. In total, he has 15 children, from multiple partners. When he left, he announced that he would no longer be paying for our schooling or upkeep. Having zero parental support was not good for me. I started acting out and my grades dropped. My eldest sister tried her best to keep me in check, but nothing she did stopped me from misbehaving. Occasionally she would ask our father for help, but he was too busy with his new family. Reflecting on it now, I can see how my choices back then have negatively impacted my life.

My mother returned to Zimbabwe in 2003. It was great to have her back, but by then the damage was done. I had lost interest in school and couldn't be told what to do. Four years later, in 2007, my parents officially divorced.

FINDING MY COMMUNITY

I knew I was different from a young age. While my school friends were becoming interested in the opposite sex, I was developing feelings for girls, although I was still too young to understand what that meant. Back then homosexuality wasn't spoken about in Zimbabwe. It is still barely mentioned today! One of my few memories of it being discussed was a rumour about a distant relative – my cousin's husband's brother. People said he was sleeping with another man for money. My cousins and I would say horrible things about him. I was one of the loudest voices, probably because I was trying to distract from my own secret. The only other time I heard about homosexuality was when Canaan Banana, our former president, was imprisoned for sodomy. That was a huge scandal.

One thing I never heard about was a woman loving another woman. I didn't know such a thing even existed. This made it hard for me to make sense of my desires. With no information available and no one to talk to, I forced myself to do what everyone else was doing. Dating guys didn't feel right, but it was what people expected. Peer pressure is hard to resist at that age.

After finishing school, I started a small business selling clothes and accessories. I would buy stock in South Africa and then take it back to Harare. One day, while sitting at my stall, I saw a butch girl walk past. I was instantly drawn to her. Before I knew it, I was introducing myself. Tariro and I exchanged numbers, and by the time I made it home we were already chatting. She confessed to being lesbian, and her words sent a shiver through my body. Tariro's revelation inspired me to disclose my own secret. I was terrified of verbalising the feelings I had been struggling with, but deep down I knew I could trust her. She was very sweet about the whole thing and made me feel totally normal. Just before we stopped chatting, she told me she would take me somewhere special the very next afternoon.

As promised, Tariro picked me up from my clothing stall. I still had no idea where we were going, but I was excited nonetheless. We ended up at an event at Gays and Lesbians of Zimbabwe (GALZ). I felt like I was in heaven. There were all types of people there: feminine guys, butch women and everything in between. I went from feeling like an alien to being surrounded by people just like me. Some of them became very close friends. One gay guy in particular became my mentor, teaching me all about LGBT life in Zimbabwe.

I went a bit crazy when I first started hanging out with LGBT people. I was like a caged animal set free. I was keen to experience as much as I could, as quickly as I could. There were lots of hook-ups, lots of parties, but what I was really doing was finding out who I am. Then, a few months after coming out, I met a girl and fell crazy in love.

A SECRET REVEALED

Coming out to my family wasn't my choice. One day, when everyone was together, my sister turned to our mum and said, 'Do you know your child is lesbian?' She had been hearing rumours about me and decided to reveal my secret out of spite (we had been arguing earlier in the day). Mum reacted like someone had died. In all honesty, it was the worst day of my life. I was disowned and kicked out of the family home.

I was so angry with my sister – more for what she had done to our mother than to me – but now, eight years on, I see it as a blessing in disguise. At the time, though, it was devastating. It broke my heart to see my mum so upset. All I had ever wanted was to make her proud and now she was devastated. I remember her saying that it was the worst thing in the world, even worse than finding out I was a murderer. It was a hard time for everyone. It was especially painful for me because I had been robbed of my coming out. I was furious at my sister for being reckless with my emotions and for hurting our mother.

All of this was going on during my first relationship. That was actually how my sister found out about me. My girlfriend was very proud and refused to hide her sexuality. If someone on the street made a comment, she would say proudly, 'Yes, I am lesbian. Get over it!' When people saw us together, they instantly assumed I was lesbian too, and that is how the rumours began.

After mum kicked me out, I went to stay with my girlfriend and her mother. I was a bit uncomfortable with the arrangement and ended up moving in with my gay friend from GALZ. I stayed with him for a couple of months, hiding my pain with drinking and partying. Then my girlfriend and I moved to her mother's plot in the rural areas. We were sick of people dictating what we could and couldn't do. We wanted to be as far away as possible from other people's judgements. We were so in love and being together was all that mattered.

About a year later, I received a call from mum, telling me to come home. Her call was a complete surprise, but it was actually perfect timing because things weren't going well in my relationship. I still loved my girlfriend, but we were fighting all the time. After giving it careful thought, I decided that repairing things with my family had to be my priority.

This was easier said than done. I tried so hard to make things work with mum, but she would snap at me for no reason. I hated the way she looked at me, like I was a huge disappointment. I couldn't take it any longer and moved into my sister's place, but that was equally bad. With nowhere else to go, I ended up back at mum's house. It was terrible: my mum became a crazy person, calling me all sorts of names and crying all the time. She even banned me from being alone with my brother's new wife. She assumed I was a sex-crazed pervert and that I would try to seduce any woman I came into contact with. My mum made me promise to never again have sexual thoughts about a woman. I was desperate, confused and hurt; I saw no other choice but to agree to her demand, even though I knew it was impossible.

No matter what I did, my relationship with my mum deteriorated. Out of desperation I called my sister who was living in South Africa. She was reluctant to let me stay with her, but then I told her about my promise to be straight and she agreed. I had never had a desire to move to South Africa, but I knew I had to get far away from mum. That is how I found myself, in October 2011, on a bus bound for Johannesburg.

DETERMINED TO SURVIVE

Desperate to change my sexuality, I started attending a Pentecostal church in Cresta. The pastor was charismatic and inspiring, and I opened up to him about my situation. He quoted lots of Bible verses, telling me that homosexuality is an abomination. He assured me that God could cure me – all I needed to do was pray harder. If I truly repented, the pastor explained, God would make me 'normal'.

Following my pastor's advice, I started dating a Nigerian guy from our congregation, but I really had feelings for a Zimbabwean woman. She identified as straight – she has since come out as bisexual – but seemed to relish the attention I gave her. She knew my boyfriend, and eventually he found out that the two of us were hanging out. It was a messy situation, but again a blessing in disguise.

Details of what happened got back to my sister and she kicked me out of her house. I found myself in a desperate situation, with nowhere to live, no income and no plan. I knew I had to start hustling if I was going to survive. The most important thing was getting money. I caught a bus back to Zimbabwe, sold my car and other belongings, and then headed back to Johannesburg. I was determined to find my own place and build a life.

I knew my money wouldn't last long, especially with the cost of rent, and so I immediately set about finding a job. Eventually I found domestic work with an Indian family. It was an awful experience. The grandfather would talk dirty and touch me inappropriately; the mother would give me almost rotten food and expect me to be grateful. Every day was a nightmare, but I put up with it for as long as possible because I was desperate. I also started selling Avon products on the side because my wage was so low. I worked each and every day, saving as much as possible so that I could apply for a work permit. The Department of Home Affairs official who handled the process said everything was above board, but he still demanded a 'processing fee'. I don't regret paying because I had no other options. I needed a permit to survive – without one I couldn't find a job, open a bank account or sign a lease.

Things remained tense with my sister. She was angry about my sexuality and refused to talk to me, let alone provide support. I was sharing a bedroom with two other women and often couldn't afford both rent and food. I was a mess, both emotionally and financially. Mum realised how bad things were and forced my sister to intervene. Even though mum was still struggling with my identity, she felt it was wrong to ignore a relative in need. My sister relented and told me about a three-month contract at her work. It was a basic customer-service role, covering for a woman on maternity leave. Somehow I am still working there today.

FINDING ME

Accepting my transgender identity took time. It was only in the last few years that I encountered trans people and was able to put a name to the way I felt. That doesn't mean my male gender hasn't always been part of me. Rather, it shows what happens when people are denied access to knowledge and services. A lack of visible role models can make it hard for young trans people to find their place in the world.

When I first learnt about lesbian women, I was overjoyed. I felt like I understood myself, that my identity finally made sense, but in retrospect I see that this was never the right label for me. Connecting with other trans folks was a revelation. I immediate felt an affinity with them, even though I didn't yet think of myself as trans. I clearly remember meeting a trans man at Jo'burg Pride in 2015. There was something about his energy and look that drew me towards him. I introduced myself and took his phone number, and later we chatted about his identity and experiences.

Our conversation inspired me to do my own research. I started reading about trans rights online and even made contact with a trans man I used to know in Zimbabwe. Back then, none of us had heard of 'transgender' and so we didn't properly respect his gender identity. Even activists used to poke fun at this guy. Eventually he fled the country and claimed asylum in Sweden. I reached out to him via social media and asked for advice. He was generous and patient, happily answering all of my questions.

The more I read and learnt, the more things seemed to click into place, yet I still didn't have the confidence to identify openly as trans. I knew deep down that I was a man, but I was hesitant to admit it because of the tension it would cause with my family. My internal conflict produced a lot of anguish. The turning point came in 2017, when I shared how I felt with my then partner, Toya. I owe a great debt to her as she accepted and affirmed my gender identity, even though it changed the dynamic of our relationship.

Acknowledging my trans identity felt great, but I was still reluctant to start on hormones. My biggest concern was how my mother would react. It had been traumatic when she discovered my sexuality and I didn't want a repeat of that drama. My mother is very conservative when it comes to gender roles; the thing she most wants is for me to dress and act like a 'normal' woman, even if I date women. I knew my body would change dramatically once I started testosterone and I was scared this would upset the delicate relationship we had worked so hard to build. My second concern was money: as a migrant, I didn't have access to public healthcare and so needed to self-fund my transition, something I didn't feel equipped to do. This is the reason why many trans migrants turn to the black market. Accessing hormones in this way is dangerous because it means there is a lack of medical supervision and quality control.

My experience with hormones began after an interaction with a trans man at the Other Foundation conference in 2017. He encouraged me to begin the process, and I am very glad that he did. I felt amazing after my first shot. Being on testosterone has changed my life: it has given me confidence and helped me feel like me. The physical changes I have undergone have allowed me to build a more positive relationship with my body, as well as improving my emotional and mental outlook. I now feel I can give myself fully to the world and am confident about achieving my goals.

My transition has garnered mixed responses. Some colleagues have been incredibly supportive. A gay friend in the IT department at work changed my email address and access card to reflect my correct gender. This made it harder for others to disregard my transition. My boss, too, has been encouraging. During one of our regular staff meetings, he instructed the whole team to use he/him pronouns when referring to me. He also intervened when some guys in the building were being transphobic. There have been a few times when people have said hurtful comments, including making assumptions about my genitals. My boss won't stand for such things and has made it clear that any reports of discrimination will be taken seriously. There are still colleagues who don't acknowledge my gender, but they do so silently because they know they will be reprimanded if they say anything directly.

It was through these changes at work that my family learnt about my transition. My sister and I work for the same company and so she was there when my boss made the announcement. She immediately called my mother and said that I was 'pretending' to be a man and demanding that people refer to me as a he. I won't lie: it has been hard navigating family reactions. My sister in the UK is very supportive, and my brother is increasingly treating me as a brother. My mum and my other sisters are still struggling.

When mum was last in Johannesburg, she expected the whole family to go to church. She freaked out when she saw me wearing formal men's clothes. In her mind, I am just being difficult; she thinks I am pushing things too far by dressing in this way. She hates the visible changes in my appearance and wants desperately for me to be a regular daughter.

That day ended in such a big fight. I told my mother and sisters that it is up to them – either they accept my gender and have me in their lives, or we go back to being estranged. They are still a long way from accepting me as a man, but for the time being we aren't fighting. Basically, they pretend my transition never happened. If not speaking about it is what they need right now, then I am happy to brush it aside. I know they love me and are trying to get comfortable with this change. That is enough for me. Sometimes we need patience and grace while our families adjust.

LOVE AND PREJUDICE

Life is a mix of good times and bad. One of the highlights of living in South Africa has been the opportunity to form strong relationships, both romantic and platonic. An example of this is my relationship with Toya. We dated for four years, and although we have now separated, I still treasure the time we spent together. That relationship helped me grow in ways I never expected. I know this wouldn't have been possible in Zimbabwe and I am thankful we were able to experience everything that we did.

Apart from a few financial challenges, life in Johannesburg hasn't been too bad. Every now and then I get harassed for the way I look, but most of the time I can handle it. I try to portray a fierce image when I walk down the street. It is a defence mechanism: I want people to know that I am not afraid. I won't tolerate being disrespected.

A few times I have had people spit at me. I have also had people freak out on taxis because of the way I look. Recently, I sat next to a woman and she gave me the filthiest of looks. It was like she was going to vomit; that is how disgusted she was by me. I didn't let it bother me, and eventually the woman changed seats. It was her problem, not mine.

I am thankful I haven't faced more serious violence. I know other trans people who have been beaten up and raped. There have been murders too. It can be especially bad if you are trans *and* a migrant. I am so tired of this shit – all the judgement, all the hate, all the discrimination. Our lives aren't anyone else's business. People need to get over their own prejudices.

The other major problem is healthcare stigma. It is almost impossible for South African trans folks to access tailored health services, and the situation is even worse for migrants. Our only option is to use the private system, but that requires money, something few of us have. Even if you do have medical aid, you are unlikely to get access to gender-affirming surgery. I know from experience how much stress and anguish this causes. You would think that medical professionals would know how to support us by now, but many are openly transphobic. There are some doctors who are sympathetic and knowledgeable, like Dr Dulcy at Park Station, but they can't be responsible for all trans healthcare.

FAITH AND STIGMA

Even though it is been a while since I have attended church, I still consider myself a religious person. When I was young, I went to Mass every Sunday, but I stopped as soon as mum moved to the UK. I didn't think much about religion after that, but I never gave up on my faith. God has always been in my heart, and spirituality continues to play a role in my life.

When the pressure from my family to be 'normal' became too much, I joined a Pentecostal church. That decision changed my thinking about religion. Pentecostal services are very different from Catholic ones: a Catholic Mass has a few verses and a homily, whereas Pentecostal ones go really deep with the Bible. I learnt so much about scripture during that time and was even inspired to read the Bible at home.

At the same time, there were many aspects of Pentecostalism that made me uncomfortable. Every time I attended a service, I would be brought up to the front. The preacher would say the Spirit was calling on him to save me. There would be the laying on of hands, speaking in tongues and other stuff like that. The preacher saw me as a woman trying to be a man and was obsessed with 'fixing' me. I hated it, and I would always try to avoid being taken up front. I just wanted to pray, not to be touched or made an example of.

I also struggled with the discriminatory preaching. The pastor would say all sorts of nonsense: that LGBT people are possessed by evil spirits, that we are going to hell, that we will never see the gates of heaven. It got so bad that I stopped going. Looking back, I should have left sooner, but my need for spiritual fulfilment kept me there.

Since then I have been considering whether to attend Catholic services again. But, to be honest, I have lost interest in institutionalised religion. These days I am more of an at-home prayer warrior. That way I don't have people telling me how I should look, how I should pray or how I should express my faith.

JOINING THE LGBT MINISTRY

I first heard about the LGBT Ministry from a friend back in 2015. I was apprehensive about joining a church-based group, but Toya and I decided to give it a go. I remember being shocked when we arrived. Our friend hadn't warned us that the group was male dominated; the three of us were the only women (I hadn't transitioned at that point). Everyone was friendly and welcoming, but I didn't know if it was the right space for me. Now I am glad I stuck with it: the group has helped me learn about myself, and over the years I have formed close friendships with the other members.

For me, the LGBT Ministry functions primarily as a therapeutic space. When I first started going, I didn't think I had anything to talk about, but over time I have learnt the value of opening up emotionally. That is why I go back. I have shared things with the group that no one else knows.

As well as helping me better understand myself, the LGBT Ministry has been a great source of support. It is reassuring to know that others have had similar experiences to me. I haven't needed direct support because I have a job and a house, but I have witnessed how the group helps those in crisis. What the group has given me is a network of people I can trust and lean on.

One thing I have struggled with is how the LGBT Ministry spends so much time discussing challenges, rather than taking action to make people's lives better. Some people in the group are really suffering – they are dealing with poverty, violence, homelessness, depression, and so on. Most LGBT migrants are in a hopeless situation: very few of us have the qualifications needed to find work. What we need are entrepreneurial skills, not just a space to sit around and talk.

Even though I think improvements can be made, I recognise there are limitations in what the group can do. The LGBT Ministry offers a particular type of support – it is not an NGO, a crisis service or an educational provider. I actually had a great conversation with Ricus about this. He explained that the LGBT Ministry is, first and foremost, about spiritual care. But at times I still get frustrated. We need action, not just words. I guess I need to remember that people are at different points in their journeys.

DREAMS FOR THE FUTURE

We need to push for religious spaces that are more diverse. Right now churches are using the Bible to attack us. For many people in Africa, the Bible is their foundation, their moral compass, and if they keep hearing negative scriptural interpretations, they will continue believing that LGBT people are satanic. This is a dangerous lie.

The Bible doesn't give people a licence to mistreat us. It has one simple command: love. God is the only one who can pass judgement. Religious leaders need to make sure they preach this message clearly. Yes, I might be gay or lesbian or trans or whatever, but no one has the right to discriminate against me. I am simply living the life God has chosen for me. People need to focus on being tolerant and kind, not wasting time on hatred and discrimination. The Bible is also my foundation, and it makes me angry when people try to take it away from me. I don't believe God makes mistakes; He made me who I am for a reason, and I am proud of being trans.

Society will only change once churches are more open. Every person – regardless of what they look like – should feel welcomed and included. I find it unbelievable that church leaders say we must forgive rapists and murderers, yet they tell people to hate the LGBT community. It is madness! We deserve love and acceptance. Also, the more open and supportive our churches are, the more open and supportive our families will be.

We need to find ways to shift people's negative perceptions of migrants. Most South Africans think we are out to steal their jobs and money. If only they could understand why we really left our homes. We are here because we have to be, and most of us want to contribute to South Africa. LGBT migrants are at a double disadvantage: we have to deal with both homo/transphobia and xenophobia. The economic crisis in Zimbabwe is one of the reasons I came here, but it is not the whole story. If I could live freely and openly in Zimbabwe, I would do so, but that isn't possible right now. People like me are trying to build a better life. We are peaceful and loving; if given a chance, we will be constructive members of society. I believe in the South African Constitution because it recognises and protects all people. I know other LGBT migrants feel the same way. We must all work together to make sure the spirit of the Constitution imbues every aspect of our lives.

Since participating in this project, Thomars founded the Fruit Basket, a community-based organisation dedicated to supporting trans migrants, refugees and asylum seekers. The Fruit Basket works closely with the LGBT Ministry at Holy Trinity.

6

SEXUALITY IS A BEAUTIFUL GIFT FROM GOD

Narrated by Dancio (Zambia)

I am a 41-year-old gay man from Zambia. I first came to Johannesburg to study, but since completing my degree I have stayed and built a life. I now have permanent residency, a steady job and a strong friendship network. Migrating to South Africa opened up many opportunities for me, including the chance to explore my sexuality. Growing up in a Catholic family, I found it difficult to accept my desires, but over time I have come to believe that God made me this way for a reason. Coming to terms with my identity wasn't easy because I had heard many negative things about LGBT people. Zambian politicians are openly homophobic and their comments take a heavy toll on young minds. Thankfully, things are starting to change there now. The younger generation is more open and accepting, even when the government refuses to change the law. I hope one day LGBT Zambians won't feel pressured to leave their country, but I suspect that is still a long way off.

A COMFORTABLE CHILDHOOD

I was born in Kitwe, a large city on the Zambian Copperbelt. We lived there because my father was a manager at one of the mines. Like most Zambians, I was raised in an extended family. I have one sister and three brothers, but as a young boy I was surrounded by cousins. It was a great way to grow up, in that I was never short of people to play with. It also meant there were lots of adults looking out for me. My parents both worked full-time, but my siblings and I were never left unsupervised. There was a community of uncles and aunties who cared for us; we knew there was always someone to assist if need be.

'The animal that best describes me is a dog. I like the way a dog looks after her pups. That is similar to me: I am nurturing, loyal and protective. I try to bring everyone together. My family and friends are very important to me. I will do anything to keep them safe.'

Back then we filled our days with different games. We would play soccer, watch movies, visit friends and generally get up to mischief. There was the normal sibling rivalry that brothers have, but most of the time we got on with each other. Any fights were quickly forgotten once there were new adventures to be had.

My family was comfortable financially. We always had a roof over our heads, meals on the table and clean clothes to wear. My father's job came with many perks, such as having our private school fees covered by the mining company. My parents were aware of their privilege and made sure to support our less fortunate relatives. They took in some of their nieces and nephews, paying for their education and upkeep, as well as assisting others in the community. They saw it as their Christian duty to provide food and shelter to those who were struggling.

My early education was a positive experience. I appreciated both the academic and social aspects of school, and took pleasure in learning new things. I particularly enjoyed subjects like English, social studies and religious education, but also did well in other areas.

When I was 15, I transferred to an all-boys boarding school in Lusaka. My parents thought it would help me concentrate on my studies. By then I was starting to misbehave, hanging out with friends at night and going to parties. I guess it was their way of reprimanding me, but I didn't see it as a punishment. I actually loved boarding school. Living in such close quarters over many years, you inevitably form a special bond with the other guys. It is like being part of a brotherhood, and many of the friends I made back then are still part of my life. Strangely enough, it also helped me feel closer to my family. Being away for months at a time made me appreciate their love and support. As the saying goes: absence makes the heart grow fonder.

While I enjoyed school overall, I wouldn't describe it as the easiest period of my life. I couldn't tell my friends about the inner turmoil I was experiencing. I could no longer ignore the fact that I was gay, but I was terrified of my desires. In retrospect, I can see this was a period of transition, one that would take many years to complete.

A PERSONAL AWAKENING

I became aware of my sexuality very early on, probably when I was about eight or nine years old. At that time it was more a fascination with boys than a physical urge. There was something that drew me to them in a way that was different to girls, yet I was still too young to know I was gay. In fact, I didn't even realise my feelings were different to those of other boys.

My desires intensified when I hit puberty. By the time I was at boarding school, I was experiencing very strong attractions to other guys. My friends were obsessed with finding girlfriends, but I didn't feel the same push. Realising you are different is scary and isolating. I became aware that my desires were not something that would be accepted by society. It is also hard to be attracted to people who will never love you back. I started to worry that I would never have a 'normal' life and so I tried my best to be like everybody else. I had three or four girlfriends, simply because it was expected; all the boys my age had girlfriends, and I didn't want to be any different. It was more a tick-the-box exercise than genuine romance, even though I was fond of my partners.

Every now and then, a fellow student would comment that I was slightly feminine, but this was said flippantly, more of a joke than a slur. Looking back, I suspect there were aspects of my personality, possibly even some of my mannerisms, that puzzled my peers. Not enough to prove my sexuality, but enough to make them pause for a second or two. It never progressed into bullying or violence. By then I had learnt how to mask things that might raise suspicion.

SEX, POLITICS AND FAITH

In Zambia, there is a lot of pressure to be heterosexual. Parents expect children to follow a particular life path – find a partner, get married, buy a house, have children, and so on. You learn these expectations very early on and that makes the possibility of being gay even more terrifying.

In my case, a lot of social conditioning happened at church. Religion was an important part of my upbringing: my siblings and I attended Mass every week and were raised according to Catholic values. This wasn't something I minded. I loved going to Mass and was honoured to serve as an altar boy. Later, when I was a teenager, I was active in different church structures, such as the parish youth group.

I quickly learnt that homosexuality isn't tolerated by the church. I remember hearing sermons about the collapse of Christian morals and family values. The priests would point to gay men as evidence that society had strayed from God's path, referencing Leviticus to bring home their point. The argument was always the same: two men having sex is an abomination in the eyes of Christ and therefore being gay is inherently anti-Christian. These statements caused me great anguish. I became convinced that there was something wrong with me and began to question my moral character.

It wasn't just religious leaders who made homophobic comments. Attacking LGBT people has long been a favourite sport of Zambian politicians. They like to refer to gay men as dogs, implying that we are filthy animals incapable of controlling our urges. Politicians spread all sorts of lies – for example, they say that anal sex ruins a person's rectum and so gay men can't control their bowel movements. They also portray homosexuality as a foreign disease, something that goes against African traditions. The takeaway message is that homosexuality is sinful and disgusting, something that no Christian should tolerate. Ordinary folks, especially men, follow the lead of these politicians. When I was younger, I would hear people in the community say that gay men have a sickness that makes them behave like women. Being exposed to these myths caused me a lot of pain. It also made me confused: I didn't feel sick or dirty or possessed, and I certainly hadn't been corrupted by any foreigners. My desires seemed natural, yet everything I heard about LGBT people was negative.

FIRST GAY EXPERIENCES

Although I felt conflicted about my faith and my sexuality, I began to experiment with other boys. Such things aren't uncommon in a single-sex boarding school. We would often share beds and, occasionally, something would happen. Mostly it was just cuddling, but sometimes we would kiss and touch each other. These forms of intimacy were tolerated because there were no girls around, but they weren't something you could admit in the light of day. It didn't take me long to realise that these experiences meant something different to me. For the other boys, such encounters were casual, an experiment, something you did until you found a girlfriend, but for me they had an emotional dimension. But I still knew better than to acknowledge or act upon my feelings.

ADULT LIFE IN ZAMBIA

I finished secondary school in 1996. After returning to Kitwe, I began working on a church-led HIV project. My colleagues and I ran workshops with local youth, building awareness and promoting healthy behaviours. Our takeaway message was to be safe in each and every situation. We also ran a research project, tracking households where both parents had passed away. Doing outreach work was important to me. My sense of community has always been strong, and I was motivated by my faith to make a difference in people's lives. Like Jesus, I wanted to help the poor and needy.

Church was a big part of my life during those years. I was a committed member of the parish youth group and would eagerly participate in meetings, retreats and other activities. The youth group spent a lot of time talking about positive relationships, in line with the church's teachings. The message was clear: the only relationships with real value were heterosexual ones, and always in the context of marriage. We never spoke openly about homosexuality, but everyone knew that such things were 'sinful'. It was impossible not to feel conflicted: I respected and adhered to the church's teachings, yet I was experiencing 'immoral' desires that felt perfectly natural to me.

Even though I hated being gay, I found myself experimenting. When I was 19, I had an intimate encounter with a guy from the local community. We had been at a party and it was too late for me to go back to my parents' house. He suggested I stay at his place because he knew my parents were strict. I had always found him attractive, but never acted on my feelings because I assumed he was straight. Halfway through the night, we found ourselves making out. It was thrilling. Afterwards, we didn't speak about what had happened – I guess we were both nervous – but we did hook up a few more times. Those encounters gave me a lot of enjoyment, although I was still a long way from accepting my sexuality. It seemed impossible that I could ever reconcile what the church was saying and what I was feeling. The only thing to do, I figured, was to suppress my desires and pray to be like everyone else.

BIG CHANGES

The year 2000 was a turning point. It was the year my father passed away, an event that deeply affected me, as well as the year I left my country. The original plan was for me to study in the UK, but the value of the Zambian kwacha had plummeted and there was no way my family could cover the school fees. The next best option was South Africa. Back then the internet was just becoming a thing and I used it to research life in my new home. That is how I learnt about South Africa's laws. I couldn't help but feel a tingle of joy. I hardly dared admit my excitement: perhaps, I thought, I could finally be me – the *real* me.

I tried to put this discovery out of mind, but my curiosity got the better of me. I was intrigued about living in a country with gay clubs and events. South Africa seemed like another world. I was particularly excited by the possibility of meeting other African men like me. My sexuality was never the primary reason for my leaving Zambia – I was still far from comfortable with my desires – but it was a happy coincidence that I was going somewhere with a visible LGBT community.

I knew there was no space for such things in Zambia. Just a couple of years earlier, some Zambian activists had formed the Lesbian, Gay and Transgender Association (LEGATRA). The government crackdown was swift and fierce. I remember ministers, including the president, denouncing the organisation and ordering the arrest of anyone advocating for LGBT rights. The media started publishing personal details of LEGATRA members, fuelling public hostility. One of the group's founders was forced to flee to South Africa because of the violence he suffered. Not long after that the government increased the penalty for 'crimes against nature'. It wasn't a good time to be coming of age as a gay man. Having the opportunity to relocate to South Africa was a relief.

When it was time to leave, I boarded a bus in Kitwe. We drove for almost 24 hours, travelling first to Lusaka, then Harare and on to Johannesburg. I remember having mixed emotions: I was sad to say goodbye to friends and family, and was nervous about being in a foreign country, but I was also excited about having more freedom. By the time the bus arrived at Park Station, I was ready to begin my new life.

A SENSE OF BELONGING

For my first year in Johannesburg, I stayed with relatives. We got on well and so it wasn't a bad living situation. However, staying with family meant living two lives: at home, I was straight; out on the streets, I was exploring my sexuality. It was a slow process: over time I met some other gay men and began to feel more comfortable with my identity. I still wasn't out to friends at school or church, and certainly not out to my family, but I was slowly figuring out what it means to be a black gay man.

It was at this time that I had my first serious relationships. Looking back, I can see that these were an important part of my personal development. Like everyone in their 20s, I was working out what I wanted in life. Back in Zambia, I could never have imagined that committed relationships like these were possible, not just because of the law but also because of how gay men were talked about. People never spoke about love or commitment in connection with homosexuality, just myths about sickness and perversion.

The other thing that had a big impact on me was attending my first Pride parade. What struck me was how diverse the crowd was: there were white people, coloured people and black people from all across the continent. It was a day I will never forget. For the first time in my life, I felt absolutely comfortable with being African and gay. I was around people just like me and that gave me a sense of belonging. Later, when we partied in Braamfontein, I felt totally happy, totally free, totally me.

A PERMANENT HOME

When I first moved to South Africa, my plan was to finish university, gain some work experience and then take my skills back to Zambia. As time went on, and as I built up my social networks, I started to think about staying permanently. Many of my formative experiences had happened here in South Africa and that made me question whether I should return home. Also, I had secured a part-time job in my final year at university and had the option of moving to a full-time position. Back then it wasn't difficult to transition from a study visa to a work permit. In fact, the company's HR department took care of everything.

After being on a work permit for a few years, I had the option of applying for permanent residency. That, too, was a relatively pain-free process, although it still took a long time for my permit to be processed.

Having lived in South Africa for close to 20 years, I feel very settled. I have a strong network of friends who come from all over the world – Southern Africa, East Africa, West Africa and Europe. I love being around people from different cultures and backgrounds.

Life in South Africa hasn't been too hard, but I know that is because I am in a fortunate position: I have permanent residency, a steady job and a solid support network. In the last decade, xenophobia has become much more of a problem. There are a lot of dangerous stereotypes floating around. When someone realises you are foreign, they treat you differently. Sometimes they will make a derogatory comment, but most often they are just stand-offish. I don't think it is always on purpose. In a way, I understand where the attitude comes from. So many South Africans are struggling to survive and that can breed resentment, but blaming foreigners is a dangerous slippery slope. You see this casual xenophobia all the time. I have had police officers be very mean to me when they realise I can't speak fluent Sesotho or isiZulu. These sorts of encounters make migrants nervous about seeking help.

I have been lucky in that I haven't faced much direct prejudice. Most of the homophobia I have encountered has come from other migrants. I have overheard guests at Zambian social events say bigoted things about LGBT people. It all stems from ignorance: if you grow up hearing negative comments, you are likely to internalise those beliefs. In Zambia, very few people are exposed to positive representations of LGBT people and end up believing the myths and stereotypes.

EVOLVING FAMILY RELATIONSHIPS

In coming to accept my sexuality, I have had to navigate family expectations about my future. I am out to a number of cousins, especially the younger ones, and they are very supportive. Someone outed me to my brother, but he didn't make a big deal of it. He doesn't think it is his place to interfere in my affairs. His view is that I should live my life in whatever way makes me happy. The rest of my family has adopted a 'don't ask, don't tell' approach. To an outsider, it might seem like my family doesn't accept my sexuality, but the reality is more complicated. My relatives make it clear that they love and care for me, even if they don't have the language or confidence to speak openly about my personal life.

These different responses mirror current attitudes in Zambia. My younger relatives have no problem with LGBT people. They don't see it as a choice or a sin, and they accept different ways of being and loving. It is, thankfully, an attitude that many people their age seem to share. The younger generation is definitely more progressive, probably because they access information online.

Older Zambians are unlikely to change their opinion, especially as the government is determined to maintain a hard-line stance. Even those older people who are willing to accept an LGBT relative won't speak out publicly. It is still regarded as shameful, something that must be kept hidden. But I understand their caution: they have seen what happens when people go public about their sexuality. Older people remember what happened with LEGATRA, as well as more recent controversies. A few years ago, for example, an activist was arrested after advocating for LGBT rights on Zambian television. More recently, a gay couple was sentenced to 15 years' imprisonment. Such cases create a culture of fear and silence.

A STRONG SENSE OF FAITH

Religion has played a big role in my life, and my faith continues to be strong. My belief in a higher power shapes how I understand myself and how I interact with others; it guides my actions and provides a sense of purpose. I am an active member of a congregation here in Johannesburg. Being part of that church gives me great joy and pleasure.

My faith has evolved over my lifetime. If someone had asked me about it ten years ago, they would have received a very different answer to what I give today. When I was younger, I saw my faith as conflicting with my sexuality. While my desires seemed natural to me, I still believed I was defying the church's teachings. It is impossible not to feel like that when you have sat through sermons on Sodom and Gomorrah. I clearly remember hearing priests describe LGBT people as an abomination and a threat to society's moral fabric.

In more recent times, I have come to regard my sexuality as integral to my spirituality, and vice versa. I had the good fortune of attending a religious retreat in Europe about a decade ago, where I was reunited with a priest I had met in Zambia. I opened up to him about my sexuality and he assured me that there is nothing wrong with being gay. I was shocked by his words. Instead of chastising me, he asked if I could remember the moment when I decided to be gay. I said no, and he assured me that this was because God had made me this way. I remember feeling an incredible sense of lightness. Up until then, I had been carrying around so much guilt and shame. Suddenly I had a different way of understanding my identity.

It might seem strange, but it hadn't occurred to me that my desires were given by God. They had always been there, but I had associated them with sin. Your psyche takes a blow when you are constantly told that you aren't normal. Having someone from inside the church tell me that I was okay made a huge difference.

Since then I have given my sexuality a lot of thought. Now I see it as a gift. It is something God wants of me, and I have a duty to honour this aspect of my being.

While I am now totally comfortable with my sexuality, I appreciate that others are still grappling with issues of diversity. I don't openly identify as gay at my regular church, not because I am ashamed but because I know it will cause friction. I don't feel the need to announce it publicly. God knows the faith I carry in my heart and that is all that matters.

FINDING HOLY TRINITY

It was by coincidence that I learnt about the LGBT Ministry. I was attending a course in Amsterdam and one of the guest speakers was Ricus, the group's founder. He had my attention the moment he described himself as a gay Catholic living in Johannesburg. I went up to him and introduced myself. He gave me all the details of the LGBT Ministry and, once I was back in South Africa, I went along for myself.

The strongest emotion I felt that first day was excitement. It was such a pleasure to meet everyone and hear their stories. It was unlike any other religious space I had encountered. Never before had I been surrounded by LGBT migrants who wanted to talk about spirituality. So many LGBT people are excluded from churches and so it is wonderful to find a parish that openly welcomes us. It means that LGBT people don't have to sit at home alone on a Sunday, struggling with shame and guilt.

In joining the group, I hoped not only to meet other LGBT Catholics, but also to give something back to my community. I have been lucky in life: I have had an opportunity to develop life skills, build a career and become independent. At work, I am a member of the company's LGBT group and that has allowed me to learn useful things that can be passed on to others. Most of the LGBT Ministry members are younger than me and I would like to help them where I can. Whenever I hear about their journeys to South Africa and their daily struggles, I am reminded of the blessings in my own life. I see it as a moral obligation, both as a Catholic and as a gay man, to give back where I can.

We desperately need more spaces like the LGBT Ministry. Faith plays a big part in the lives of Africans, and churches have the potential to transform attitudes. We have seen the positive influence that religious institutions can have (for example, in the fight against HIV) and we need them to do the same with LGBT rights.

The other reason we need affirming spaces is because LGBT people crave spiritual nourishment. If you grow up feeling isolated and afraid, you miss out on important life skills. Many LGBT people don't have positive role models, or they don't get exposed to healthy relationships, or they don't learn to love themselves and their God. Many are first exposed to 'gay life' on the streets and as a result end up in trouble. We need spaces that build up people's faith, that give them access to information, that help them grow and thrive. A church should be a home, a place where a person can be nurtured and healed, but that isn't happening right now.

HOPES AND DREAMS

First and foremost, I want to see society become more equal. LGBT people just want respect, not special rights. In the same way that a poor person shouldn't be treated differently to a rich person, an LGBT person shouldn't be treated differently to a straight person. Every human – gay or straight – is a reflection of God's love, and we must rejoice in the gifts that God has given us. He has put a certain type of love in my heart and it is my duty to use that love. Discrimination and judgement are the real sins, not loving the same sex. Our churches must return to the mission of Jesus Christ and follow His call to protect those on the margins of society.

I also hope for change in my home country. There is less hostility among younger Zambians, but it is still going to take time for things to meaningfully change. Those in power refuse to accept diversity. I hope that one day my fellow LGBT Zambians won't have to run away. We should be safe and free in our homeland.

I think the winds of change are blowing. Activists in Angola, Botswana, Mozambique and other countries are using the courts to make things better for LGBT people. We are also seeing changes in the Catholic Church. Pope Francis is trying to make it more open and welcoming, both for LGBT people and for migrants. Only a few days ago, the Holy Father called on Catholics to show compassion for LGBT people. He even compared homophobic politicians to Hitler! To have the head of our communion say that homosexuality is not an illness or a sin is truly remarkable. Hopefully his message of tolerance will be taken up, because the church really does need to be reformed – the child abuse scandal is proof of that!

Change is also needed here in South Africa. We have wonderful role models speaking out in support of LGBT rights – Archbishop Emeritus Desmond Tutu, Justice Edwin Cameron, even Cyril Ramaphosa – but there are still dangerous lies circulating in the community. Ordinary people tend to be scared of things they don't understand. LGBT migrants are particularly vulnerable. They are struggling with the basics – food, shelter, healthcare – and urgently need support.

On a personal level, I want to continue to grow. The last two decades have been an incredible journey. There was my physical journey from Zambia to South Africa, but also my emotional journey towards self-awareness and self-acceptance. I am thankful to this country for letting me find myself and for helping me mature into the man I am today. Hopefully, in the next few years I can find the love of my life and get married, but we will have to wait and see. In the meantime, I will continue to give back however I can.

7

THIS IS WHERE GOD WANTS ME TO BE

Narrated by Mike (Zimbabwe)

I was born and raised in Bulawayo. I left for South Africa in 2015, when I was 25 years old. I have been living in and around Soweto ever since. There are many things I like about my life here: I am part of a supportive community and am free to chill with my LGBT friends. But I also face many difficulties, especially in relation to employment, housing and documentation. Not having a stable income makes it hard to pay rent and buy food. The LGBT Ministry has helped me deal with these challenges, while also providing a safe space for me to express my faith. I am a devout Catholic and was overjoyed to discover a church that is welcoming of LGBT people. Being part of an affirming faith community has made a big difference to my life.

THE FAMILY PERFORMER

I am the eldest child in my family: I have one younger brother and two younger sisters. Growing up, I had a lot of responsibilities. My family wasn't well off and so both of my parents had to work – my father as a technician for a communications company and my mother as a domestic worker. My mother would only arrive home at 8 o'clock in the evening and so it was up to me to look after my siblings. My father would finish work earlier, but he would go straight to a tavern and drink. He didn't take his family responsibilities seriously. My mother cared for us very much, but she had to work long hours so we could get by. When she did arrive home, she would make sure we had everything we needed, no matter how exhausted she was from her workday. She has always been a kind and generous woman, and I am still close to her today.

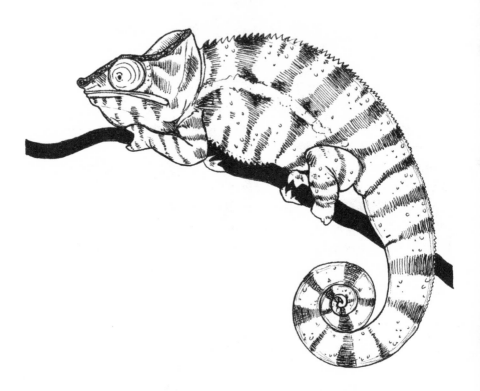

'Chameleons change colour when they need to fit in, and that is just like me. I can adapt
to any situation. This is how I am able to deal with so many challenges. I am good at
blending in with my surroundings and, when I need to, I can hide my true identity.'

Even though I had a lot of responsibilities, I never felt overwhelmed. My grandmother stayed nearby and would help out when needed. Later, after my parents separated and my mother migrated for work, my siblings and I moved in with our aunt. There was always an adult nearby whom I could turn to for help.

My childhood was very happy. I was mischievous and would often get into trouble at school. I would sing and dance in class, much to the annoyance of my teachers. It wasn't that I was naughty per se; I just had a lot of energy. I actually enjoyed going to class and never bunked off. The problem was that some teachers didn't know how to handle my personality. They wanted me to be like the other boys.

Most of my energy went into after-school activities. I was in a choir, a dance group and a theatre club. I *loved* performing. Even when I was very young, I would put on shows for my family. I was always drawn to feminine parts, although I am not sure why. I would sing in a soprano voice or act out a female role. This wasn't a conscious decision; I just did what felt natural. I also used to love dressing up. Sometimes I would wait for my mother to leave and then sneak into her room and try things on. Back then I wasn't frightened of my femininity. I was always more comfortable around girls, and I hated sports like rugby and soccer.

This changed as I started to grow older. People would say negative comments that made me self-conscious. I remember guys making jokes about me being a girl. By the time I realised I was gay, I knew better than to reveal this part of myself. I would regulate my behaviour because of the stigma associated with being feminine. I even thought about giving up singing and dancing, but these were my main social outlets. Instead, I tried to behave in a more masculine way, hoping I wouldn't draw attention. I was frightened that people would find out about my sexuality and treat me badly.

A RELIGIOUS CALLING

I left school in 2006. I failed my O-levels and had to drop out because my family didn't have enough money for me to repeat. I couldn't find a job and spent the next year contemplating my future. After a lot of thought, I decided to enter a seminary. I was very religious and felt a calling to the priesthood. I spoke about it with my parish priest and he urged me to follow my heart, but he also warned against rash decisions. He encouraged me to re-sit my O-levels and even helped raise funds for my school fees.

After passing my exams, I entered the seminary. It caused a lot of friction in my family. My mother was very supportive, but my father was firmly against it. He wasn't religious and couldn't comprehend my decision. He even threatened to disown me.

I only stayed at the seminary for a year. I don't regret joining because it helped me connect more strongly with my faith, but leaving was the right thing to do. My decision to drop out was motivated by two factors. First, there was a lot of family drama going on. After my parents split up, my mother moved to South Africa to find work. She was supporting my siblings on her own because my father wasn't fulfilling his financial responsibilities. I was concerned about the pressure she was under and wanted to contribute more to the family. Second, I had doubts about taking the vows. I didn't know if I could suppress my sexual desires and live the life required of a priest. The vows are incredibly serious, and I couldn't take them if I had any uncertainty. Leaving was a hard decision. I still wonder if the priesthood is my true vocation.

After exiting the seminary, I went to live with my father. I wasn't in a great place, emotionally or financially. My only income came from the church: I was helping out at the youth centre and doing administrative work for one of the nuns. The work was irregular and I barely made enough to survive. Most of my days were spent looking for a full-time job. My father decided to teach me a lesson by not providing any assistance. I would spend the whole day in town looking for work, often without enough money for food. I even had to borrow transport money from friends and relatives. Eventually I landed a retail job. It was such a relief to have some stability. Most importantly, it allowed me to move out on my own.

PEOPLE LIKE ME

It was only after leaving the seminary that I allowed myself to explore my sexuality. I was very discreet and was reluctant to admit my feelings, even to myself. I was scared of what would happen if people found out.

One day, Mpumelelo, a friend from church, invited me back to his place and confronted me: 'You are gay, aren't you?' he asked. 'Don't worry because I am too.' Up until then I had no idea he was gay, and I am still not sure how he knew about me. He ended up inviting me to a party at the Bulawayo branch of Gays and Lesbians of Zimbabwe (GALZ). I was initially apprehensive, but Mpumelelo assured me it would be safe: 'There is good security,' he said. 'No one, not even the police, will bother the people inside.' The GALZ centre was in an upmarket part of town, far from my friends and family, and that helped put me at ease.

The party was so much fun: there was drinking, dancing, people making out. The first time you attend an event like that, you are considered hot property – everyone wants to get with the new guy. It was amazing being around people like me, just chilling and having fun. What surprised me was how many faces I recognised.

After that I started regularly attending GALZ events. As well as going to parties, I would participate in workshops and dialogues. We discussed so many issues: health and HIV, safety and security, the law and our rights. These sessions were really helpful because they were my main source of information. I was still largely in the closet and didn't have access to many resources. At GALZ events, I could ask questions and learn from other people's experiences.

It was around this time that I had my first relationship. It was with a guy from church, but not Mpumelelo. Once I became involved with GALZ, I started finding out about other gay guys, including people I had known for years. All it takes is one connection and then you are part of the community. It was through these links that I found my first boyfriend.

Even though I was meeting more and more LGBT people, I mainly socialised with my straight friends. This seemed like the best way to hide my sexuality. I was scared of being ostracised or attacked if people discovered my secret. Zimbabweans can be very conservative and don't always react well to LGBT people.

One night, when I was at a club with friends, a very drunk femme guy came up and started dancing with me. He was moving his body like Shakira and getting a lot of attention. People started taking photos of us together and that made me uncomfortable. I wanted to run away, convinced that my photo would end up in the newspaper. That didn't happen, but the incident shows how afraid I was back then.

And I was right to be nervous. In 2013, the GALZ Christmas party was raided by the police. They surrounded the venue and started assaulting anyone who tried to leave. Some people were arrested, myself included. It was mainly drag queens and people wearing political T-shirts who were targeted. Luckily, someone was able to call the Sexual Rights Centre and they sent their lawyers to the police station. They were able to negotiate our release, though we still had to pay a fine. I was terrified when we were taken into custody; I was sure our names would be splashed across the media. I couldn't stop thinking about how my family and church friends would react. But, much to my relief, nothing serious happened. I am still grateful to those lawyers for protecting our privacy.

A NEW BEGINNING

I stayed in Bulawayo for a year after the raid. I was unemployed, directionless and struggling to get by. I only survived because my boyfriend, Sindiso, owned a small business. One day he proposed an idea: I should travel to South Africa and source stock for his shop. The plan was to buy accessories and other things that weren't readily available in Zimbabwe. I jumped at the opportunity because it would allow me to visit my mother. By then she had been working in Johannesburg for almost seven years. I missed her desperately and wanted nothing more than to see her.

It wasn't long after arriving in Johannesburg that I decided to stay. The city was a shock at first – it was *very* different to Bulawayo – but it was also exhilarating. There were so many different kinds of people, all doing their own thing, and I knew there would be a better chance of finding work in such a big city. It was also getting scarier to be LGBT in Zimbabwe: police raids were becoming more common, and every few months a government minister would say something homophobic. Going from this hostile environment to one in which LGBT people could openly show affection was amazing. It seemed like everyone here was happy and carefree. That is exactly how I wanted to be. The hardest part was telling Sindiso. We had been together for a couple of years, and I loved him dearly. Still, I knew that staying here was the right thing to do.

Sindiso didn't take the news well. He was constantly calling my phone, and even started posting inappropriate comments on Facebook. He sunk into a deep depression and threatened me with suicide. He made it clear that I would be responsible for his death. At one point, when he was very drunk, he took a bunch of sleeping pills. He called and told me what he had done, and I immediately contacted his aunt. Thankfully, his family was able to get him to hospital in time. In the end I had to change my phone number and block him on social media.

However, that didn't stop him from outing me. One day, quite out of the blue, he called my mother. He told her we had been dating and that I had deserted him. My mother stayed calm and told him it was our private business. He begged my mother to send me back to Zimbabwe. Again, she emphasised that this was something for us to work out. After the call, she asked me if there was anything I wanted to tell her. I pretended not to know what she was talking about. We still haven't had that conversation, but I think she has come to tolerate my sexuality. My father still doesn't know, and I doubt he ever will. He would kill me if he found out. I suspect my siblings have guessed, but I don't know for sure. I am a private person and my siblings know not to pry. I have told my sisters off in the past for snooping into my affairs and now they wouldn't dare raise such a topic. It is not that I am embarrassed or ashamed; I just like my personal business to remain private.

TRYING TO SURVIVE

When I first got to South Africa, I stayed with my mother in Hillbrow. In less than a month, we moved to Robertsham, where my mother's cousin lived. We soon moved again, this time to Regents Park, and a little while later my mother left for Mpumalanga. I decided to stay in Gauteng and found a back room in Soweto. I have been living in the township ever since. Housing has been something I have struggled with because I haven't always had a steady income. It is nearly impossible to find a job without documentation.

I first entered South Africa on a visitor's visa. That wasn't a problem because I had a passport and was only planning to stay for a month. Once I decided to relocate permanently, I had to find a way to renew my visa. This meant getting someone to have my passport stamped on my behalf every three months. That wasn't hard: there are always truck drivers who are willing to help – for a fee, of course! I did this for a while, but wanted a more permanent and stable solution. I decided to apply for asylum based on my sexual orientation. The South African government claims that this is a straightforward process, but the reality is quite different. In the end it took me over five years to formalise my status.

The first hurdle was getting to Marabastad. It is far from where I stay in Soweto and thus requires a lot of transport money. You also have to arrive before sunrise if you want to get inside. The area around the centre is chaotic, with criminals exploiting the lack of security; if you want to leave with your belongings, you have to keep your wits about you. There is also a lot of corruption. One time I had to pay R400 just to get through the gate and then the person who was supposedly helping me disappeared. That was the last of my money and so I had to turn around and go home. I have also witnessed the security guards being violent. Once I saw people being pulled out of the queue and beaten. Even an old man was assaulted. After a couple of attempts to apply for asylum, I decided it wasn't worth it. I couldn't face going back to that place.

Living without documentation is horrible. You live in fear of being solicited for a bribe, arrested or deported. Very few people will give you work, and those who do are exploitative. This makes it hard to lead a normal life. I did manage to hold down a job at Woolworths for a while, but that was only because I used a friend's ID book. I had to disappear once management started asking questions.

In 2017, I decided to try again with my asylum application. Marabastad was still hectic, but it was slightly more organised this time around. Of course, the guards were still taking bribes. I was thrilled when I made it inside, but then I ran into another hurdle. I told the official I was gay and applying for asylum because of homophobic persecution. She was confused and told me she had no experience dealing with such cases. She called out to a colleague and explained my case. He said they couldn't process a claim on those grounds. The officials weren't overly rude, although they did give me funny looks, but it was clear they had no knowledge of LGBT issues. They also didn't seem to know the law. I was eventually issued with a Zimbabwean Exemption Permit because it was easier for them.

It took a while after getting my permit to find a job. I went for so many interviews, but was never successful. A couple of times the business owners made rude comments about my sexuality or nationality. Not having a job made my life difficult. Landlords don't like to give rent extensions and so what little money I could raise went straight to them. I now have a hospitality job and am able to pay rent and buy groceries, but who knows how long this will last.

The other problem I face is street harassment. I have had people yell homophobic slurs at me in the mall close to where I stay. They use words like '*inkonkoni*' and '*stabane*'. This stems from a lack of education. Many people in Soweto are traditional and don't know about different sexualities or genders. They think being LGBT is evil and anti-Christian. I have even had landlords say nasty things once they discovered my sexuality. Discrimination doesn't happen all the time, but when it does it hurts.

SEARCHING FOR A RELIGIOUS COMMUNITY

My faith has always been close to my heart. When I was growing up, I would go with my mother to her church. My father wasn't religious and so never came along; he would stay home or go drinking. I enjoyed going to my mother's church, but I hated how the service went on for the whole day. As I got older, I tried out a few different denominations. I went along to Pentecostal and Zionist churches, but neither felt right. It wasn't until secondary school that I attended my first Catholic Mass and formally joined the church.

As an adult, my faith continues to play a big role in my life. I try to live according to Catholic teaching, but I am not perfect. Church helps me stay grounded; it gives me a sense of purpose and direction.

EXPERIENCE OF HOLY TRINITY

I started attending Holy Trinity not long after I moved to Johannesburg. I found it by reaching out to Dumi and asking if he could recommend a church. I had met Dumi back in Bulawayo and knew he was Catholic. He told me he was part of a church in Braamfontein and offered to take me along.

Over the years I have become more involved with Holy Trinity. Since February 2017, I have been a member of its Sacred Heart Sodality. This is a special group for those wishing to honour the compassion of Christ through community service. We are identifiable by our special blue uniforms and distinctive red rosettes. Last June, the chairperson asked for my rosette, saying she had to repair it, but later she told me I could no longer be part of the group. She said it was because of my involvement with the LGBT Ministry. I was speechless. I reported the incident, and Fr Graham offered to mediate. He explained that the two groups are separate and that my participation in one has no bearing on the other. The chairperson still doesn't like me and is visibly uncomfortable with my sexuality, but she knows better than to say anything. It was wonderful to receive that level of support. It showed just how much Holy Trinity respects its LGBT congregants.

A SPIRITUAL HOME

I was shocked when Dumi first showed me a flyer for the LGBT Ministry. I knew the Catholic Church doesn't condone same-sex relationships and had grown up hearing anti-LGBT comments. This made me even more intrigued by the LGBT Ministry. 'Perhaps this is where God wants me to be,' I thought to myself.

Although I was nervous before that first meeting, my fears vanished as soon as I met everyone. I was asked by Dumi to introduce myself, and straightaway the group made me feel welcome. That first day we watched *Noah's Arc*, a TV series about black gay men in America, and afterwards we reflected on our own experiences. It was fantastic to hear from people who have faced similar struggles to me. Since then we have covered many topics: Christian attitudes towards homosexuality, affirming interpretations of the Bible, being true to your faith, maintaining healthy relationships, coming out to friends and family – all sorts of things.

We also try to raise awareness of LGBT issues within the parish. Fr Graham supports this by inviting us to join important devotions, such as the Stations of the Cross. I always take part, not just as an expression of my faith but also to increase the visibility of LGBT Christians. It shows that we are as faithful and committed as the rest of the parish. It also provides an opportunity to pray for our LGBT brothers and sisters. I know people who are struggling to find work, or dealing with health issues, or battling with drugs. I ask Jesus to bring them peace and comfort.

Not everything the group does is serious. One of the best parts is making friends from all corners of the globe. We have had members from Botswana, Nigeria, Congo, Uganda, Zambia, South Africa, Pakistan, Holland and many other places. This means we get exposed to different experiences and points of view. I have made many close friends through the group. It is a special connection: we are always there when someone needs help, but also when they need to let off steam. If there is a special event happening, such as a Pride celebration, we go along together.

MESSAGE OF HOPE

I wish churches would be more welcoming and accepting. At the moment, LGBT people are being pushed away from God. Churches need to accommodate diverse communities. And this doesn't just mean LGBT people – they also need to welcome migrants, the disabled, the poor and others who struggle. We are all created in God's image, and we all deserve love and respect. The Bible is clear on this: we must care for one another, no matter our differences. Church leaders must read their Bibles and follow Jesus' example; they must teach the community to accept and love. That is the first step.

Communication is also very important. Church leaders have a responsibility to share accurate information with their congregations. Through educating communities, church leaders can help end discrimination. They can set a positive example by including us in church life. We should be free to worship without being exposed to hate speech. If we are told we are possessed or sick, we will feel rejected and stop coming to church; if we are welcomed and celebrated, we will feel included and want to contribute to our spiritual communities.

Holy Trinity has shown just how much impact a church can have if it promotes acceptance. I pray that other churches will follow its lead.

I also want to see changes across Africa. In Zimbabwe and many other countries, LGBT people are still waiting for freedom. We have to educate people in these places and demand our rights. We even need more education campaigns here in South Africa. I know that many locals are still misinformed, including those who are tasked with helping us. South Africans need to understand that LGBT migrants come here for protection, yet still we are suffering.

8

GOD KNOWS THE DEPTH OF MY FAITH

Narrated by Zee (South Africa)

I am 28 years old. I identify as a woman who loves women. I used to describe myself as lesbian, but now I am sick of labels. These days I prefer to focus on the loving part. I live in Vosloorus, a large township to the southeast of Johannesburg. I have always lived on the East Rand, but have moved between different places – Leondale, Katlehong, Vosloorus. Moving around isn't easy, especially when there are family pressures involved, but these days I feel settled. My life has had its fair share of drama, but I have always managed to hang on to my faith. Even when I have been isolated from my family and my church, I have kept God in my heart. The way I have been treated by other Christians shows why we need churches to be more open and accepting. Education is the first step in making that happen. I hope that one day humanity can learn to truly love all of God's children.

CHILDHOOD AND FAMILY

I am a mix of cultures and beliefs. My father is Swazi and my mother is Zulu. My father is very traditional and raised me according to Swazi customs; my mother is a proud Christian and made sure I followed her faith. This tension has been a defining feature of my life. One side has always been about African beliefs and customs, while the other has steered me towards the Bible and church. It wasn't easy balancing the two. These days I appreciate that my parents had my best interests at heart, even if it didn't seem like it at the time. My parents ended up divorcing in 2008, when I was 17 years old. It was a difficult transition, but it was definitely for the best.

'I am like a lion because I am brave and go for what I want. Lions are also family-orientated and protective, just like me. I always protect those who are close to me.'

I come from a large family. There are nine children in total, and I am the second-born. Only four of us are from mum and dad's marriage; the other five are from my dad's second marriage. My big sister is ten years older than me and so we don't have much in common. I love her, but we aren't close. I get on very well with my two other sisters from mum and dad's marriage. They are quite a bit younger than me – one by eight years and the other by ten – but we have always been close. I don't know my other siblings so well, but they are still an important part of my life.

My mother and I have always had a strained relationship. She was more like a distant relative than a maternal figure. From the ages of five to nine, I was raised by my maternal grandmother. After that I was raised by my aunt, with help from my dad. Whenever I saw my mum during that period, the conversation would be stilted. I don't think we ever said more than a passing 'Hi, how are you?' There just wasn't a bond between us. My dad and aunt were definitely the most important figures in my life. I am still very close to my father; my aunt passed away in 2008. I miss her very much. One of my biggest regrets is not telling her about my sexuality. I know she would have stood by me, no matter what.

After my aunt passed, I went to live with my mum. I stayed there for a couple of years, but the situation became unbearable after I came out. Since then I have been trying to give my mother space to work through her emotions, but her words and actions test my patience. Our relationship remains strained.

FINDING A VOICE

I attended a Catholic school, even though I was baptised in the Lutheran Church. It was a typical religious education: very conservative, very rigid. But there were also many positives. My school instilled in me a strong belief in the Catholic virtues, like hope, charity and justice.

I was an introvert at school, preferring to watch and listen rather than be the centre of attention. The thing I most struggled with was the uniform policy. It was mandatory for girls to wear dresses in summer, and I absolutely hated it. I used to feel exposed and insecure. Winter was easier because girls could choose between pants or a skirt. At least for those months I felt comfortable in my skin.

I am grateful to my teachers for helping me recognise my talents. My English teacher, in particular, was instrumental in helping me find my voice. She nurtured my love of poetry and encouraged me – in the face of great reluctance – to share my writing. Her support had a profound impact on my life, and even today I use writing to express my emotions.

FAMILY TENSIONS

There were signs of my sexuality from an early age. I was always a tomboy: I refused to wear skirts and dresses, and I loved to play boisterous games. When I was young, possibly eight or nine, I announced to my mum that I would never carry my own child. That wasn't necessarily evidence of my sexuality, but it did show that I was uncomfortable with traditional gender roles.

I was young when I first acted upon my desires. I started 'dating' a girl from next door, in the way that young kids do. We had grown up together; I was ten and she was eight. We didn't have a name for what we were feeling, but we definitely knew what we were doing. Our fling didn't last long – but long enough for me to think about what I wanted in life.

In secondary school I dated guys. This was due to peer pressure rather than genuine feelings. I still experimented with girls, but I was always expected to have a boyfriend. It was a confusing period: I was unsatisfied being with guys, but I didn't have another option – at least that is what it felt like to me. When I was 14, I fell pregnant for the first time. I miscarried after three months, an experience that left me feeling empty and depressed. Four years later, I fell pregnant again, but this time I decided to have an abortion. It was a painful decision, but certainly the right one.

I haven't technically come out to my father, but I don't think that matters. It is not something I have to tell him. My father realised I was special when I was still very young and he has never tried to change me. He treated me differently to my sisters, almost like a son, and encouraged me to follow my interests. He even bought me boy clothes because he knew they made me feel more comfortable. He would give them to me without saying a word. There was no judgement, no disapproval, no anger.

I remember once being out with my father when we ran into one of his friends. My father introduced me as his child, rather than his daughter, and his friend greeted me as if I were a boy. He panicked when he realised his mistake. '*Ngiyaxolisa!*' he said, red with embarrassment. Other fathers would have been angry, but my dad laughed it off. He didn't see it as an insult. He never cares how I dress or act. And he definitely doesn't worry about other people's opinions.

The person I did have to tell was my mother. I came out to her in 2011, when I was 20. I had hoped my honesty would bridge the gap between us. I had always dreamed of having a special mother–daughter bond. Regrettably, that isn't how things turned out. It blew up into such a drama. My mother went on and on about the Bible, quoting this and that verse at me. She said I was possessed by a demon. 'You must end this sick and perverted lifestyle!' she screamed. She told me flat out that she would never condone my sexuality because she didn't want to join me in hell.

For weeks we fought constantly. I would be sitting down, minding my own business, and suddenly my mother would storm in and start yelling about Sodom and Gomorrah. She would accuse me of going against the Bible and violating God's natural order. Sometimes she would be distraught, crying uncontrollably, and then she would fly into a rage. Other times she would preach, begging me to heal my ways. The stress was relentless.

In 2012, almost a year after coming out, I realised I had to escape. By then I had found a job and was in a position to be financially independent. It all happened very quickly: I told mum I was leaving on the Monday and I was gone by the Saturday. It was one of the best decisions I have ever made.

My relationship with my mother continues to be tense. I am always on edge when I visit her because I never know what she will say. I had hoped things would improve with time, especially now that LGBT issues are more openly discussed in South Africa, but she is adamant that I am going to hell. Her attitude has made things very difficult for my sisters. They know about my sexuality and are generally supportive. My older sister once told me to live the life that makes me happy. It is hardest for my younger sisters because they still live at home. They know I have a partner, but they can't mention her in case it upsets mum. We all know the topic is off-limits. It makes me sad because I want to share my life with them.

BUILDING A HOME

When I first left home, I moved to eBasothong in Vosloorus. I was staying by myself and was worried that my landlord – an old man – would have a problem with my sexuality. I didn't say anything to him, but my clothes were enough to give me away. In the end he became a father figure; he was very protective and would regularly check to see that I was okay. He proves that you can't judge a book by its cover.

In 2014, I started having a WhatsApp conversation with my girlfriend, D.C. We had been introduced by a mutual acquaintance and immediately hit it off. I was in Durban at the time, but quickly decided to head home. D.C. and I have been together ever since.

We have moved around a lot since then. We started off in Doornfontein, but moved to Yeoville, then Soweto and finally back to Vosloorus. We have now lived in a couple of places around Vosloorus. We once had a landlord who had a real problem with our relationship. She would give us dirty looks and make negative comments. Thankfully, we now live somewhere where we feel welcome and accepted.

Vosloorus is a relatively safe place to be an LGBT person. It hasn't had as many hate crimes as other parts of the East Rand. Someone on a taxi might give you a funny look or say something under their breath, but most people don't care. They let us go about our business without much fuss. When someone does say something, I don't let it upset me.

SURVIVING AGAINST THE ODDS

The biggest challenge in my life has been unemployment, not homophobia, although the two have occasionally gone hand in hand. One time I went for an interview at a restaurant. I am a trained chef and was more than qualified for the job, but the manager seemed more interested in my appearance than my work experience. He said he doesn't like 'women who try to be men' and that I wasn't suitable for the position.

I know other LGBT people who are really struggling. They are being mistreated because of how they dress, or speak, or act. I am not as butch as some lesbians and haven't been on the receiving end of violence, but I know it is a problem for others. I am proud of how I look, and I refuse to change. Over the last few years I have finally made peace with myself. But

I still know what it is like to be rejected by loved ones. That is why I want young LGBT people to have strong role models.

NEGOTIATING FAITH

To me, faith is deeply personal: it is about an individual's relationship with their God. It is not right for me to tell people how to practise their faith, nor should anyone criticise my beliefs. I am not interested in other people's opinions. All I know is that my faith is an important part of who I am. I get so annoyed when people tell me how I should pray or waste my time with rules about how a 'good' Christian woman should behave. What matters is the love I have in my heart. Only God knows the depth of my faith, and only He can judge my actions.

Church was a big part of my childhood. There was a mandatory Mass every Friday at school, and on the weekends I would attend a Lutheran church with my aunt in Katlehong. After I moved back in with my mum, I started attending her Pentecostal church in Leondale.

I was forced out of our Pentecostal church when I came out. My mother made such a big deal about my sexuality. She would go on and on and on about it to the pastor and congregation. I couldn't take the comments and stares; leaving seemed like my only option. I lost a part of myself that day. My faith community was very important to me, and suddenly it was gone. Church had always made me feel uplifted, but it ended up being a site of pain and abuse. It is hard to go from being loved and welcomed to being shamed and excluded.

The worst part was the deliverance ceremonies my mother dragged me to. She was convinced that my 'demon' could be exorcised. Eventually, I couldn't take it any more. My mother and pastor were busy organising another deliverance, but I decided not to go. I had been dreading it for weeks, praying to God for guidance, and after much soul searching I realised the problem was with the church, not with me. 'Why am I being forced to be someone I am not?' I asked myself. 'Why should I change when this is how God made me?' Looking back, I am thankful to God for giving me the courage to stand up for myself.

This all happened in 2013, and it wasn't until 2016 – three years later – that I again set foot inside a church. Some might say it was my choice to leave my old church, but that isn't the truth. The congregation had made it clear that I would never be accepted. I had to make a decision: either surrender who I am, or leave for good. When I did leave, I found myself without a key support network. I suddenly lost the people I would turn to in difficult times. I went from having a community to being isolated and lost.

A RELIGIOUS HOMECOMING

I first heard about the LGBT Ministry in May 2016. D.C. and I went along as a couple. We were initially apprehensive, but it turned out we had nothing to fear. Everyone was friendly and kind, and both of us enjoyed the conversation. Since then, D.C. and I have been regular members. I have come to see the group as a nurturing space. It is a place where we can be ourselves without fear or shame. There is no need to hide – just be you, be happy and be free.

While our fortnightly meetings are a big part of what we do, they are only part of the story. The best thing about the LGBT Ministry is that members are always there for one another. We like to stay connected via social media. This helps us respond quickly when someone is in trouble. People in our group face serious issues – family breakdowns, health complications, homelessness, poverty, to name a few – and they often feel overwhelmed. There is rarely a quick solution to these problems, but as a group we can offer love and support.

Being part of the LGBT Ministry has helped me cope with my family drama. Other members have gone through similar things and can give first-hand advice. I have now accepted that my mother is in shock. It can't be easy having a child who is different to your expectations. I have to give her time and space, even if it hurts me.

A FRIENDLY ENVIRONMENT

I don't attend Mass at Holy Trinity – these days I express my faith in more personal ways – but I have had interactions with the parish. One encounter left a huge impression. It was a meet-and-greet event designed to connect the church's different ministries. Each group, including the

LGBT Ministry, had a stall where we could share information and answer questions. It soon became clear that parishioners were frightened to be associated with us. I could see people looking at the LGBT Ministry table out the corner of their eye, but then they would scuttle past without picking up a flyer. It seemed to be more embarrassment than prejudice, but it still hurt. I explained the situation to Dawn from the Parish Council and she put some of our flyers on her stall. Suddenly people were picking them up and reading. I really appreciated what Dawn did that day; it is amazing to know we have that level of support.

I make an effort to help out at special events. Last year, the LGBT Ministry participated in the annual feeding of the poor (when the church provides a free Christmas lunch to hundreds of homeless people). Each of the church's groups is tasked with managing a table, for two sittings. Our group pooled our money so that we could prepare food and buy small gifts, like soap and toothbrushes. I was part of the cooking team; the others had to decorate our table and wrap the gifts. It was an honour to provide care to those who are suffering. The people we fed looked like they hadn't had a warm meal in a very long time. Our participation proved that LGBT people can give back to society. The best part is that we didn't have to hide: we decorated our table with a Pride flag and wore our LGBT Ministry T-shirts.

A GOSPEL OF LOVE

Christianity needs to be more open and inclusive. When I came out, I no longer felt welcomed in my church. The things that were said and done to me made it impossible for me to practise my faith. Being excluded took a heavy toll on me, and I don't want other LGBT people to suffer the same fate. Learning to accept oneself is hard enough. The last thing LGBT people need is for faith communities to turn against them.

I strongly believe that we are *all* made in the image of God. LGBT people are God's creation, just like everybody else, and we deserve respect. The Bible tells us to look at each other with an open heart, yet so many preachers have closed theirs off to us. When we are driven by love, we see God inside others, no matter how different their lives may be from our own.

Religious leaders who say hateful things need to go back to their Bibles. In Matthew 22, Jesus instructs us to 'love thy neighbour as thyself'. Yet so many Christians refuse to show us love. All we are doing is living God's plan for us. I don't consider my loving another woman to be unnatural. So why am I being judged? Since when was loving a sin? Again and again the Bible warns us against judging others, but still people treat us like we have done something unforgivable. When I read the Bible, I see a simple message of love. At the end of the day, we are all God's children. He doesn't make mistakes, and it is not for me or anyone else to criticise His plan.

A WORLD DRIVEN BY LOVE

I dream of a society that recognises the dignity of all people, regardless of their sexuality, race or gender. We need to get to a place where LGBT people are accepted. I am just like any other person – I am someone's daughter, someone's sister, someone's lover. Most importantly, I am *someone*. People need to remember my humanity before they judge me. Straight people also need to accept that they will one day have an LGBT person in their family. That is a fact. How are they going to feel then? How will they behave?

I also hope that every LGBT person finds a family that treasures them. Sometimes the most loving families don't share the same genes. The LGBT Ministry is an example of that. I am lucky to have people who care for me: I have my partner, my father and my sisters. I also know in my heart that my mother cares for me, even if she struggles to express it. Whatever happens, I know I can reach out to my chosen family: the LGBT Ministry.

I think a lot about the pain that LGBT youth carry. Coming to terms with one's sexuality isn't easy, especially with all of the intolerance in this world. There are young people right now being told they are satanic, that the love they feel is evil. I hope they know that there are people out there who won't judge or hate them. LGBT people have to stay strong; we can't let society break us. All we can do is stay true to ourselves and live for our own happiness.

9

I CAN SERVE GOD, NO MATTER WHO I LOVE

Narrated by Sly (Nigeria)

I am a 39-year-old gay man. I am originally from Nigeria, but have been living in South Africa for 11 years. Being gay is an important part of who I am, but it is not my defining feature. I want to be known as a kind and loving person who is committed to spreading the word of God. I believe that our biggest duty as Christians is to show love and compassion to all people. I have been part of the LGBT Ministry for many years and have seen how it is helping to challenge prejudice, both in the parish and in the broader community. The group shows what can be achieved if churches open their hearts to LGBT people. I want religious leaders of all faiths to draw on Holy Trinity's work and start including LGBT people in their activities. They must lead by example. Only then will we see positive change in society.

EARLY YEARS

I was born in Enugu, a small city in the south-east of Nigeria. My family is originally from Nnobi, but my parents moved to Enugu for my father's job. We are a family of six children: five boys and one girl. I am the fourth-born child, and the third son.

I had a very normal upbringing. As a young child, I didn't feel any different from my brothers. I enjoyed sports and being active, and had similar interests to other boys my age. My sexuality wasn't even on my radar back then.

My parents were relatively well off and were able to send their children to one of the city's best secondary schools. It was there that I first started to suspect I was different, though I certainly didn't identify as gay. It was an all-boys school and my social group – there were perhaps six

'I am like a dove. It is a gentle and kind creature, just like me. It also represents purity. That is something I have always strived for: purity of soul and purity of heart.'

of us – were all considered effeminate. Boys like us were called 'mummy's pets', but in an endearing rather than homophobic way. My friends and I were generally accepted by our peers, and even had school 'husbands'. This was more of a running joke than a sexual or romantic thing. On the whole, we were regarded as an amusement. People just assumed we would grow out of these 'games' as we developed.

AN INTERNAL STRUGGLE

It was in 1993, my matric year, that my sexual desires became too strong to ignore. Realising I was gay made me rethink my mannerisms. I didn't necessarily think it was wrong to be feminine, but it no longer felt like me. I was playing a part, rather than being true to myself. I decided I wanted to act more like a man. Perhaps it was just internalised homophobia. Whatever the reason, changing my behaviour made it easier to conceal my sexuality. That was a relief, as I was terrified of being found out.

Being from a Christian family, I struggled to accept my desires, especially in those early years. There was no way I could admit my feelings to the important people in my life. I suspect my mother knew, perhaps even before I did, but it was not something we could discuss. Interestingly, out of all the boys in my family, I was the only one allowed to have female visitors. My parents didn't seem to care. The funny thing is that my brothers' girlfriends had to pretend they were visiting me when really they were there to see my brothers.

I have always been very close to my family; even now I talk to my parents most days. I also have a strong relationship with my siblings. Despite our closeness, we never speak about my private life, and I doubt we ever will. There is an unspoken agreement that the topic is off-limits. I am not angry about my family's attitude: it doesn't mean that they love me any less, or that I love them any less. Sexuality is a complicated topic in Nigeria, even more so for religious people, and I respect my family's beliefs and values.

A STRANGE NEW WORLD

After secondary school, I enrolled at a university in Calabar, a city close to the border with Cameroon. My mother was concerned about me living in the student residence and forced me to move in with her sister. But that didn't stop me from getting out and about. This was long before the internet or smartphones and so it was a lot harder to find other LGBT people. There definitely weren't any gay bars in Enugu or Calabar!

I first met others like me at the start of my second year. I had to pay my fees at the registrar's office and the guy assisting me was very camp. His name was Hakeem, and I suspected immediately that he was gay. I am not sure how he knew about me; I guess my sexuality was more obvious than I thought. After he finished serving me, Hakeem slipped me a piece of paper with his address, telling me to come and visit that evening. I didn't know how to interpret Hakeem's invitation, but my curiosity got the better of me.

Arriving at Hakeem's place was like entering a strange new world. There were ten or so LGBT people sitting around in one room. Everyone was chatting, laughing, having a good time. It was mainly men, but also a couple of lesbian women. What struck me was the diversity of the guests: some were feminine, others butch, but all were different to regular folks. At first I felt awkward and uncertain, but then I realised that this was my introduction to gay life. That night was a turning point: from then on I regularly visited Hakeem's house, meeting new people and exploring my sexuality. It was through this network that I met my first boyfriend. I am still very thankful to Hakeem for taking me under his wing.

Even with this exposure to LGBT people, I struggled to accept my sexuality; I would have done anything to be straight. Back then I thought it was impossible to be gay and Christian. My faith was central to my identity and I was unwilling to give it up. I was searching for answers, but nothing I found put me at ease. It was a very confusing time. On the one hand, I was beginning to explore what it means to be a gay man; on the other, I was doing anything I could to change. So much of my time was spent praying. I would plead with God to make me 'normal'.

GAY LIFE IN NIGERIA

When I was coming of age, there wasn't a visible LGBT community in Nigeria. There weren't any LGBT activist groups or services, and there definitely weren't open discussions about homosexuality. The only regular event I remember was a party called the Night of All Nights. It was put on each year by a guy living in Port Harcourt. It was always a big occasion – almost every gay guy in Nigeria would attend, no matter how much travel was involved. The location wasn't announced in advance and so people would congregate at the local taxi rank until the venue was revealed. It was always a huge celebration, one wild night of fun, and the next day everyone would pack up and travel home. I remember seeing my first-ever drag pageant at one of those parties. 'Wow, this is so great!' I thought. There were other contests too, such as Mr Big Dick and Mr Macho.

I also remember attending a gay party in Enugu – something I never expected to happen! It was organised by a group of guys known as the Goddesses. There were seven of them and each one had a special name: the Goddess of Light, the Goddess of Seduction, the Goddess of the Moon, and so on. The Goddesses were quite popular in the community; they weren't subjected to discrimination or violence. People would refer to them as mummy's pets – just like at my school – but that was just what feminine guys were called. It wasn't a derogatory or hateful term.

Being gay in Nigeria wasn't a huge problem back then. Obviously it wasn't legal, or encouraged, or even spoken about, but it was rare that a person would be arrested or attacked. LGBT people were mostly left to their own devices. The key was discretion and sticking to the 'rules'. It wasn't even a big deal when I used to act feminine. Most people, including my relatives, found it entertaining. However, there was a clear expectation that I would grow out of such behaviours. Camp mannerisms might be amusing from a young boy, but they would be met with suspicion from a grown man. The standard attitude was contradictory: gay men were welcomed at certain times and places, but were still regarded as unnatural and abnormal. People certainly didn't want their children to turn out that way.

A CHANGE IN DIRECTION

In 2008, just as I was turning 30, I started chatting with Bobby, an African-American guy living in South Africa. We connected on Gaydar and soon became friends, messaging and flirting regularly. It wasn't long before he starting inviting me to visit him, but I was nervous about travelling all that way. After a few failed attempts to convince me, Bobby decided to visit Nigeria instead. He arrived just before Christmas and spent three weeks with me. I quickly realised I had strong feelings for him. Four months later, I decided to take the plunge and travel to South Africa.

That trip was my first time leaving Nigeria. I was shocked when I arrived in Johannesburg; it didn't look anything like home. It was like being in a European city: there were smooth roads, working traffic lights and modern buildings. It didn't take long for me to fall in love, both with South Africa and with Bobby. I desperately wanted to stay. At the time, Bobby was working for an education NGO called Tshepo Trust. He said he could organise a voluntary teaching job for me and also help me out financially.

There were a couple of reasons I decided to stay. There was my relationship, of course, but there also seemed to be more opportunities here. I had been struggling to find work in Nigeria, despite having a tertiary qualification, and it made sense to live somewhere with better employment prospects.

The other big factor was my sexuality. Even though I hadn't experienced direct discrimination in Nigeria, I still wasn't able to be myself. When I arrived in South Africa, I was amazed by how free people seemed. Homosexuality wasn't even mentioned back home, yet here I saw LGBT couples being affectionate on the street. I remember my first Jo'burg Pride like it was yesterday. It was a life-changing moment. More than anything, it made me determined to live my life as a proud gay man. South Africa presented the possibility of being free, and I was determined to make the most of the opportunity.

I should say that things in Nigeria weren't as bad when I first left as they are currently. I didn't face direct persecution, but then again only a few trusted friends knew about my sexuality. Back then you could get by as an LGBT person if you kept your head down. You might encounter the occasional slur or rumour, but rarely violence or persecution. That changed once former president Goodluck Jonathan amended the law in 2014. Suddenly political and religious leaders were making a big fuss about LGBT people. After that police raids become a very real threat. Discrimination also become more frequent, spurred on by nonsense stories in the tabloid newspapers. These changes make me apprehensive about returning home. My country is very unsafe for LGBT people, even if we are discreet.

TOWARDS ACCEPTANCE

Moving to South Africa changed my life, but living here hasn't always been easy. I have faced my fair share of challenges, though as an economic migrant my struggles are different to those of people fleeing violence. Having seen the way my LGBT brothers and sisters have suffered, I can say that I am lucky. I have always had a strong support network, both here in Johannesburg and back home in Nigeria.

Getting my documentation sorted out was my biggest hurdle. I was initially on a tourist visa, but once I started volunteering at Bobby's organisation, I tried to switch to a work permit. The director of the organisation wrote a letter explaining the situation, but my application was rejected on the grounds that a South African could be doing the work. I tried to explain that it wasn't a formal paid position, but the Department of Home Affairs (DHA) wasn't interested.

A short time later, Bobby and I broke up. I knew I had to act quickly to formalise my stay and decided to start a small business importing Nigerian cooking products. I had enough capital to get started, but still needed a work permit. I applied again and this time – when the official hinted that a 'processing fee' was required – I gave in. I am not proud of this, but I had no choice. What other option is there when the system is broken and corrupt? DHA officials won't even look at your application if there is nothing in it for them.

Things have been easier since getting my work permit. About four years ago, I was able to start a second business: I now do up old cars and sell them for a profit. I have always enjoyed mechanical work and so it is the perfect job for me.

Fully accepting my sexuality was another challenge. When I first arrived in South Africa, I was still trying to reconcile my sexuality with my faith. I sought out different churches, desperately looking for reassurance and guidance. For a long time I was angry with God for not 'curing' me. My attraction to men felt so normal, but I couldn't get past the idea that I was living in sin. Thankfully, with the help of my networks, I have now come to terms with my identity.

Being an LGBT migrant is generally hard. Most migrants can lean on their country networks for support, but LGBT migrants have to isolate themselves if they want to be free. For me to live openly as a gay man, I must separate myself from my Nigerian countrymen. Word travels fast in the diaspora and there is always a risk of your family finding out about your sexuality. I have many friends who are forced to remain in the closet. One Nigerian friend stays with his older brother and lives in constant fear of his sexuality being discovered. He would love to be independent, but he doesn't have the financial resources to make that happen. And so he continues to live a lie, terrified of being disowned or worse. My situation is nothing like that, but I still avoid Nigerians for my own safety.

Of course, it is not just Nigerians who are homophobic. Since living in South Africa I have come to realise that the country isn't the safe haven I first imagined. LGBT people here are mistreated and abused – on the streets, in clinics, in schools. Some are even being killed. When xenophobia is added to the mix, things can turn ugly very quickly. I know I am better off than many LGBT people because I have an education, an income and a house, but all of us are struggling in some way.

I also consider myself lucky because I have a loving and supportive partner. I have been married since 2011. My husband is the most important person in my life. We are best friends and would do anything for each other.

A TEST OF FAITH

Church has always been a big part of my life. My parents are staunch Catholics and raised their children according to the church's teachings. We were baptised, sent to catechism, underwent confirmation – everything that is expected of good Catholic children. I loved going to church: it provided a sense of community and made me feel closer to God.

Growing up, I didn't hear negative preaching about homosexuality. It simply wasn't mentioned in our church. I knew the story of Sodom and Gomorrah and the prohibitions in Leviticus, but I never heard our priests talk specifically about homosexuality. As I started to notice my sexual desires, I became more aware of society's attitude towards LGBT people. It dawned on me that homosexuality is regarded as a sin by most people.

This realisation caused me great anguish. I didn't think it was possible to be both Christian and gay; my sexuality and my faith seemed at odds. In desperation, I sought help from a Pentecostal pastor. He was someone who regularly spoke out against the 'dangers' of homosexuality, referring to it as a form of possession and calling on LGBT people to repent. I underwent several deliverances in the hope that I could be free of my 'demon'. Nothing changed, of course – I had exactly the same feelings before and after each exorcism.

When I moved to South Africa, I continued attending Pentecostal services. This time I decided not to tell the pastor about my sexuality. I was finally starting to feel comfortable with myself and didn't think it was any of the pastor's business. Back in Nigeria I prayed and prayed and prayed to be straight and yet I stayed the same. Eventually I realised that God had made me this way. This shifted my whole perspective and attitude: I began to see it as my duty to accept the special love that God had placed in my heart.

After Bobby and I broke up, I stopped attending church. I was fed up with it. I had started seeing religious leaders as hypocrites: they were always saying one thing, but doing another. Yet, even with this anger, I didn't lose my faith. I just felt there was no longer a place for me within formal religion.

That all changed when I discovered Holy Trinity. I first heard about the church from Ricus and was shocked to learn about its LGBT Ministry. The group seemed inconceivable, but I was fascinated and desperate to learn more.

The first meeting I attended was in 2011. I had so many thoughts running through my head. Is this the right place for me? Should I bother going? What are people going to say? Will I be asked invasive questions? Although I was feeling more comfortable with my sexuality, I still felt uneasy discussing it in public.

Upon arrival, I was relieved to see another Nigerian guy – a brother from another mother – as that made me feel more at home. By the end of that first meeting, I knew the group was going to be an important part of my life. I have now been involved for eight years – first as a regular member and later as the secretary – and the group continues to play a big role in my life. I consider the LGBT Ministry to be my family: we are always there for each other, no matter what happens.

PRIDE IN ACTION

The LGBT Ministry has impacted my life in many ways. First and foremost, it has helped me come back to God. Now I use my experience to help others do the same. I regularly meet LGBT people who have given up on church because of the bad things that have happened to them. I challenge them to come along to the LGBT Ministry and not feel the love of God. I know how much our community is struggling, especially those of us who are migrants, and I firmly believe that things will only improve once we open our hearts to God.

One of my fondest memories is the day we screened *For the Bible Tells Me So*, a documentary about how literal interpretations of the Bible drive intolerance. We invited the whole parish to come along and had some fantastic conversations. Some of our most outspoken critics even admitted to having their beliefs challenged.

But the best experience was undoubtedly the 2012 Jo'burg Pride. The parade was on a Saturday and Fr Russell, our parish priest, organised an ecumenical service, inviting different religious communities to bless our participation. I remember Fr Russell preaching a message of love and acceptance. He explained how the destruction of Sodom and Gomorrah is not a condemnation of homosexuality, but rather a lesson on the importance of hospitality. I can't stress enough how great it felt to hear those words: I felt welcomed; I felt included; I felt inspired to serve God.

The parade itself was amazing. We carried a large wooden cross, onto which we nailed the names of LGBT people who had been murdered. We all wore T-shirts showing we were from the LGBT Ministry. Some people were shocked to see a Christian cross at a Pride parade, but most people celebrated our involvement. A couple of journalists even asked us for interviews! The positive reception shows just how much LGBT people are desperate to reconnect with their faith. After the parade, we took the cross back to Holy Trinity, where it was displayed during Mass.

Raising the visibility of LGBT Christians has always been a big part of our work, but it is not our primary focus. The LGBT Ministry's main objective is to provide spiritual care to those who are denied it. This happens mainly through our fortnightly meetings. I have great memories of us sitting together and discussing our lives. Having a safe space where we can support each other is really important.

Talking through our day-to-day struggles is useful, but it is our faith-based discussions that are most important to me. We have had many lively debates about what it means to be an LGBT Christian. I remember us talking about the dangers of reading the Bible with a closed mind. People always get so worked up about Leviticus, saying it proves that homosexuality is wrong, but then they disregard the surrounding text. They claim that other commandments, like not wearing clothes of mixed fibres or selling daughters into slavery, are no longer relevant to the modern world.

Learning about different ways of reading the Bible has helped me make peace with my sexuality. It has taught me that the most important thing is my personal relationship with God.

THE NEED FOR ACCEPTANCE

Holy Trinity serves as an example of a kind and loving church; it shows what can be achieved when there is a commitment to diversity. Churches should be places where love is put into practice, not just spoken about.

Here in Africa, church is the place where people learn what is right and wrong. Church leaders have a responsibility to embody Jesus' message of unconditional love. They need to recognise the power they hold and set a positive example by welcoming *all* people – without judgement, without prejudice, without fear. Discrimination will continue unchallenged if communities keep being exposed to homophobic preaching.

I will definitely stay involved with the LGBT Ministry. I hope it will continue growing so that we can have a bigger impact. My dream would be for us to start a crisis centre. Then we could really help our brothers and sisters in need. It breaks my heart when I see LGBT migrants living on the street or abusing drugs. We need to address these problems while also offering spiritual support.

I also hope we can continue our outreach work. We need to keep working to dispel myths about LGBT people. Too many people still think we are sick or crazy, but none of us chose to be this way. People also need to know that LGBT migrants aren't coming to South Africa to cause problems. Some are fleeing terrible situations, but when they arrive here they experience more suffering, more pain, more hopelessness.

I am truly grateful to South Africa. It is been a privilege to build a new life here. I am most thankful for the chance to work with and support the LGBT community. I hope other LGBT migrants get the chance to give back, just like I did.

10

DON'T LET THE HATE GET YOU DOWN

Narrated by Tino (Zimbabwe)

I am a 39-year-old gay asylum seeker from Zimbabwe. I migrated to South Africa in 2007, when I was 27 years old, and since then I have lived in many different locations. Right now I am back in Johannesburg. I won't lie: life in South Africa has been tough. I thought my problems would be solved once I crossed the border, that I would be free and happy, but life doesn't always go as planned. I have faced violence, homelessness, unemployment and many other challenges, yet I try to stay positive. The LGBT Ministry has been a great source of support, although there were periods when I couldn't attend meetings because of my personal circumstances. I know I will always be welcomed back and that gives me comfort.

FAMILY EXPECTATIONS

I had a happy childhood. I grew up in Mutare, a city in the east of Zimbabwe, close to the Mozambican border. We were a big family – nine boys and one girl; I am the second-youngest son – and all of us got on well with each other. We had many relatives staying nearby so there was no shortage of cousins to play with. My favourite was my cousin-sister. We used to love playing dress-up. Sometimes we would even play with our mothers' make-up. We would walk around and pretend to be grown-ups, all the while howling with laugher. I was very young at the time and so my family didn't see anything wrong with these games. Everyone saw it as a bit of fun. Looking back, I can see that being gay was always part of me, even if I didn't have a name for it at the time.

My mother was the most important person in my life. She loved me unconditionally and would encourage me to express myself. Things were

'I am like a chameleon because I am very good at disguising myself. When I was young, I learnt to hide my sexuality so I could fit in with the people around me. Sometimes I still have to camouflage myself in order to be safe. I am not hiding because of shame. It is more about survival. In my heart, I am always the same person. When I hide myself, it is because of other people's hate and discrimination.'

different with my father. He realised early on that I wasn't like other boys and that made him furious. He had a narrow view of how sons should behave. I tried hard to fit in, but couldn't hide the fact that I was different. The only time he was proud of me was when I did well at school. Then he would tell everyone how smart I was. But most of the time he seemed disappointed. At one point he even started saying I wasn't his son. This caused a lot of conflict between my parents. My mother couldn't understand how he could say such a thing. He died soon after – when I was still in primary school – and so he never saw the man I became. My mother died a few years later, in 1996, when I was in Form 2. I was devastated when she passed, and I still miss her terribly.

My family was deeply religious and our Christian faith played a big role in our lives. I grew up in the Zion Christian Church, but as a teenager I started attending Pentecostal services. I loved going to church – it would uplift my soul and make me feel closer to God. When I was young, church seemed like a place of unconditional love. As I grew older, I began to feel uncomfortable with some of the messages coming from the pulpit. We would hear about Sodom and Gomorrah, about how gay people will burn in hell, about how Christians must resist this 'moral sickness'. Yet we were also taught that God made humans in His image and that He loves each and every one of us, sins and all. Hearing these contradictory messages made it difficult to come to terms with my sexuality.

SEARCHING FOR ANSWERS

Primary school was a positive experience. I was known for being fastidious in how I presented myself. Other learners would comment on my cleanliness and how I always smelled of soap. Sometimes the other boys would joke that I was like a girl, but it wasn't anything serious.

Things changed when I went to secondary school. I still did well academically and had close friends, but more and more people started noticing my mannerisms. This was the time of the sodomy scandal involving Canaan Banana, Zimbabwe's first president. It was all over the news, and one of the impacts was that people became more familiar with homosexuality. I remember seeing coverage of the trial on TV. My siblings were also watching and were revolted. 'This guy is so disgusting!' they yelled. 'How could anyone do such a thing?' My internal monologue was very different: 'He is just like me! This is what I am – gay.' I knew from the other reactions that being gay was a bad thing. Kids at school also made the connection and started to tease me, but I always denied it. Some relatives started becoming suspicious too. I had an effeminate friend and that upset my brothers. They would ask why I was hanging out with such a person. 'He is a good friend,' I told them, 'and it is only right that I visit him.'

By the time I was a teenager, I knew for sure that I was gay, but I didn't dare act on my feelings. At first I was confused: I thought other boys were experiencing the same desires as me, but then they all went girl crazy. It was all they would ever talk about. I felt alone and confused. Eventually, after much peer pressure, I started dating girls. I hoped I could change if I tried hard enough, but deep down I knew it was impossible. The Canaan Banana scandal had shown me who I was, but it also taught me to keep my identity hidden. All the stuff I heard about gay people – from church, from family, from the media – reinforced the idea that something was wrong with me. It was a distressing time.

To find out more about being gay, I reached out to Gays and Lesbians of Zimbabwe (GALZ). The organisation didn't have an office in Mutare, but I was still able to register as a member. GALZ used to send out pamphlets and newsletters, and I would read them from cover to cover before quickly disposing of the evidence. One day, after I arrived home from school – I was about 17 at the time – my sister-in-law told me I had mail and handed me an opened envelope. Inside was a letter from GALZ. I stood there, frozen. I swear I could hear my heart pounding. I thanked her and went to my room, terrified she would tell my brother. She never did. I now realise how much she was protecting me. Later, when relatives started to question my sexuality, my sister-in-law would defend me. She would tell my brothers off for listening to rumours, reminding them that I was family. My sister-in-law was always on my side – not once did she betray me, not like the other people in my life.

A DIFFICULT HOME ENVIRONMENT

A few years later, when I was still at college, a relative tried to out me. He was my sister-in-law's nephew and he had come to stay with my family after his mother passed. We had known each other our whole lives and were very close. One night, when we were looking after my uncle's house, we got drunk and passed out in the same bed. Nothing happened between us – nothing ever did – but for some reason he told my brother I had tried to sleep with him. That morning I woke up to so much drama. My eldest brother was already there, yelling and making a scene, demanding to know whether the accusation was true. My sister-in-law came to my defence and, luckily, calmed my brother down. That incident caused a lot of problems for me. Our neighbours found out what had happened and started treating me differently.

Things became strained with my family, even with the protection of my sister-in-law. More and more rumours were circulating about me in the community and this was making things difficult for my brothers. They didn't confront me again, but I could see they were frustrated and angry. That is when I started to think about leaving Mutare.

By then I had finished my accounting diploma and was working as a clerk. My job brought neither happiness nor fulfilment. Online dating sites became my only escape. I used Gaydar and PlanetRomeo to connect with guys in different countries. I started chatting with Jaco, a South African guy, and we immediately hit it off. Jaco owned a farm in Limpopo and encouraged me to come and stay with him. He said he could organise a work permit and would pay for my bus fare. All I had to do was apply for a travel document. I knew it was legal to be gay in South Africa and so I jumped at the offer. Jaco kept his word and sent me all of the paperwork, as well as money for my ticket. I told my family I had found work in South Africa. They were happy but surprised. Obviously I didn't mention the real reason: that I was going to live with a guy I had met on the internet. In the days leading up to my departure, I couldn't stop thinking about my new life over the border.

NEITHER FREE NOR HAPPY

When my departure date finally rolled around, I was filled with excitement. I caught a bus to Musina and then a train to Mokopane, where Jaco was waiting as planned. Once we arrived at the farm, Jaco showed me around: there was the main house, a small guesthouse and restaurant, and sleeping quarters for the farmhands and domestic workers. Jaco showed me where I would be sleeping and told me to rest up. That night I slept very well.

The next day I found out Jaco already had a long-term partner. They had been together for almost ten years! I was confused and angry. He explained that they were in an open relationship and we could all be boyfriends. I was shocked because I had never heard of such a thing. The idea made me uncomfortable. I suggested we forget about the relationship part of our plan and that I just work on the farm. Things were okay for a while, but every now and then tensions surfaced.

Only a few months after I arrived, Jaco snuck up to my room and spied on me. I was just chilling with another Zimbabwean guy, but seeing us together sent Jaco into a jealous rage. There was a lot of drama that night! Word soon spread among the workers that I was gay. I felt trapped and isolated; I couldn't handle the strange looks I was getting. About a week later, I demanded my pay and said I was leaving. Thankfully, there was someone driving to Gauteng. That is how I found myself – alone and confused – in downtown Johannesburg.

My first thought was that I would have to go home. This was something I wanted to avoid at all costs: Zimbabwe was a mess, and the last thing I wanted to do was go back into the closet. I only knew two other people in South Africa: my cousin-brother, who was living in Cape Town, and a friend from church, who was now based in Bloemfontein. I tried repeatedly to contact my friend, knowing that he was closer, but couldn't get through. In desperation I called my cousin-brother. Not long after that I found myself on a bus to Cape Town.

My cousin-brother was waiting for me at the bus terminal and took me back to his place in Gugulethu. I was shocked: he was living with five other guys in a shack. I had never seen such a thing and told him he couldn't keep living like this. I still had my wages from the farm and offered to help him find better accommodation. I agreed to cover the rent if he found somewhere suitable.

Once we were settled in the new place, I made contact with a white couple I had met in Limpopo. They were very kind and had taken a liking to me. They were shocked to hear about my situation. The man said he could give me work in the warehouse of his tile company in Brits. I didn't really want to travel across the country again, but it was too good an opportunity to pass up. I told my cousin-brother what had happened and left him money for rent. Then, before I knew it, I found myself on yet another bus.

As well as giving me a job, the couple organised a place for me to stay. It was a one-bedroom flat on the same property as the warehouse. I was initially sharing with a South African guy – he slept in the bedroom and I took the sitting room – but this arrangement only lasted a few months. After the South African quit, I was asked to take over his job, which meant I was now responsible for opening and closing the warehouse.

This was a great period in my life: I had a job, an income and friends looking out for me. I stayed in Brits for two-and-a-half years, only leaving when my contract expired. I was sad to leave, but also grateful for the opportunities I had been given.

TO THE CITY

In June 2010, I found myself without a job or a home. I had been chatting for a while with a guy in Hillbrow and decided to try my luck there. I had heard rumours about Hillbrow ever since arriving in South Africa. It sounded like hell on earth. It is so dangerous, people would say, that you will be robbed even in the daytime. Riding the taxi to Johannesburg, I was nervous and afraid, unsure what would greet me at the other end. My friend met me at Park Station and we walked back to his apartment. The streets were crowded and chaotic, with people rushing everywhere, but it was nowhere near as scary as I had imagined. I was just happy to have somewhere to sleep. Having a friend who knew the area helped because he showed me how things worked.

Life in Johannesburg has been a mixture of good and bad. One of the biggest challenges has been finding a stable job. I have had work on and off, but usually it is only casual. Finding work was my priority when I first arrived in Hillbrow. I immediately set about forging personal connections, as that is the best way to hear about opportunities. Most businesses aren't looking to employ foreigners – especially gay ones – and so you have to rely on your personal networks. My first job actually came about through a hook-up. I met a guy at the Carlton Centre and we got talking about my life.

I told him I was new to Johannesburg and struggling to get by. He offered me few hours of admin work each week. It wasn't much, but it was something. Later, I met another guy at Gandhi Square, and through him got a job at a fish-and-chip shop in Cresta. That was my longest job in Johannesburg: I worked there for almost two years, until the shop closed down.

A NEVER-ENDING STRUGGLE

Living without an income is a nightmare. I have tried so hard to find a permanent job, but nothing ever works out. I am not the sort of person who can sit around and do nothing, and so I decided to reach out to some LGBT organisations. I had attended a few workshops with the GALA Queer Archive and thought it would be a good place to gain work experience. I spoke to the director, Anthony, and he invited me to become a part-time volunteer in the library. I did that on and off for two years. It was a great experience and, importantly, I learnt many new skills.

Another big challenge has been accommodation. I have lived in lots of places: Hillbrow, Yeoville, Cresta, Freedom Park, Orange Grove, the West Rand and more. Some of these places have felt like home. I once lived in a cottage in Yeoville and have great memories of hanging out there with my friends. Other places have only been temporary, either because they turned out to be dangerous or because I couldn't cover the rent. It is hard to find something long-term when you don't have a steady income. There have been a few times when I have been kicked out because the landlord found out about my sexuality. Sometimes they are outright homophobic, but mostly they just make up an excuse. There was one landlord with whom I had a great relationship, but that changed when I came out to her. The very next day she told me I had to leave because her brother was moving in. Situations like that have led to periods of homelessness. Living on the streets is scary. I have to hide my sexuality for my own safety. There have been times when other homeless people have found out and threatened me. You also have to watch out for the police. They love to harass homeless people – some want a bribe, but others do it for fun. It is even worse if they suspect you are gay.

Discrimination has been a regular occurrence in my life. Strangers regularly use hate words or make rude jokes. People will shout things like 'faggot' or 'stabane'. There was one group of guys in Yeoville who always harassed me. 'Look at that dirty gay!' they would yell. 'You can tell he has been busy getting shagged.' They would mock me in Shona, my home language, which made me feel even more ashamed.

I have even faced discrimination from those who are meant to protect me. There have been numerous times when police officers and nurses have used homophobic slurs. One time, when I went to Charlotte Maxeke Hospital, the nurses were both homophobic and xenophobic, first saying that migrants were taking all the medication and then laughing when I explained about my sexuality.

When I finally applied for my asylum permit, I had a terrible encounter with the Department of Home Affairs (DHA). Like everyone else, I had to bribe the security guards just to make it through the gates. Then, after I had filled in the paperwork, the official asked me very personal questions in front of other Shona men. She forced me to say out loud that I was gay, outing me in front of my ethnic community. When I explained about my sexuality, I was met with a look of disgust. Other DHA officials then came to laugh at me. 'This one is just pretending to be gay to get asylum,' they said, scornfully. The officials processed everyone else's permits while I just sat there. Eventually, after a few hours, my asylum documentation was issued, but only after I had been humiliated.

It doesn't take much for slurs to turn into violence. Once, when I was enjoying a few beers at The Base, a bar in Hillbrow, I was beaten up by one of the bouncers. I remember him saying homophobic things as he punched me. Some other patrons were able to pull him off and then helped me get to the nearest clinic. Another time I was attacked at Time Square in Yeoville, but this time no one intervened. I am most scared of violence when I am homeless. The police and security companies will wake you up and tell you to move on. If they happen to be angry or bored, they might push you around. One time I had my belongings set on fire.

Right now I stay in Orange Grove, where I survive by selling clothes on the street. It is not an easy way to earn a living, but I don't have another option. I regularly experience homophobia, both from passers-by and other traders. Occasionally the police come by to harass street hawkers. If you can't bribe them, you have your goods confiscated; if you are very unlucky, you will be arrested and deported. I know I am at risk because my permit has expired, but I don't have enough money to go back to DHA. I am also scared of being mistreated again.

HELP AT LAST

Although I have struggled in South Africa, I have also experienced kindness. The people who work at GALA, the Jesuit Refugee Service and the African Centre for Migration and Society have assisted me in various ways, offering helpful advice and a friendly smile.

One of the most important support structures has been the LGBT Ministry. My Christian faith has always been important to me, and I was incredibly happy when I heard about an LGBT-friendly church. I had enjoyed my Pentecostal church back in Zimbabwe, but in the end it wasn't right for me. Church is meant to be a place where you connect with your community and with God, a place where your spirit is nourished and uplifted, but that was no longer happening for me. The Pentecostal preachers back home would go on about Sodom and Gomorrah, encouraging people to pray for the 'evil' of homosexuality to leave our country. Hearing that stuff took a toll on me. I couldn't understand why being attracted to other men – a feeling that God had given me – was a sin. As far as I understood, God doesn't make mistakes. Even though I was feeling disconnected from the church, I didn't lose my faith. I still went along to services, but no longer felt uplifted. Churches should be caring places, but so many of them make LGBT people feel unwelcome.

I first went along to the LGBT Ministry in 2010. It was with my friend from Hillbrow. He had been going along for a while and had told me all about it. I was excited to join, but also a little anxious. I had never been to such a group and didn't know what to expect. That first day we each talked about what it means to be an LGBT Christian. It was an issue that I had long struggled with and I appreciated hearing other people's experiences.

The LGBT Ministry became a critical part of my life. It has taught me that there is nothing wrong with me, that I can be gay and Christian. It has also given me many close friendships. We are more a family than a support group; we try to help each other as best we can. It is truly a blessing.

A MESSAGE OF HOPE

I believe each of us belongs to God – no matter if we are gay or straight – and we should all be welcomed at church. We must be free to explore our spirituality without hiding who we are. The Bible teaches us to love each other, but that isn't being practised in our communities. Our pastors must stop sowing the seeds of prejudice. Saying just one homophobic thing can turn LGBT people away from God.

Churches have a role to play in changing attitudes. Our communities need to realise that people who seem different are not necessarily bad. This applies to everyone who might be struggling – it could be an LGBT person, a homeless person or someone from another country. People like me need love and support not hate and violence. South Africans also need to know that migrants come to their country for different reasons. No one wants to leave their home, but many of us are forced to do just that. LGBT people come to South Africa to survive, because here we can fight for our rights. In our home countries we face violence and discrimination, but sometimes we find ourselves dealing the same problems here. All of us need to work together to create a peaceful society. We must act with love and kindness – just like Jesus.

11

I AM NOT WILLING TO LIVE A LIE

Narrated by Angel (Uganda)

I am a 32-year-old asylum seeker from Uganda. It is been just over two years since I joined the LGBT Ministry. Having a space where I can connect with other LGBT migrants has made a big difference in my life. The other people in the group have gone through similar things to me and hearing their stories makes me feel less alone. I came to South Africa to be free; it is dangerous to be gay in Uganda. I love that there are laws protecting LGBT people here, but that doesn't mean life is easy. There is a lot of violence and corruption in South Africa. Still, I would rather be free here than living a lie back home. I just wish I wasn't so far away from my family. I pray that things will change in Uganda. LGBT people shouldn't have to run away from their country just to survive. We deserve love and support, just like everyone else.

A LOVING HOME

Growing up, I was happy and content. Like all children, I sometimes fought with my family, but most of the time I lived a carefree existence. My parents were kind and always treated their children with respect. I was especially close to my mother. One of my favourite things to do as a child was to listen to her stories. Some nights, while preparing the evening meal, my mother would share memories of her childhood. I would sit beside her, transfixed by her soft, gentle voice. She would also teach me her favourite songs and then we would sing them together while doing chores. It was from my mother that I learnt what is right and wrong. There were two important lessons she taught me: first, always aim to be a better person; second, always act with kindness. My mother passed in 2007, when I was

'My spirit animal is the lion. I like how tough it is. When people look at me, they don't think I am tough, but in my heart I have the strength of a lion. I have overcome a lot in my life. You don't have to look scary to be brave.'

20 years old. Even though my mother is no longer a physical presence in my life, she continues to guide and protect me.

I have five siblings in total: three brothers and two sisters. As the second-oldest child and the first-born boy, I had to take on extra responsibilities. When my parents were busy with work or church activities, it was up to me to care for the young ones.

I was, and still am, close to my siblings. My last-born brother and I have a special bond. If I am struggling with a problem, I ask him for advice, and he does the same with me. He seems to get me more than my other siblings. He still doesn't know about my sexuality – it is the one topic that is off-limits – and that makes me sad. I honestly don't think he could handle the truth, even though he loves me dearly. Maybe that will change one day, but for now I must keep my sexuality hidden.

My elder sister and I also have a strong relationship. We are close in age and have always been there for one another. I still help her as much as possible, such as by sending money for her children's school fees. Even though we care deeply for each other, we rarely talk about my private life. If she ever asks me a personal question, I find a way to change the subject.

Despite being close to my siblings, I have always known that I am different. I was young – around five or six – when I started to have feelings for other boys. It wasn't necessarily a sexual attraction. There was just something that drew me to them. As I grew older, the feelings became more intense. I soon realised that other boys my age weren't experiencing the same desires.

THE CLASS CLOWN

My parents were relatively well off and were able to send their children to good schools. I have great memories from that period of my life. I was well liked by the other students because I could make people laugh. I was never that interested in the academic side of things, but I loved being creative. The highlights for me were music and sport, both of which I excelled at.

I was never bullied or excluded at school. Ugandans tend to be private people – we rarely share our innermost thoughts – and that helped me hide who I am. I buried my sexual attractions deep inside me and tried my best to act like other boys. The only hint I might be different was my close friendships with girls. I was reasonably popular with both boys and girls, again because I was good at making people laugh, but my strongest relationships were with girls. They liked me because I was nicer and more approachable than other boys. I will never know if they suspected I was gay, but they certainly didn't say anything. Homosexuality wasn't mentioned back then and so I doubt it was on anyone's mind.

I quit school after Standard 4, when I was 16 years old. I wasn't keen on academic subjects and didn't see much point in carrying on. What I craved was independence and real-world experience. So, once I had written my exams, I set about looking for a job.

SECRET DESIRES

As I said, I was very young when I was first attracted to other boys. That is how I know my sexuality has always been there. Because I was so young, I didn't understand what was happening or why. If I shared a bed with a male friend – in the normal way that children do – I would get a special feeling inside. It was a warm, fuzzy sensation and it would make me feel both excited and nervous. These feelings grew stronger as I became a teenager. Suddenly I found myself thinking about kissing boys.

Hearing my brothers talk about girls made it clear that I was different to them. It was confusing because my desires felt natural to me. I had felt like this, in some form or another, my whole life. Still, I was scared about telling people. Difference is not always welcomed in Uganda, and I knew better than to disclose what I was feeling. The best thing to do, I decided, was to stay silent.

INDEPENDENT, BUT NOT FREE

After leaving school, I got a job in Munyonyo, on the northern shores of Lake Victoria. It is an upscale part of Kampala, with lots of resorts and function centres. I was employed as a housekeeper at a hotel. I loved interacting with the foreign guests. They would all compliment my bubbly personality and high standard of work. I have always been a tidy person – some might call me obsessive – so housekeeping was the perfect job for me.

It was around this time that I had my first relationship. I met Emmanuel, my boyfriend, at a restaurant. He saw me waiting for my dinner companion and decided to introduce himself. I liked him straightaway: he was cute and a sharp dresser, just like me. We chatted and flirted and soon made a plan to hang out again. We ended up dating for over a year, right up until I left for South Africa. He was a simple, easy-going guy, the type who never fights or causes trouble.

I quit my housekeeping job not long after meeting Emmanuel. I have always had an entrepreneurial mind and decided to start my own business. I began travelling to Tanzania to buy goods at different markets and then transported them all the way to the border with DR Congo. It didn't take long for my business to grow, and after a few months I had saved enough to buy a small plot of land. I should have been happy at this point – I had a great job, a loving partner and a supportive family – but I felt miserable. I knew I could never be free in Uganda; the thought of being in the closest forever was suffocating.

ALWAYS HIDING

Very few of my friends knew about my sexuality or my relationship. I mainly hung out with straight people and didn't feel comfortable telling them about my private life. The one person who knew was my gay friend, Isaac, and that was only because he had confronted me. One day, out of the blue, Isaac asked if I had ever slept with a woman. I told him off for asking such a question, but Isaac stood his ground. 'No,' he said. 'You are my friend and it is only right that you tell me about yourself.' He then opened up about his own sexuality, revealing his feelings for me. After much prodding, I divulged my secret, but I emphasised that I was already in a relationship. It felt good to tell someone, but I was nervous about what would happen if others found out. I guess I trusted Isaac because he was living with the same secret.

I didn't come out to others because I hated the idea of being the subject of gossip. Perhaps my friends would have come to accept my sexuality, but I definitely couldn't risk my family finding out. I knew how LGBT people were treated in my country and was scared of being rejected or arrested.

Ugandans are not as accepting as South Africans. My country can be a dangerous place if people discover your sexuality. LGBT Ugandans face all sorts of problems: they are beaten, ridiculed, extorted, even sent to jail. The police and government make life very difficult. That is why most LGBT Ugandans keep to themselves. If you stay hidden, you are less likely to end up in trouble. I don't want to think about what could have happened if my sexuality was revealed.

Most Ugandans think homosexuality is a sin. People say that two men can't make a baby and therefore being gay is against God's natural order. They only think about sex, never the love between two people. Uganda is a Christian country and people take their faith very seriously. When a priest or pastor says that LGBT people are against the Bible, he is believed. It only takes one powerful person to say something prejudicial for people to get into a frenzy. However, most of the time people don't think about LGBT issues. It is not a topic of conversation, especially among regular people. It only became an issue when the president changed the law in 2014. After that newspapers started publishing photos of LGBT people on their front pages. That caused a lot of pain and suffering. Some LGBT people were even killed. The most famous case is David Kato.[1] I am thankful I was able to get out when I did.

Pretending to be something you aren't is exhausting. It was a bit easier for me because my income gave me the luxury of privacy. As time went on, I found it harder to cope with the stress of hiding. Living in a state of anxiety is unhealthy. I was never able to relax because I was always worried about being caught. That is why I decided to leave Uganda. It wasn't an easy decision because I loved my boyfriend and my family, but I also had to consider my future.

A LONG JOURNEY

I chose South Africa because I knew it was legal to be gay. For LGBT Ugandans, South Africa seems like the Promised Land. People are aware of the Constitution, but know little of the violence and discrimination that happens here. Personally, I knew nothing about the negative side of things.

The first person I told about my plan was my father, although I didn't share my real reason for wanting to leave. Instead, I said that I had a school friend in Johannesburg who could set me up with a job. It wasn't a total lie: I did have a school friend here, but I didn't have guaranteed work. My father was reluctant at first, but I assured him that everything would be okay. The South African economy is strong, I explained, so moving makes sense financially. In the end my father gave me his blessing. He knew me as an honest, trustworthy and hard-working son, and he had confidence in my abilities. He even offered to cover some of my transport costs.

The next step was breaking up with my boyfriend. That was much harder. I cared for Emmanuel very much and didn't want to abandon him, but I also knew this was too good an opportunity to pass up.

I set off for Johannesburg in November 2012, when I was 25 years old. The journey was long and boring, but my excitement made it bearable. Whenever I felt exhausted, I would imagine the new life waiting for me. I travelled the whole way by bus: I caught the first one to Kenya, then another one to Tanzania, and so on through Malawi, Zambia and Zimbabwe. As a Ugandan, I didn't need a visa for the transit countries and so I could cross the borders without drama. The entire journey took ten days, and more than once I felt alone and afraid. There were even times when I thought about giving up, but then I would dream of being free.

Things turned bad when I arrived at Beitbridge. I didn't have a visa for South Africa because I was planning to lodge an asylum claim. I was unsure about the process and must have looked lost. Some locals asked if I needed assistance, but they turned out to be criminals and robbed me. It was dark and they were armed. I had no choice but to hand over my belongings. I lost so much: clothes, shoes, jewellery, money. I remember feeling helpless and scolded myself for being so stupid. My only comfort was that I still had my most valuable possession: my passport.

When I finally made it to the immigration counter, I told the South African official about the robbery. He was sympathetic but said there was little he could do. I was granted a transit permit and told to lodge an asylum claim once I got to Pretoria. I have heard stories of people having a tough time with border officials, but the guy I had wasn't mean or corrupt. I think he took pity on me because of how upset and exhausted I looked.

By now it was early morning. I was tired, hungry and afraid; I had no plan, no friends, no food and barely any money. I stood on the street, not far from the border, and cried. After a while, a kind woman asked if I was okay. She was very generous and took me back to her place. After I had washed and eaten, I explained what had happened.

That woman had the heart of saint. She said I could stay with her for as long as I wanted. I think she was lonely and wanted a son, but I didn't want to live in the rural areas. I needed to get to the city so that I could earn money and build a life. The woman helped me make contact with my father, who agreed to send more money. Once it had come through, I repaid the woman and boarded a taxi to Johannesburg. I am not sure I would have made it without her generosity.

As we pulled into Park Station, I was overcome with excitement. I had finally made it! The first thing I did was phone Victor, my old school friend, but my calls went unanswered. I tried again and again, but the same thing kept happening. Victor and I had spoken before I departed Musina and so he knew I was on my way. By now I was worried. With no other option, I sat on a bench outside of Nando's and prayed that he would make contact soon.

I waited and waited and waited. Eventually, my phone rang. To my surprise it was Charles, not Victor. I knew Charles from back home, but considered him more of an acquaintance than a friend. He explained that Victor was no longer willing to 'babysit' me. Charles thought it was wrong to abandon a countryman in this way and decided to collect me himself. He told me to wait where I was until he could make it to Park Station.

Charles turned out to be a lifesaver. He let me stay at his place in Rosettenville and helped me get a job. In all honesty, I wouldn't have survived without him. We became close friends, but that also meant going back into the closet. Charles knew my friends and family back home and so I couldn't risk divulging my secret.

FINDING A COMMUNITY

When it came time to get my own place, I found a room in the southern suburbs. I was sharing with other migrants and had to keep quiet about my sexuality. I busied myself with work and tried to save as much as possible. My life at that time wasn't bad, but it wasn't what I had dreamed of. I certainly wasn't happy or free.

In 2015, I moved to Johannesburg CBD. Living downtown allowed me to explore LGBT places and meet new people. This is how I made my first gay friend, Daniel. We met at Buffalo Bills, a bar at Park Station that used to be popular with gay guys. I was having a drink at the bar, minding my own business, when Daniel came up and asked if I was alone. He flashed a big smile and said he would be my friend. We ended up getting very drunk that night. What I liked best is that he didn't pry into my background. I knew instantly that we would become good friends.

It was only later that Daniel asked about my sexuality. He had invited me over for dinner and the conversation turned to love. I was still scared about disclosing my sexuality and denied being attracted to men. Daniel could see I was uncomfortable and didn't push the issue. It took a few more weeks before I trusted him enough to come out. Looking back, I am not sure why I was so scared – Daniel was openly gay and wasn't in any way connected to Uganda. We became very close friends after that. It was only when Daniel moved home to Durban that we lost contact.

Since then I have met many more LGBT people. One important friend is Thabiso, whom I met while working at the KFC in Park Station. He had come in a few times and was always very nice. One day, after leaving a good tip, Thabiso said he wanted to be my friend. We exchanged numbers, and the next weekend he invited me to a party in Hillbrow. That was my first time attending a gay party – and I loved it!

A few weeks later, Thabiso took me to a party in the northern suburbs. It was like being on another planet. Everyone seemed so comfortable and happy. When we first arrived, the host gave me a Hunter's Dry and told me to enjoy myself. It didn't take long for me to join in the fun: I sang and danced and flirted all night. I finally felt like I had the freedom I had been craving. Later, after we had left the party, I thought to myself, 'If only my country was more like South Africa.'

ISOLATION AND INSECURITY

South Africa is great because you can be yourself, but life is still hard. My biggest challenge has been employment. I have had a number of jobs since living here – some were only ever temporary, while others I quit due to mistreatment. There have even been times when I was forced to work without pay. If you complain, you are threatened: 'Do you want this job or not?' the manager will say. 'There are plenty of others who will do the work.' Employers exploit foreigners because they know we are desperate.

There have been a few occasions when I have stood up for my rights, but this usually means getting fired. Finding a new job is a headache. It can take four, five, even six months before you have an income again.

Unlike other LGBT migrants, I haven't faced direct violence. I am a very discreet person and like to keep to myself. Growing up in Uganda, I learnt to hide who I am, a skill I still use today. I have to really trust someone before I open up about my sexuality.

Still, the negatives of life in South Africa don't outweigh the benefits. I am freer here than I ever was in Uganda. I miss aspects of home, but I am not willing to live a lie. Even if the law back home were to change, people's attitudes would remain the same, at least for the foreseeable future. Change is slow in my country. That is why I want to stay here in South Africa.

A LIFE ON HOLD

I applied for asylum back in December 2012, just after I arrived. One of the hardest parts was getting to the Refugee Reception Office. I was still struggling to navigate Johannesburg, let alone make it to Pretoria on my own. When I finally got to Marabastad, I was given forms to fill in and told to wait. The guy interviewing me asked lots of questions about why I had come to South Africa. I told him I couldn't stay in my home country because of my sexuality. I explained that Uganda doesn't have the same protections as South Africa and that it is very dangerous for LGBT people. 'I was scared for my safety,' I said. 'That is why I came here – for protection.'

Surviving on an asylum permit isn't easy. The renewal process is usually a nightmare: the guards demand bribes, or the tsotsis rob you, or the computer system is offline. I am lucky, though, because I haven't encountered homophobia. Some of the Department of Home Affairs officials have been rude and inefficient, but none have said anything mean about my sexuality. Perhaps they know how bad the situation is in Uganda. My friends have been less lucky. Some have had personal information shared without their consent, or been called names like 'moffie' and 'stabane'. One was even accused of lying about his sexuality in order to get special treatment.

It is been over seven years that I have been on my asylum permit. Not having any certainty is exhausting, and it is a real hassle travelling back and forth to Pretoria. I have no idea when a determination will be made on my case. All I can do is hope that I will soon be classified as a refugee.

RELIGION: A COMFORT AND A THREAT

I am a proud Christian. My faith is central to who I am; it gives me strength and helps me stay focused. When I am feeling alone and confused, I ask God for guidance. Praying gives me a sense of calm because I know everything will be okay. When I pray, I feel God's mercy and wisdom. Communing with Him helps me better understand my life. For me, faith is like a map; it shows me which path I should take. Only God knows what I must do to overcome my problems.

I grew up in a strict Catholic family. We attended church every week and were raised according to Catholic values. My favourite part of church was the music. Singing hymns with my family would fill me with joy and make me feel close to God. I also enjoyed being an altar server. This meant I would prepare the church and assist during Mass. I was proud of my role, and each week I looked forward to being useful.

When I was young, I didn't hear much about homosexuality. It was a taboo topic back then. Things have changed in the last few years. Now there are Ugandan religious leaders who are obsessed with LGBT people. They say we are possessed by demons and sabotaging God's plan for humanity. Most of them supported the president when he brought in the anti-gay laws because it would 'protect' the country's morals. These religious leaders have created so much fear and anger. They tell their congregations all sorts of lies – for example, that we are rapists and child molesters. These lies make people hate us.

A SURPRISING DISCOVERY

I found out about the LGBT Ministry through my friend Samuel. We were hanging out and he mentioned a meeting he was attending. I couldn't believe such a group existed, especially at a Catholic church! Samuel said it is a place where LGBT people can meet and talk, and so I decided to go along. At that point I didn't belong to a church and was feeling unfulfilled.

That was back in 2017. I still remember my first meeting. The people were friendly, and it didn't take long for me to make them laugh. That day everyone shared about their lives. People were very open, telling the group about challenges with their families, their relationships, their faith – all sorts of things. Hearing about their joys and struggles was very special.

I go along to the group whenever I can, but I wouldn't call myself a regular member. I work weekends and that makes it difficult to attend meetings. But I always have fun when I do go along. What I like most are the stories people share. I feel less alone when I know that others are facing similar problems. Not because I take pleasure in their suffering, but because it helps me grow as a person.

THE POWER OF ACCEPTANCE

Churches need to be more tolerant of LGBT people. All we ask for is kindness and respect. Most religious people don't have compassion for us: their words and actions cause us pain rather than comfort. Many of us would like to participate more in church life, but don't feel accepted. A lot of LGBT people feel a strong connection with their faith, but struggle to express it because they can't be themselves at church. We should be free to worship as LGBT people and to thank God for the precious gifts of life and love. Imagine if we were all valued and included. That would be such a great feeling! I just want to have the chance to do what everyone else does: have a wedding, raise a family, be a part of the community. This needs to happen everywhere, but I most want to see change in my home country. Instead of spreading hate, Ugandan pastors should preach love for all. They are the ones causing trouble, not LGBT people.

HOPES AND DREAMS

I try not to think too much about the future, but when I do I dream about giving back to society. Sometimes I imagine all of the things I would do if I had the chance. My biggest dream is to help children in need. I sympathise with their lives: even though I have a loving family, I sometimes feel like an orphan because I can't be honest with my relatives. I can't share the things that make life worth living. Even if I found my perfect man and had a wedding, I couldn't invite my family. Some people think that being gay is a choice, but no one would choose such a lonely life. That is why I want to help other people in need. I know how hard it is to survive on your own.

I hope South Africans can learn to accept and love migrants. All of us need to work together to build a better society. The government needs to stop spreading lies about us. There would be positive impacts for all South Africans if the government provided better support. We hear all the time that migrants are stealing jobs and keeping locals poor, but this isn't true. Migrants can make a positive contribution to the economy. We want to work and give back to this beautiful country.

The most important thing to remember is that all of us – locals and foreigners, heterosexuals and homosexuals – are facing the same challenges: poverty, violence, crime, unemployment. Turning on each other is not going to solve anything. Instead of blaming migrants, the government should fix these problems. We aren't here to make things hard for people. In fact, most of us would go home if we could. I would love to be safe in Uganda, but that is only a dream. My country is still too dangerous for LGBT people. For now, I have to live in South Africa. Only here do I have my freedom.

12

LOVE IS ABOUT HEARTS, NOT PARTS

Narrated by Toya (Zimbabwe)

I am 28 years old. I grew up in Harare, where I had a carefree childhood. It was only in my late teens that I started to suspect I was different. For many years I struggled to make peace with my sexuality. I was confused by the way I felt. My desires seemed natural, but my religion regarded them as sinful. By then my mother and younger sister were living in Johannesburg. I came to stay with them in 2009. At first I didn't know how long I would be in South Africa, but now – over a decade later – I consider it home. I don't think I could return to Zimbabwe. Here I can walk down the street holding my partner's hand. That would never be allowed back home. I am grateful for the freedoms and opportunities I have in this country. Living here has allowed me to understand and express my lesbian identity.

NOT A GIRLIE GIRL

I was a tomboy as a small child. At the time, my parents put it down to me always being around boys: I have five older brothers, and we all used to play together. Even on school holidays, when all the cousins would stay together, I would play with the boys. We were always climbing, chasing and fighting. I was never interested in Barbie, despite my mother's best efforts. She desperately wanted a girlie girl and would always buy me flouncy dresses. It just wasn't me. I was more comfortable wearing shorts and getting dirty. In 1995, when I was four, my parents had a second daughter. That took some pressure off me because my sister was happy to wear dresses and play with dolls.

My childhood was very normal. My mother was a stay-at-home mum and my father worked as a boilermaker. We moved around a lot, mainly

'I am most like a cat. It takes a while for me to feel comfortable around someone, but once I do I am totally loyal. At first I seem shy and quiet, but in reality I am very caring. There are many ways I show affection. I will also defend my territory if threatened.'

due to financial pressures. Money wasn't a huge problem when I was young, but it became an issue when I got to secondary school. By then my father had started his own business and it wasn't always easy to make ends meet. Things were bad for everyone back then: Zimbabwe's economy was falling apart and jobs were scarce. When things weren't going well, my family would move into a cottage on my granny's property. The toughest period was when my father was wrongly arrested for a bad business deal. He was the family's breadwinner and we struggled without him. Thankfully, the police caught the real culprit and my father was released.

The worst thing about moving was having to change schools. I attended three primary schools and two high schools. My first high school was a single-sex college. That wasn't great for me because I was starting to have feelings for other girls. In Form 1, when I was about 13, I developed a crush on my best friend. I told her how I felt and she didn't take it well. Word spread, and I soon became a target of gossip. I begged my parents to send me to another school. They eventually conceded, much to my relief. The new school was co-ed. I felt much more at ease there. I was still attracted to girls, but this time I knew better than to disclose my feelings.

In 2007, my mother moved to Johannesburg in the hope of finding work. By then the Zimbabwean economy was in free fall: there were fewer and fewer jobs, and our currency was practically worthless. It made sense for my mother to move this side and look for domestic work, especially as my eldest brother was already living here. A year later, my mother came back and collected my little sister. She begged me to migrate with them, but I wanted to stay with my friends and finish matric. In the end it was decided that I would live with my aunt because my father was too busy with his business.

A KINDRED SPIRIT

As a child, I felt a lot of pressure to behave like a typical girl. My family is very traditional, especially when it comes to gender roles. My parents were elders in our Pentecostal church, and being the child of elders comes with certain responsibilities. My siblings and I were expected to be model Christian children: pious, obedient, courteous, punctual. We were always seated in the front pews during services and never missed Sunday school. My father even insisted we memorise Bible verses.

While my parents tolerated my tomboy tendencies when I was young, they put a stop to them when I became a teenager. I was expected to dress in a feminine way, especially at church, and to take on the roles and responsibilities of a daughter. By then I knew for sure that I was attracted to other girls, but I didn't have the words to describe my feelings. People in Zimbabwe didn't speak about such things. Not having access to information about LGBT people made me feel isolated. I was convinced I was the only person with these feelings. I began to think there was something seriously wrong with me.

When I was 17, I made friends with a butch girl called Danai. Her mother and my aunt were close friends, and Danai would be dragged along on her mother's visits to our house. My aunt would always complain about Danai as soon as they left. She would go on and on about how it wasn't right for a girl to dress like that. I would just laugh it off. Over time Danai and I became close, and one day she confided in me that she was lesbian. I was so happy: 'Wow, there is a name for this feeling. It is a real thing, not just in my head.' I told Danai that I was also attracted to girls. It felt great to say it out loud. For the first time in years I didn't feel ashamed or crazy.

Danai was a player and knew lots of LGBT people. She was my inroad to the community: once you meet one person, you soon meet others. These new acquaintances were always trying to hook me up with their friends. Even though I was becoming more comfortable with myself, I wasn't yet ready to act on my desires. I was still involved in church and felt guilty about my sexuality. Things got even worse when my father invited our pastor to live with us. I was expected to look after him, basically serving as his PA. After the pastor moved in, my family started hosting all-night services on weekends. By then I was feeling more and more distant from my faith. For the first time in my life I started questioning what I had been taught. I still believed in God, but I was struggling to see my place in Christianity. It was all very confusing.

It didn't take long for my family to notice changes in my behaviour. In a matter of months I had gone from being heavily involved in church activities to having no interest. My aunt and father put it down to Danai. They were worried she was tempting me into her 'sinful' lifestyle. Little did they know that I was lesbian long before then!

In 2009, just before my 18th birthday, my parents insisted I move to South Africa. I had mixed feelings about migrating: I didn't want to leave my friends, but at the same time I was eager to finish matric, something that was no longer possible for me in Zimbabwe. I also knew I had a better chance of finding work here.

LOST AND CONFUSED

My mother and sister were overjoyed when I arrived, and I felt exactly the same way. However, my mother didn't waste any time in laying down the law. She said my father had warned her about the people I had been hanging out with and that she wouldn't tolerate such behaviours under her roof. It was clear that she had a plan to make me a 'normal' daughter.

After a few months, my travel document expired. I had to sort something out, but I was frightened to go to Home Affairs. At that time Zimbabweans were flooding into South Africa and there was a lot of xenophobia. I decided to wait and try my luck. Life without documentation is hard: you are always worried about being arrested or deported. If you see the police, you immediately cross the street and hide.

I lasted a few months without a permit, but then I couldn't take the stress any longer. I decided to apply for asylum and headed to Pretoria. It wasn't an easy process: there was a lot of violence, corruption and exploitation at the Refugee Reception Office. The queues were long and scary; I had to sleep on the street so I didn't lose my place. After lodging my asylum claim, I was issued with a six-month permit. I was already dreading having to renew it.

My first year in Johannesburg didn't pan out as expected. My mum wasn't earning enough to send both me and my sister to school. I tried my best to find work, but couldn't land a job. The constant rejections made me feel directionless.

I am not sure if it was out of boredom or just to please my mum, but I started dating a guy. Perhaps I was also trying to prove something to myself. Whatever the reason, I forced myself into a relationship that didn't feel natural. It didn't last long – but long enough for me to fall pregnant.

I was actually in Zimbabwe when I realised my situation. I had gone home to apply for a passport since that was the only way I could formalise my migration status in South Africa. Instead of stability, however, I found myself pregnant and broke. By then my father was also living in Johannesburg and so I couldn't even turn to him for help. In the end he had to travel back to Harare and rescue me. He brought enough money to sort out my passport and buy two tickets back to Johannesburg. When we got back, I applied for and was granted a Zimbabwean Special Dispensation Permit. It was a relief to finally have some security, but I still had no idea what to do about my pregnancy.

LIFE IN SOUTH AFRICA

One day, not long after my return, I was busy getting dressed for church. My mother, father, sister and I all shared one room and so there was very little privacy. My mum looked over at me and said, 'You are pregnant!' I froze on the spot. I had no idea what to say. I had been dreading telling her in case she forced me to get married. My parents are both conservative and expected me, as the eldest daughter, to find a nice man, have a lobola ceremony and start a family. Even though my mum was in shock, she was also relieved – a baby born out of wedlock was still better than a lesbian daughter!

Eventually I found the courage to tell my ex-boyfriend. Straightaway he insisted we get back together. His family belonged to the Zion Christian Church (ZCC) and there was a lot of pressure for us to marry. I stood my ground and told him I didn't want a relationship. I didn't divulge the real reason because I didn't have the energy to fight about my sexuality. What was most surprising was my parents' support of my decision.

I finally found a job as a nanny and used my wages to prepare for the baby's arrival. I worked right up until the week of the birth. I had my son in June 2011, when I was 20 years old. It was a big change, but I was ready for it. It felt wrong to cut out the father completely and so I told him he could visit, but stressed that we wouldn't be getting back together. About five months after the birth, my ex was deported to Zimbabwe. At first he stayed in contact, but as time went by I heard from him less and less. Every now and then he sends a WhatsApp message, asking for pictures or an update. Sometimes it annoys me. I wouldn't mind if he was contributing, but he doesn't play a role in my son's life. They are basically strangers.

I returned to work as soon as possible after the birth. After six months I had saved enough to move out. I wanted to have my own space and more freedom; no one wants to be living with their parents in their 20s!

I started looking around for a better job and found work as full-time dental assistant. It was a good wage, but it meant being separated from my son during the week. I would drop him off with my parents each Monday morning and collect him again on Friday night. It was hard being apart, but I had no choice: I had to keep earning. Through this job I met a woman who ran a catering company. I expressed interest and she said I could come and work for her.

It turned out I had a natural talent for cooking. I wanted to do it properly and so enrolled in a culinary school, and it was there that I discovered my passion for baking. Never in a million years did I imagine I would work with cakes and pastries. After graduating, I was hired at a bakery in Fourways. It was a good job, but it meant travelling across town every day. By the time I paid for transport, rent and groceries, I had no money left. I decided to start selling my own cakes to earn extra cash. It was a small-scale business run out of my kitchen, with most of my clients coming from word of mouth or Facebook. My boss at the bakery found out and was irate, accusing me of stealing his customers, despite the fact that I was working on the other side of Johannesburg. The bakery closed a few months later and so I was glad to have my own business to fall back on.

A SPECIAL RELATIONSHIP

It was only once I was living independently that I came to fully accept my sexuality. I had known for ages that I liked women, but the pressure from my family to be 'normal' was too much. When I had first arrived in Johannesburg, I had seen LGBT people on the street and that had made me feel less alone, but I still didn't have a support network to lean on. This changed once I moved out from my parents' place.

One of my neighbours in Kenilworth had some lesbian friends. Whenever they visited, they would tease me, but in a friendly way. I was astonished by how open and proud they were. Their confidence inspired me to confront my own anxieties. I finally stopped believing I was sick or broken.

My first lesbian relationship was with another Zimbabwean woman. This was back in 2014, when I was 23. My girlfriend was a university student in Masvingo and could only visit during semester breaks. She came down for the December holidays and we decided to attend her friend's New Year's Eve party. That is when I first saw Thomars. The attraction was instant; there was just something about his energy. (This was before Thomars' transition. At the time, he identified as lesbian and used female pronouns.)

My then girlfriend clicked that something was going on. We had a fight, and in the end I went home with Thomars. We spent the next couple of days together and it was clear to both of us that this was something special. A month later, Thomars moved in.

A CHANGE OF COURSE

Thomars and I separated in 2019. It was very tough on both of us, since we still have love and respect for each another. I struggled for a long time after our break-up. I could barely function: I was having trouble eating, sleeping, working, even doing the most basic of tasks. It got so bad that I was fired from my job for taking too many sick days. My boss thought I was trying to take advantage, but in reality I was in mourning.

Recently, I started work as head chef for a café chain. As well as cooking, I move between the franchises, running trainings, supervising staff and helping build up the stores. The job has opened up a lot of opportunities for me, including travel to different parts of the country. It is nice to feel a sense of purpose again. The only problem is the long hours, which make it hard for me to care for my son. He is now back with my parents and doing Grade 2. It is painful being separated from him, but I know it is for the best. Sometimes I feel like a failure because I am not always around, but then I remind myself that I work hard to provide for him. School fees, food, medicine – none of this is cheap.

NAVIGATING STIGMA

Life is good in South Africa, but it is not without its bumps. The best part is that people can be openly LGBT, even if there is a risk of violence. Sometimes you have to be careful because there are people – especially men – who truly hate us. And then there are those who hate foreigners.

Being Zimbabwean and lesbian can be especially dangerous because you are a double target. I tend to slip by unnoticed because people think I am a boy, but I still worry something bad will happen to me or my friends.

There were a few occasions when Thomars and I were taunted on the street. Thomars is trans and attracts more attention than me. People would mostly stare, but occasionally someone would make an ignorant comment. Just stupid questions like 'What *are* you?' or 'Why are you trying to be a man?' There will always be idiots who refuse to accept LGBT people. I try my best to ignore them. I am happy with who I am, and I don't need to waste time on bigots.

I have also encountered discrimination in my professional life. Some employers don't like it when women dress butch. I have had job interviews where negative things were said about my clothes, even though I was wearing a formal shirt and suit jacket. Clients occasionally react badly too. If someone calls about having a cake made, I direct them to my online portfolio, only to have them freak out over my profile picture.

There is a difference in how discrimination plays out in Zimbabwe and in South Africa. People here are more used to seeing LGBT people. Yes, there is a lot of violence, but most of the time people let you get on with life. In Zimbabwe, people are shocked and outraged if they see an LGBT person. I would never walk hand in hand with a partner back home. People just wouldn't cope. They are all brainwashed by what they hear in church. They take the Bible too literally, yet only in relation to homosexuality. People don't seem to care about other sins. Part of the problem is the reluctance to talk about sex and sexuality. It is a no-go topic in Zimbabwe and that means people remain uneducated.

I have witnessed the positive changes that can happen when people are exposed to LGBT folks. Even my family's attitude has improved. A few years back, when I visited Zimbabwe for Thomars' mother's birthday, I caught up with some relatives. I was dreading seeing my aunt, but her reaction was really sweet. I expected her to preach at me, or at the very least tell me off for my appearance, but instead she embraced me, crying, and told me how happy she was to see me. She even said, 'Where is your person?' It might not have been the best wording, but that is irrelevant. What matters is that she acknowledged my relationship without malice.

I have also had positive experiences with my brothers. One is heavily into church and used to preach at me when he lived here in South Africa. When I visited him in Harare, he and his wife were chill: they didn't say anything nasty about me or my partner. I also visited the brother closest to me in age. He designs T-shirts and made me a special one with 'Love is about hearts, not parts' printed on it. His workshop is a shared space with a hair salon. When he gave me the T-shirt, everyone in the salon – both workers and customers – stared at me like I was crazy. But neither he nor I cared about their reaction. It is nice to have the support of my siblings. My parents have also come around, to a degree anyway. We still don't openly discuss my sexuality, but they also don't make negative comments.

A DIFFICULT RELATIONSHIP

Ten years ago, back when I was zealous about church, I could never have accepted my sexuality. I had internalised too much shame. Now I am in a much better place. I understand that I can be Christian and lesbian.

I have a problem with preachers who stir up hate. They quote Bible verses in ways that mislead and confuse. People need to learn the true message of the Bible, rather than fixating on statements like 'God made Adam and Eve!'

Since living in Johannesburg, I have occasionally gone with my mother to her Pentecostal church. I did it to please her and never felt comfortable. I also tried a few different churches with Thomars, but they never worked out. The pastor would always notice us, especially Thomars, even when we were sitting quietly at the back. They would call Thomars to the front and pray over him. All we ever wanted was to enjoy the service, but we were always singled out. I guess the pastors thought they were doing God's work. Soon we stopped going altogether.

SPIRITUAL SUPPORT

Thomars and I first heard about the LGBT Ministry in 2016. It was our friend Tafadzwa who told us about it. I was a little disappointed when we first arrived because there were no other lesbians, but the gay guys were super friendly. They welcomed us with open arms. It was just nice to be around people whose lives I could relate to. I remember thinking, 'Yeah, I definitely want to come back here.'

I have been attending on and off since then. The problem for me is that I often work weekends. When I do make it to meetings, I inevitably have a good time. It is nice to catch up with friends, and I always enjoy the conversation. We mainly discuss religion, love, coming out, staying healthy and day-to-day challenges. It really helps to talk through these problems.

The LGBT Ministry has built up my confidence. Most important of all, it allowed me to confront the shame I was still carrying. I finally understood that there was nothing wrong with being a lesbian Christian. I always felt I had to choose between these aspects of my being. Now I understand that God made me this way for a reason.

This only happened after Fr Graham addressed the group. We were discussing the church's stance on homosexuality and Fr Graham spoke about Jesus' love for all His children. It was a fascinating conversation. Fr Graham's take was so different to the attitudes of preachers I had grown up with. He assured us that God listens to all prayers, no matter the person's gender or sexuality. I still remember him saying that hate and judgement are the true sins. Hearing this was one of the best moments. To have a priest affirm my right to be Christian was very special. Everyone in the LGBT Ministry was moved that day.

Another strong memory is a session about families. I left the discussion with much more empathy for my parents. I realised I sometimes push too hard, expecting them to miraculously accept my life. I now appreciate that my parents' struggle isn't because they hate me, but because they don't yet understand. That discussion taught me to take things slowly, to look for ways to educate my parents, and our relationship is much improved since then.

CHANGING THE NARRATIVE

One of my biggest hopes is that the LGBT Ministry will get bigger and stronger. I don't think enough people in the community know it exists. There are so many LGBT people who would benefit from being involved. And not just migrants – there are South Africans who are struggling because of homophobia and transphobia.

We need to spread the message that it is okay to be LGBT and Christian. There are too many discriminatory pastors out there. They are pushing LGBT people out of churches. All it takes is one homophobic or transphobic comment for intolerance to flourish. The more we have honest and informed conversations, the more we will shift community attitudes.

Some pastors need go back and study their Bible. At the moment they pick out verses to suit their own agendas. They seem to overlook the part about being non-judgemental. It shouldn't matter if someone is attracted to the same sex or the opposite one. After all, love is a gift from God. What counts is how you treat others.

HOPES FOR THE FUTURE

There are a lot of things I look forward to. I want to continue providing for my son and to raise him to be a good man. I also want to continue strengthening my relationship with my parents. Despite our earlier challenges, my parents have come to accept me, and for that I am grateful.

Professionally, I want to open my own restaurant or café. If that happens, I will use the business to train and employ others LGBT migrants. Right now too many LGBT migrants are turning to drugs out of boredom or desperation. I want to inspire the people in my community.

I also want things to improve here in South Africa. There is too much xenophobia, too much homophobia, too much hate. People need to understand that LGBT migrants don't leave their countries by choice. We would all rather be at home, but it is too dangerous. Our lives aren't easy, and things are even harder when locals discriminate against us. We are thankful that South Africa has protections for LGBT people and want to pay back the country that has saved us. I know things are tough for many South Africans, but that doesn't justify violence or murder. The T-shirt my brother made for me says it all: love is about hearts, not parts. More people need to hear this message.

13

STOP CALLING US SINNERS

Narrated by Nkady (Lesotho)

I am 26 years old and I identify as lesbian. I grew up in Lesotho, but have lived in South Africa for many years. I have faced many hardships, but I stay positive. One big obstacle was coming to terms with my desires. When I was young, I thought that being lesbian was a form of satanism, but now I know that it is completely natural. The LGBT Ministry helped me make peace with my sexuality. I hate it when people say that the love I feel is sinful or sick. God made me this way, and I must honour His plan for me. People should concentrate on their own lives, not waste their time and energy judging me. In my opinion, education is the key to overcoming discrimination. The more people know about LGBT lives, the more they are likely to accept us.

ALONE AND AFRAID

I was raised in Ha 'Malesaoana, a small village in Leribe District. It is a very rural and traditional part of Lesotho. My parents were too poor to raise me and so I was sent to live with my father's uncle. I lived with this man, whom I referred to as grandfather, from the ages of two to ten. My brother, who is two years older than me, stayed with my parents, while my sister, who is two years younger, went to stay with other relatives.

This period of my life was incredibly tough. My grandfather was a traditional healer and was well respected in the community, but he was a domineering and frightening figure at home. He was very quick to anger: no matter how well I behaved, I always ended up being flogged. Like many children in Lesotho, I was expected to contribute to the household, which meant lots of chores and work. Some days my grandfather would lock me in the house, only letting me out if he needed help. This meant I

'I am fierce and brave like a lion. I have been through a lot and am still fighting. People assume I am weak because I am small and soft-spoken. But if someone threatens me, they will hear my loud roar. I am not violent, but I will defend myself. That is what survivors do.'

didn't have much chance to play with other kids my age. My grandfather's own children – my aunt and uncle – were much older than me and so I often felt alone. That being said, my aunt was very kind. She felt a sense of responsibility towards me and would often refer to me as her child. Even today we share a special bond.

When I was in Grade 1, a family friend began raping me. He threatened me into silence, saying that no one would believe me if I reported him. One day, my aunt – who was in Grade 11 at the time – came home from school and found the guy on top of me. She fought him off and went to tell the family, but my grandfather didn't take it seriously. 'What are you talking about?' he asked. 'A girl her age can't do that with a man. She is just seeking attention.' And so the guy continued to rape me, confident that he would never be punished. The assaults continued for over a year. I was only seven when it started, not even close to being an adult.

I barely saw my parents during this period because they lived in another village. I was able to visit them once or twice a year, but never for long. It was always tense when I saw them. 'How could they have given me away?' I used to think. 'Did they not love me?' As an adult, I understand that my parents were poor and had no choice, but as a child I couldn't help feeling abandoned. At one point, my father got a job at the mines in Gauteng, but he still couldn't provide for his family. Whenever he came back to Lesotho, he would drink away his pay cheque, leaving nothing for his wife or children. Often his visits would be accompanied by violence.

The physical and emotional abuse I endured affected all aspects of my life. At school, I got into fights, mainly because I didn't know how to socialise with other children. The other reason I was bullied was because I was a tomboy. I mainly hung out with boys and I enjoyed physical activities, such as playing soccer or climbing trees. I was athletic and strong, with a talent for running. 'This one must be a boy,' the other students would tease. 'There is no girl who can run like that!'

My grandfather also noticed something different about me. Sometimes he would send me out to mind the livestock. That is very unusual in Lesotho – normally boys watch the herds, while girls do domestic chores. I would also be sent to fetch things with a donkey, something most girls wouldn't be allowed to do.

REUNITED, BUT STILL DISTANT

When I was ten years old, my mother left my father. She was fed up with his drinking and his temper. Desperate for us to be a family, my mother brought my brother and sister to live in the same village as me. It was our first time living in the same place.

After a year, we all moved to Botha-Bothe, another district in Lesotho. We lived there from when I was 11 years old to when I was 16. Even though I was happy to be with my mother, I struggled to build a relationship with her. I was haunted by the memory of her giving me up. No matter what she said or did, I couldn't accept that she loved me. The fact that I had been raped during those years added to my sense of abandonment. A real mother would have protected her child, I reasoned, yet my mother had left me to be abused. Looking back, I can see that these thoughts were unfair, that my mother was doing her best, but that wasn't how I saw it as a teenager. I was craving love and security, but all I could feel was sorrow.

I never told my mother about the rapes. I didn't want to add to her suffering. I knew she was also a victim of abuse and couldn't bear to worsen her pain. I knew it would break her heart if she found out. Keeping quiet seemed like the best thing for everyone.

Life in Botha-Bothe was hard. My mother had no money and was forced to accept a job as a domestic worker in Rustenburg, in the North West Province of South Africa. This was the only way she could earn enough for our upkeep, but it meant splitting up the family again. I was sent to live with my mother's aunt, while my little sister went to stay with my mother's older sister. By then my brother was old enough to live by himself. Again, my mother's actions seemed like a betrayal. I felt disposable and unlovable.

At first, the woman I lived with was kind, treating me just like her own children. But it didn't take long for her to start using me as a servant. She would wake me up early in the morning and demand that I make food for the others. Then, later in the day, I would clean up and prepare for the evening meal. Taking on these household responsibilities meant that my school attendance suffered.

I actually enjoyed secondary school and was disappointed when I couldn't give it my full attention. I had lots of friends, unlike in primary school, because by then I had learnt how to fit in. I had stopped running, in spite of my natural talent, because I didn't want to stand out. Gender roles are strong in Lesotho and there are consequences if you do things that are considered abnormal. That is why I started acting more feminine. Yet some people were still suspicious. One reason was my preference for baggy clothes. I wasn't comfortable with my body, and I certainly wasn't interested in dressing sexy. My clothing choices seemed perfectly reasonable to me, but my peers found them strange.

HOPES OF A NEW BEGINNING

In 2009, I failed my Grade 10 exams. By then I had started to misbehave at school. Things were difficult at home, and I found it impossible to stay focused or control my temper. When I heard that I had failed, I called my mum and said I wanted to leave Lesotho. She was working as a live-in cleaner and so I couldn't stay with her in Rustenburg. It was decided that I would live with her stepbrother in Orange Farm.

In early 2010, when I was 17 years old, I left my country. Like many Basotho, I naively believed that South Africa was the Promised Land. I was convinced that my situation would be transformed once I crossed the border: I would have a big house, eat nice food, find a high-paying job and live happily ever after. Little did I know that life doesn't work out like that.

Migrating was easy. I was granted a one-year permit and had no problems crossing the border. Once in South Africa, I caught a minibus taxi directly to Orange Farm. It was a little scary because I was making the journey alone, but my strongest emotion was excitement.

I stayed with my uncle for the whole of 2010. Living with him was an awful experience. He and his wife only wanted me there so I could care for their newborn. They regarded me as free labour. All I wanted to do was finish Grade 10, but I kept missing classes because I was expected to babysit. When I did make it to school, I was focused and determined, and by the grace of God I passed.

At that point, school was the only enjoyable thing in my life. It was my first time being around people from different ethnic groups and I was excited to learn about these new cultures. My school had isiZulu, isiXhosa, Sepedi and Sesotho speakers; I loved hearing these different languages.

Although I enjoyed my new school, it took a while for me to feel fully settled. Some boys used to follow me around and repeat everything I said, exaggerating my accent. With time, however, I found a social group. There were three girls who came up and said they would be my friends. That was very sweet, and we are still close even today.

In 2011, I moved in with my mother's stepsister. She lived close to my uncle and so it was easy to relocate. I still live there, even though my aunt has now passed away. I currently live with my two cousins, my brother and my sister, though when I first arrived it was just me, my aunt and my cousins. My mother passed on the same year as my aunt. Losing two influential figures at the same time was hard. I now consider it a turning point, in that I had to start taking on adult responsibilities.

Balancing school with my family responsibilities was tough. I am grateful to have had the support of my friends and teachers. My Life Orientation teacher was an angel. One day she saw me crying and asked what was wrong. I explained that my mother had been dead for months, but her body was still at the morgue. My father had gone to identify her, but just took her passport and left. He told the staff he would come back and pay the bill, but he never did. When the mortuary staff didn't hear from him, they started calling me, demanding that I do something. I tried to explain the situation: 'I am a teenager,' I said. 'I don't have money.' But they kept calling and calling. I was riddled with guilt, ashamed that my mother's body had been dumped. On the day my teacher saw me crying, I had been informed that my mother would be buried in a pauper's grave if I didn't pay up. My teacher helped me organise an affidavit and gave me money to travel to Rustenburg. My brother and sister were still in Lesotho at this point and so I had to take care of everything myself. It was an overwhelming experience for an 18-year-old orphan.

A CONFRONTING REALISATION

It was in secondary school that I first noticed my attraction to girls. For the first couple of years, I tried to put it out of my mind. 'No, this can't be happening,' I told myself. 'This is not acceptable.' The mere thought of being lesbian was too much. I was under the impression that same-sex relationships were a form of satanism; I was determined not to involve myself with such things.

The problem was my lack of knowledge. The things I 'knew' about LGBT people were picked up here and there, and almost all of them were incorrect. As a child, you are taught what is right and wrong by other people. Most of your values come from family, but you also learn things at school and church. My school was very strict when it came to gender norms. There were some girls who were rumoured to be lesbians because they wanted to wear Dickies. The principal wouldn't allow it and forced them to wear skirts instead. Seeing reactions like this made me police my own behaviours. The last thing I needed was a rumour about me.

Desperate to fit in, I started dating boys. This was what was expected of me: all my friends had boyfriends, and not doing the same would have attracted unwanted attention. All you want as a teenager is to fit in. I prayed my relationships would make me straight. I did like the boys I dated – some were very kind – but never romantically or sexually.

My first lesbian experience was in 2012. I had gone to stay with a close friend's family because I was having trouble at home. One night, my friend and I fooled around, kissing and touching each other. The next morning we agreed that our actions were wrong and must never happen again. For her, it was a way of experimenting, of exploring her body, but for me it was something deeper. It felt great to be with another woman. Of course, realising you enjoy something is very different to accepting it.

Coming to terms with my sexuality was a long process. I was terrified of what people might say. There are so many misconceptions out there – for example, that lesbians are possessed, or diseased, or trying to be men. I was scared that people would think those things about me. I couldn't stand the idea of being an outcast.

Religion was the other reason I struggled with my sexuality. I knew that LGBT people weren't welcomed or accepted in Christianity. My relatives in Orange Farm were churchgoers and were steadfastly against same-sex relationships. They believed that LGBT people should be cured through exorcisms. 'God created Adam and Eve, not Adam and Steve' was a popular saying in the house. Such comments weren't necessarily directed at me, but hearing them still hurt. I didn't want my family to think of me as evil.

TRYING TO MAKE A LIFE

I wrote my matric exams in 2012, but failed because of problems at home. By then I was undocumented and that made it hard for me to re-enrol. I spent the next few months at home, with nothing to do and no hope for the future. Then a miracle happened: the South African government announced an amnesty for Basotho living here illegally. We were allowed to cross the border and apply for a Lesotho Special Permit. This document allowed Basotho to work or study in South Africa, meaning I could finally re-sit my exams. And so I headed to Lesotho for the first time in almost three years. It took just over two months to get everything sorted. It wasn't a difficult process, but it took time because so many people were applying.

Once I passed matric, I started looking for work. I found a job at a shebeen in Germiston, where I lived with the owner and a few other women. Our boss was very demanding, forcing us to work long hours for little pay. She made us do all the manual labour ourselves, like changing the kegs and packing crates.

I lasted at that job for almost two years. In the end, I couldn't take the conditions any longer. Quitting made me happy, but I was worried about my financial situation. In addition to supporting myself, I had to send money to my little sister. She wanted to join me in South Africa, but lacked the financial resources. In the end I took a job as a live-in babysitter in Benoni. I worked there from 2016 to 2017, only losing my job because the child started crèche. Without work, I found myself back in Orange Farm, depressed and bored. By then my siblings had also moved into the house. Living with that many people is tough. We fight, just like all relatives, but at the end of the day we are family.

Since 2017, I have been supporting myself through casual babysitting jobs. This income isn't regular, but it is enough to get by. I would love a better job, but unemployment is a huge problem in my area. Even if I do find a steady job, I will have to share my earnings with my relatives. Family obligations can make it difficult to plan a future.

TOWARDS SELF-ACCEPTANCE

I was 19 when I began to confront my sexuality. It had become clear to me that I wasn't going to change, no matter how many boyfriends I had.

By then I had started to search out information on sexuality. Learning about LGBT people made me feel better, but it still took a while for me to identify openly as lesbian.

In 2017, I met a woman through a WhatsApp group chat. Someone on the group had mentioned a woman in Free State who was looking for a partner and I asked for her contact details. My sister was also part of the group and was shocked when I said this. She immediately sent me a private message: 'Are you serious? Do you like women?' That was actually how I came out to her. She didn't have a problem with my sexuality, much to my relief. I think it is easier for women to accept lesbians. Men are threatened by the idea of us.

So I started chatting with this woman on WhatsApp. After a few weeks, I went to visit her in Free State. It was a very short relationship – only a matter of weeks – but it was a positive experience overall. It made me realise that happiness is possible within a same-sex relationship, even if that one didn't work out.

My next relationship was with a woman from Diepsloot. We met on a Facebook group for lesbian women. A few months into the relationship, I invited her to the house in Orange Farm. By then everyone in the family knew about my sexuality. The person who struggled the most was my brother. He just couldn't wrap his head around it: 'You were always normal,' he said. 'How can you be like this now? It isn't right! You must find a nice man and settle down.' Like many people from Lesotho, my brother is conservative. He used to believe that LGBT people go against nature and the Bible. He was battling with a lot of emotions: embarrassment, shame, confusion, perhaps even fear. He was concerned about what other people would say; he didn't want our family to become a target of gossip. But I stood my ground, telling him that it is my life. I hoped that bringing my girlfriend to the house would force him to confront my sexuality. I wanted him to see how happy the relationship made me. My plan worked – luckily!

My cousins also struggled with my identity. They were raised in an evangelical church and had been taught that LGBT people are possessed. With time, however, they have come to accept me, although we rarely discuss my sexuality.

FINDING A COMMUNITY

Once I had come to terms with my sexuality, I began seeking out other LGBT people. In 2018, I went along to Orange Farm Pride and to Vaal Pride. These were my first experiences of LGBT politics. It was amazing being surrounded by people just like me.

This year, I went to Soweto Pride for the first time. It was much bigger than the other events I had attended. I was blown away by the number of people and the joyous atmosphere. Seeing that many black LGBT people was inspiring. It is a great feeling to be with people who truly get you. And then there was the after-party! Everyone was relaxed and enjoying themselves: drinking, dancing and hooking up. It was one of the best days of my life.

Being active in the LGBT community has helped me build a network of friends. Now I even know LGBT people in my area. Most of the time we just hang out, but occasionally we go to a tavern that is welcoming of LGBT people. Even the straight people at that tavern love us! On the whole, Orange Farm isn't dangerous. People on the street will occasionally use a slur like 'stabane' or spread a nasty rumour. There have been a few times when friends have been threatened by guys who think they can 'cure' lesbians, but such cases are rare. Thankfully, most people in the area are kind and accepting. I even have neighbours who encourage me to invite my LGBT friends over because they like them so much.

REFLECTIONS ON FAITH

When I was young, I was an active member of a Catholic parish. My grandfather was a traditional healer and wasn't interested in church, but he sent me along to honour my mother's wishes. I enjoyed going to Mass, not just because of how it made me feel but also because it was an escape from the troubles at home. It was the one place where I felt happy.

Religion continues to play a role in my life. I feel a strong personal connection with God, and my faith helps me understand and express my love for Him. I believe that my sexuality and faith can exist side by side. Both are central to who I am. I didn't always feel this way, but now I believe that being true to my sexuality is an important expression of my faith. The Bible tells us that love is the most important thing, that we can't know God if we don't know love, so for me it is important to honour the desires that God has blessed me with. If God didn't want me to be lesbian, He wouldn't have created me like this. I am here because of God, and to deny my sexuality would be to reject God's plan for me.

It wasn't easy to reach this point, especially when so many churchgoers are against homosexuality. Growing up, I used to hear that LGBT people are sinners in need of salvation. Even my relatives would say this. One aunt, for instance, was very upset when I came out. She told me that she would pray for me to find Jesus and be healed. Her reaction made me very angry: 'If you are so desperate to help,' I said, 'then pray for me to find a hot girlfriend.' She is more accepting now. Like many religious people, my aunt's negative attitude was born out of ignorance. What she needed was education and exposure. These days she is much more comfortable with LGBT people.

AN ADOPTED FAMILY

I was introduced to the LGBT Ministry by a friend. I was stunned when he first mentioned it. How could such a group be possible, I wondered, when Christianity disapproves of same-sex relationships? Most churchgoers come at us with scriptural quotes, trying to prove that homosexuality is demonic, and so I couldn't conceive of an LGBT-friendly parish.

I went along the very next week. There were lots of people at the meeting – more than 20 – and everyone seemed so confident and well spoken. I couldn't help feeling shy. I decided to sit quietly and learn from the others. There was no shortage of conversation: people talked and talked and talked and talked. It was so interesting to hear what people had to say.

I decided to stick with the group because it could help me grow. I see the LGBT Ministry as a space for learning. It is one of the few places where I feel fully supported. What I like best about the group is that everyone is valued and treated equally. There is so much love there.

A few months ago we all went to a retreat in Bela-Bela. That was a very special experience. We talked through some tough emotional stuff. There were a lot of tears, but afterwards everyone felt a sense of lightness. It was good to share things buried deep inside my heart. But the best part was hanging out and being free. Once our sessions had finished for the day, we would jump in the pool and relax. I felt like I finally belonged.

A PRAYER FOR CHANGE

As a migrant, I am very worried about the recent xenophobic attacks. I wish people would remember that we are, first and foremost, Africans. We are stronger when we stand together. We must love and support all our brothers and sisters, no matter where they were born.

I would also love for South Africa to accept LGBT people. We deserve respect and support. The same is true for Lesotho. The government there needs to provide better services. LGBT people are part of Basotho society, whether our leaders like it or not. Things are slowly starting to change back home, thanks mainly to the work of Matrix Support Group.

Churches in both countries must become more open. Right now, LGBT people are being forced to set up their own churches. While I understand the reason for this, I don't think it is the best way forward. If we want to be accepted by society, then we need to be part of the same churches as everyone else.

Religious leaders need to start accommodating LGBT people. They can set a positive example by being kind and welcoming. If I were to meet a bishop or cardinal, I would tell them that we are regular people, just like them. LGBT people shouldn't be feared. We are good people, and we are living our lives in line with God's plan for us. We don't choose our sexuality or gender, and there is nothing wrong with us. I would ask them to open their hearts, to take the time to listen and learn, and then help share a message of love. Things will only get better if church leaders take a stand. They must tell people that we are human beings: we love, we have fun, we work hard, we make mistakes and we hurt.

Picking and choosing Bible verses is dangerous because it misrepresents Jesus' message. Rather than fixating on rules, religious leaders should preach the gospel of love. Stop calling us sinners. People should concentrate on their own deeds, rather than attacking us. If I am sinning – which I don't think I am – then I am prepared to meet my maker and face the consequences. I get so angry when people say that the love I feel is somehow worse than murder or rape. Politicians and religious leaders must stop spreading lies!

14

I PRAY FOR STRENGTH AND GUIDANCE

Narrated by Tinashe (Zimbabwe)

I am a 32-year-old gay man from Zimbabwe. I used to have an asylum permit, but it expired a few years ago and now I am afraid to renew it. There is too much corruption and violence at the Refugee Reception Offices. Coming to terms with my sexuality was a long process. I was scared to admit that I was attracted to guys and spent many years supressing my desires. It eventually became too hard to keep the lie going. These days I am proud of my sexuality, although I am still cautious about who I tell. It is not easy being a gay Zimbabwean. Our culture and religion teach us that LGBT people are unnatural, and many people back home are horrified by the thought of same-sex relationships. Our politicians don't help the situation and continue to spread lies. I was coming of age when Mugabe was saying all sorts of homophobic stuff. It was a scary time. It took leaving my country for me to finally feel comfortable with myself.

AN UNBREAKABLE BOND

I grew up in Mutare, a small city in the eastern part of Zimbabwe. I had a difficult but not unhappy childhood. My parents separated when I was eight, and I lived on and off with both of them. My father and I fought a lot. He remarried, and I had a strained relationship with his new wife. I regarded her presence as a slight against my mother. I had always been close with my mother; she was very supportive and encouraging. My mother also remarried, and her new husband became a father figure to me. Although I am my parents' only child, I have many siblings: on my father's side, I have seven sisters; on my mother's side, I have four brothers and one sister.

'I am like a leopard. It is a strong yet graceful creature. It depends only on itself for survival, waiting patiently for the right moment to strike. I, too, have had to learn patience and perseverance.'

I have very fond memories of my mother. We used to do so many things together, like go to the market and prepare food. When I was very young, she would let me comb her hair, something I loved doing. Sometimes my siblings and I would argue about my close relationship with our mother. They would say that she spoilt me because I was her favourite. In reality, my mother was protecting me because she could see I was different.

My mother became seriously ill in 2005. By then I was the only person around to care for her. My stepfather had died a few years earlier, and my mother's siblings had rejected her because of her disease. I stayed by her side throughout her sickness. I used to go with her to the clinic and would feed and clean her. When she was on her deathbed, she asked me to take care of my siblings. I promised her I would. She died when I was 19.

AN UNCOMFORTABLE REALISATION

I enjoyed school, even though it was difficult at times. I was a boarder and would only see my family on weekends. Most of these were spent at my grandmother's farm, where I would help with various chores. I loved my grandmother very much and always looked forward to these visits.

By the time I reached secondary school, I was already battling with my sexuality. I knew there were girls who liked me, but I didn't feel the same way about them. It was other boys who caught my attention. I didn't know what to make of these feelings; I worried that I was sick or evil. My sexuality was confirmed in Form 3, when I had my first sexual encounter. I had been hanging out with a cousin, Kudzai, and another cousin's boyfriend, Takudzwa, drinking beer and having fun. When we got back to school, I crashed in Takudzwa's bunk. We fooled around, and that is how I knew for sure that I liked guys.

The next morning I felt embarrassed. I left as soon as I woke up, afraid that Takudzwa would be angry or blame me for what had happened. It turned out that he was struggling with the same feelings. He confessed to liking me, but I didn't reciprocate his feelings. I was still riddled with shame. We both had girlfriends, and I was not even close to accepting my desires. I was scared that if I admitted to liking Takudzwa, I would be gay for the rest of my life. I was also afraid of being found out. 'What if this is a test?' I worried. 'It might be a trap. Perhaps he will demand money or tell my family.'

I ended up having heterosexual relationships and eventually married a girl. We dated for many years and, after she fell pregnant, our families pressured us into marriage. It wasn't what I wanted, but my father insisted. He was traditional and had strong opinions on how a Shona man should behave. He said it was my responsibility to get married, earn money and be a good husband. He worked at the Ministry of Transport and was able to organise a job for me. I raised enough to pay lobola and that was that. I was only 20 when we married.

TOWARDS ACCEPTANCE

I loved my wife, but we had a strained relationship – and not just because of my sexuality. After we married, we moved into my father's place, hoping to save money. My job was out of town and so I would only see her on weekends. I was struggling emotionally at the time. This was not long after my mother's passing. My mother would visit me in my dreams, making it difficult for me to sleep. It was also becoming harder to ignore my desires. I was drinking and smoking heavily, spending more and more time away from my family. This led to lots of fights, both with my wife and with my in-laws. They accused me of being a useless husband. They had a point: I certainly wasn't fulfilling my responsibilities. I couldn't bring myself to tell my wife that I was no longer attracted to her. The fact that I was having sexual urges for men made me feel even worse.

Tired of my antics, my wife initiated divorce proceedings. I don't blame her for doing so. We went to court over our son and it was decided that we would share custody. I was also asked to pay maintenance because my ex-wife didn't have an income. After a few months, it became clear that neither of us had the skills or resources to care properly for our son. We decided that he should stay with my father and stepmother.

With fewer family responsibilities, I began to explore my gay side. One day I bumped into Takudzwa. He was now married, and I was divorced. We didn't speak about what had happened all those years earlier, but it was clear that we were both attracted to each other. He invited me to have a few drinks and one thing led to another. We ended up having an affair for two years, right up until he moved cities.

After that I was keen to have a stable relationship. What I most wanted was to settle down and be happy. I met a guy living in Harare and we dated for almost two years. I was still working on the outskirts of Mutare and would travel to Harare each Friday after work. He was married when we first met, but eventually left his wife because he didn't want to keep lying. My boyfriend wanted us to move to South Africa and start a new life, keen to enjoy the freedoms of living here, but I wasn't ready for such a big change. Sick of my excuses, he packed up and left without me.

When I was 27, I met a guy in Mutare and we dated for a while. We were both straight-acting and so it wasn't hard for us to hide our relationship. This made things easier for us than they are for other LGBT people. I remember being at a bar one night and seeing some gay guys there. They were very feminine and caught the attention of the other patrons, eventually being chased out by some angry men. No one suspected anything about me or my boyfriend. I still feel guilty about not defending those guys.

FINDING A COMMUNITY

I knew a few gay men in Harare and they introduced me to Gays and Lesbians of Zimbabwe (GALZ), a local NGO fighting for LGBT rights. Before connecting with GALZ, I had no idea there were so many people like me in Zimbabwe. I was introduced to a whole range of people and got to meet important activists, such as Chester Samba and Samuel Matsikure.

I would go to GALZ events whenever I could, but always kept my movements secret from my family. The first event I attended was a Miss Jacaranda drag contest. I went along with my boyfriend and some friends from Harare. It was my first exposure to drag. I loved it! That night was so much fun: we drank, danced and laughed until the early hours.

A later GALZ event was raided by the police. That night many of us ended up in the holding cells. This was back when Mugabe was making a big deal about LGBT people. The authorities would bully us to prove a point, especially when elections were coming up. That night we were socialising at the GALZ office and suddenly the police came rushing in. It was a terrifying experience.

The next day, some GALZ supporters made contact with the government and demanded our release. They threatened to go public with details of homosexual activities involving government officials. They basically blackmailed the authorities into letting us go. The cops wanted to bring in journalists, but thankfully this was stopped before our names and photos were published. Our friends on the outside took care of us, bringing food and arranging transport money once we were released. I was so pleased to be free, but also terrified about going home in case my family had heard.

After the raid, it felt too risky to visit GALZ. When I would go to Harare, I would just visit friends like Samuel. He was always very supportive and encouraging. If I had any problems – whether it be relationship issues, family dramas or health stuff – I would turn to him for advice.

A NEW BEGINNING

In 2015, when I was 28, I started chatting online with a guy from South Africa. We met on Facebook and immediately hit it off. He was the one who encouraged me to move to Johannesburg. By then I was keen to settle down, perhaps adopt another child, and I hoped this was the guy for me. I also dreamed of coming out to my family and helping them understand who I am. Little did I know that this would happen in the worst way imaginable!

David and I chatted for a couple of months before he suggested I move to South Africa. I agreed, and we were both very excited. He would even send photos of furniture so that we could pick out things for the house. He wanted to make it our place, not just his. He was adamant that I shouldn't bring anything on my journey. He told me he would sort out anything I needed once I arrived. In the weeks leading up to my departure, David sent money so I could apply for a passport and buy snacks for the journey. I knew my father would be suspicious and so I kept the money hidden. All I told him was that I had found a job in South Africa. I definitely didn't tell him I would be staying with a white guy because I knew it would set off alarm bells.

The bus went first to Masvingo and then on to Beitbridge. We arrived at the border around midnight and it took a while for everyone to get their passports stamped. I was entering on a visitor's permit and had no trouble with the border guards. It took another six hours to get to our final destination: Park Station. I was very nervous while waiting for David to collect me. I was curious as to what he would be like in person. But when I saw him coming down the escalator, I was overcome with joy. I remember thinking: 'This is it! Here is my boyfriend.' We gave each other a huge hug, right there in the station.

This was my first time in Johannesburg and I was excited to be in such a big city. My boyfriend showed me how to use the Gautrain; I remember being astonished that it went underground. Then we went to Jet and he bought me new clothes. Our last stop was the liquor store so that we could celebrate my arrival. Later, when David introduced me to friends and colleagues, he used the word 'husband'. Hearing this word made my heart sing with joy. I was also introduced to his mother and father in Cape Town, and they told me how happy they were that I had made it to South Africa.

At first things were fantastic. I was free, happy and in love. I was so grateful for everything David had done: he had helped me get a passport, paid for my bus ticket and sent money home for my son in Zimbabwe. Later, when I became bored with staying home, he helped me get a job at Pick n Pay. I never imagined myself in such a stable and fulfilling relationship, let alone with a white guy in another country.

Before I could start the job, I had to sort out my immigration status. David and I drove to Marabastad to apply for an asylum permit. We weren't prepared for how crazy it would be. Everything was hectic and disorganised. There had been another outbreak of xenophobic violence and a lot of people were looking for protection. The queue snaked around the building and wasn't moving at all. I had no idea what to do. A random guy came up and said he could arrange a permit, but it would cost a fee. I guess he approached me because I was with a white guy. David and I discussed it and decided to take the risk, just because we knew we would never make it inside on our own. We agreed to give the guy R250 upfront and another R250 when everything was finalised. About two hours later, he emerged with my papers. The permit seemed like the real deal: it even had a watermark and an official stamp. I am not sure who this guy was or how he managed it. Looking around, I could see that the only people getting permits were those who paid.

After six months, my relationship soured. David became unfaithful and violent. We seemed to be fighting all the time. He would do all sorts of crazy stuff, like tearing up my documents. He even threated to report me to the police if I ever broke up with him. I couldn't take it any longer and packed my bags. Thankfully, I was able to reach out to a colleague and she helped me find accommodation in Tembisa, near to the Pick n Pay where I worked. All of my colleagues were supportive. My manager even intervened when my David came to the supermarket and threatened me.

In revenge, my ex outed me to my family in Zimbabwe. He even called my father and told him I was in a gay relationship. My father didn't believe him and so my ex sent photos of us together. This enraged my father, and he immediately called and confronted me. I panicked and said that David was trying to turn me gay. I had refused his advances, I lied, and now he was trying to blackmail me. It took a while, but I managed to reassure my father that I was telling the truth. It was the fact that I had a child that finally convinced him.

FINDING MY FEET

Life was hard when I first separated from my David. I had been dependent on him, both financially and emotionally. The drama with my family was particularly stressful. My ex was still sending inappropriate messages and photos, making everyone furious with me. I was especially afraid of running into my brothers who lived here in Johannesburg. I felt alone, afraid and depressed.

By chance I ran into a friend from back home. I explained everything that was happening and he suggested I move into his place in Parktown. That was when my life turned around. I reached out to some relatives and tried to help them understand who I am. My aunt on my mother's side was initially upset, but now she is quite supportive. She said my sexuality is okay, but urged me to live a stable life. By that she means finding one person and settling down, not sleeping around. My four brothers on my mother's side are aware, but aren't willing to talk about it. I have told my big sister on my father's side and she has no problem. She doesn't see anything wrong with my sexuality and has encouraged me to be true to myself. I am very close to her and her husband, even though they live back in Zimbabwe. My other sisters don't want to hear about anything gay. Their decision initially hurt me, but now I have made peace with it. The only people with whom I have never raised the topic are my father and stepmother. I know they won't understand and am scared they will cut off access to my son. I won't do anything to jeopardise that relationship.

About a month after moving to Parktown, my friend and I went to a club downtown called Egoli. That is where I met my current boyfriend, Tendai. Egoli is a straight club, but it is still possible to meet gay guys there. Tendai and I liked each other from the minute we met. We had similar histories: both of us are Zimbabwean and both of us have been married and divorced. My friend assured me that Tendai was a good guy and that I should go for it. We have been together ever since.

I lost my job at Pick n Pay about a year ago. There was no way they could keep me on because my asylum permit had expired. Tendai has supported me ever since. He is very kind and generous: if he buys a T-shirt or a pair of trousers, he will buy me something too. He even upgraded my glasses when I needed new lenses. He has been in South Africa for eight years longer than me and is a lot more experienced. He has given me lots of useful advice and introduced me to great networks, including the LGBT Ministry.

I don't like to sit around doing nothing and have been trying my best to find work. It is also important to me that I contribute financially to my relationship. I have picked up piecemeal jobs here and there, but they only ever last a couple of days. What I most need in my life is a permanent job.

I also need to sort out my documentation. I wanted to renew my asylum permit when it first expired, but the paperwork had been destroyed by my ex. I was also nervous about dealing with the Department of Home Affairs. I have heard horror stories from so many people. Most of all, I am frightened of leaving my passport there in case it disappears. It is my most valuable possession. What I currently do is pay someone to stamp my passport out every three months. This is a lot of hassle and means I never feel stable, but it is still better than being caught without documentation.

LOOKING FOR A SPIRITUAL HOME

I identify as Christian and regard my faith as an essential part of who I am. Growing up, I attended two different churches: a Roman Catholic church and an Anglican church. This is because my parents belonged to different denominations. The church I attended was based on which parent I was living with. Later, when I stayed with my aunt, I attended a Seventh-Day Adventist church. Even though I feel a connection to these different denominations, it is Catholicism that is closest to my heart. That is where I spent most of my time and where I feel most comfortable.

I continue to practise my faith here in Johannesburg, although I am not always able to attend Mass. Whenever I need spiritual guidance, I find a church and pray. I like to spend time there alone. Praying helps if I am feeling down. I ask for the strength to deal with the challenges in my life. I feel comfortable in the knowledge that God is looking after me, even when times are tough.

A CHOSEN FAMILY

It was back in 2015 that Tendai introduced me to the LGBT Ministry. He had been a member for a long time and was able to explain the purpose of the group. I was apprehensive because I didn't think it was what I needed, but I trusted my boyfriend and went along anyway. Right from that first meeting I felt included. I suddenly had a whole new network of friends.

The LGBT Ministry has taught me to keep going when times are tough. It is a source of inspiration and hope. This is partly because of the topics we discuss and partly because of the support I receive from other members. One example would be times when I am having problems with my relatives. The session we had on coming out taught me to approach family relationships with patience, understanding and grace. I have also received more practical forms of assistance. For example, the group helped me get my driver's licence so that I could improve my chances of finding employment.

My best memories are from the social events, like the Christmas parties. I remember one where we were all dancing in the summer rain. I was drunk and happy and totally carefree. There are other times when we just have a braai and swim in the pool. It is nice to have moments when you can forget your troubles.

THE POWER OF ACCEPTANCE

Everyone at the LGBT Ministry has experienced discrimination at some point. The countries we come from are very homophobic. Our politicians and religious leaders spread lies and intolerance. They tell people that being LGBT is an evil sickness that must be cured. People who don't know any better believe this nonsense. I know this from my own life, but also from my friends' experiences. There is one guy whose family took him to see Pastor Bushiri in Pretoria. He was forced to undergo a deliverance ceremony to cast out his 'demons'. The experience was deeply traumatic for my friend. There is also the recent case involving Somizi at the Grace Bible Church in Soweto. Both of these incidents show how churches are spreading hate.

This situation will only improve if religious leaders stand up for LGBT rights. They must let people know that we are born this way. It was God who made me like this and He wouldn't have done so without a purpose. It is not up to priests or pastors to 'fix' me because I am not broken. Instead, they should teach society that being gay or lesbian is perfectly normal. I wish people understood that we are Christians, that we are good people, and that we have hopes and dreams, just like them. They should accept us as we are, not go around claiming we are possessed. Society would feel differently about LGBT people if they knew the positive contributions we make.

CHAPTER 6

LOOKING AHEAD
The case for affirming religious spaces

In putting together this collection, I have come to confront some of my own prejudices about faith. As someone who works closely with LGBT migrants, I am constantly reminded of religion's contribution to the us-versus-them mentality that drives so much hatred and violence. In fact, barely a week goes by when I don't read or hear about an incident of homo/transphobia tinged with religious self-righteousness or justified on scriptural grounds. My anxieties were only exacerbated when collating examples of such incidents for the introduction to this book. How can one view religion as anything but damaging, I wondered, when faced with this litany of hurtful words and deeds? Is the antidote to the intolerance poisoning our communities not a rejection of religion, or at the very least a radical restructuring of its institutions?

However, in having the privilege of hearing the narrators' stories firsthand, I have come to think more deeply about religion's place within social justice. While my concerns about the politicisation of religious discourses remain, I have become more open to the transformative potential of faith-based organising. As the LGBT Ministry demonstrates, progressive religious spaces can open up modes of support that are simply not possible within social movements or civil society organisations (although relatable forms of connection and comfort are certainly found in these spaces). This is because progressive religious spaces have the power to heal emotional scars inflicted by their conservative counterparts. The LGBT Ministry provides its members with more than just material or psychosocial care; it represents a spiritual welcome that has long been denied, often violently.

In engaging the narrators, I was struck by the way in which they recounted the pain of being rejected by faith communities. For some, the mere expression of their sexual orientation or gender identity was enough to bring about permanent exclusion from people they had known their whole lives. The message behind such a punishment is unambiguous: you are *not* one of us, and you do *not* belong here. The anguish this causes is palpable to anyone who reads the stories. Yet, somewhat surprisingly, very few of the narrators have rejected religion outright.

Despite years of emotional turmoil, of battling feelings of shame, guilt and worthlessness, the narrators have held tight to their beliefs. I initially dismissed this as a product of socialisation, a hang-up from childhood indoctrination, but over time I have come to realise that something more transgressive is at play. These individuals aren't seeking reluctant inclusion so much as meaningful recognition, and for many this means developing alternative forms of spirituality. It also involves rethinking what it means to have and express faith. With churches and mosques unwilling to provide safe spaces, the narrators have had to look elsewhere for healing – in their hearts, in their minds, in their relationships, in their dreams.

I was also deeply affected by the way in which the narrators have made sense of faith within their lives. After being exposed to years of homo/transphobic preaching, the narrators began to question dominant scriptural interpretations and to formulate understandings that align with their own needs and values. The frequency with which the narrators referenced the biblical imperative to act with compassion is testament to the ways in which LGBT people draw strength from scripture in spite of orthodox teachings.

For the narrators, the essence of Christianity – that is, its directive to express faith through acts of love – is far more important than its performative rituals. It is on this basis that they seek to hold religious leaders to account for their role in perpetuating hate. As Sly, a gay migrant from Nigeria, says, 'Church leaders have a responsibility to embody Jesus' message of unconditional love.' Faith leaders' obsessive denouncements of LGBT people are recognised by the narrators for what they are: an effort to maintain hetero-patriarchal authority, both within religious institutions and within society more broadly. It is not, and never was, about being generous, kind, charitable or just.

My biggest takeaway from this project has been the enormous potential of churches to catalyse positive social change. The way in which the LGBT Ministry has transformed the lives of its members, in both a material and a spiritual sense, evidences the very real impacts of affirming faith practices. And, as the narrators rightly point out, individual religious leaders have an important role to play in shifting public perceptions. This is something that Dancio, a gay migrant from Zambia, feels strongly about:

> Faith plays a big part in the lives of Africans, and churches have the potential to transform attitudes . . . We have seen the positive influence that religious institutions can have (for example, in the fight against HIV) and we need them to do the same with LGBT rights.

Beyond recognising this potential, we must ask what an inclusive religious space looks like in practice, as well as how such a thing might be realised. Is it simply a matter of adapting the content of sermons, or is there a deeper shift that needs to take place?

In reflecting on this question, the narrators offer many words of advice, suggesting everything from visible acts of solidarity, such as establishing dedicated LGBT groups or displaying posters with affirming messaging, through to more subtle responses, such as slipping in positive references to diversity whenever possible. All agree on one simple yet necessary action: for religious leaders to personify Jesus' directive to love without distinction.

For Nkady, a lesbian migrant from Lesotho, religious leaders have a duty to embody inclusive principles at all times:

> If I were to meet a bishop or cardinal, I would tell them that we are regular people, just like them . . . We are good people, and we are living our lives in line with God's plan for us. We don't choose our sexuality or gender, and there is nothing wrong with us. I would ask them to open their hearts, to take the time to listen and learn, and then help share a message of love. Things will only get better if church leaders take a stand.

In addition to welcoming some of the most marginalised people in South Africa, the LGBT Ministry serves as a model for religious institutions opposed to discrimination. The clergy at Holy Trinity have shown what is possible when faith leaders take a stand against prejudice and open up institutions to those who are normally excluded.

'At the heart of the ministry of Jesus is a mission to build a community of inclusion,' Fr Russell says. He continues:

> As soon as people are excluded from the table, we have ceased building a community of the common good . . . We are all brothers and sisters because of our humanity. Addressing homophobia, xenophobia, racism and sexism must be central to what we do as a church.

As a starting point, he suggests finding ways to promote open dialogue:

> The first step is always creating moments in which dialogue can take place, where people in a congregation can listen to and learn from other people's experiences . . . There is something so powerful in the act of sitting with and hearing another person's story. When we listen with open hearts, we recognise that this other person is, in essence, the same as us, even if we may have travelled along very different paths.

But he also concedes that dialogue is not enough, especially when culturally sensitive issues are involved. When it comes to justice, he says, religious leaders have a duty to challenge communities, even if only gently at first. Leading by example and holding others to account are essential steps towards change, as Fr Russell argues:

> I am wary of just standing up and preaching stuff. I believe the experiential stuff is more valuable when trying to shift feelings on an emotive topic. A person might leave such an encounter feeling angry or confronted or confused, but when these feelings have dissipated they might reflect on what they have seen and heard. Physical encounters tend to trigger a strong response, hopefully bringing something to a person's consciousness that wasn't there before . . . Everyone, including clergy, must be willing to put in the effort to listen, reflect and learn.

Ricus, too, believes that religious institutions must be at the helm of creating safe spaces: 'Promoting inclusion must be a core activity of our mission as a church.' Like Fr Russell, he encourages religious leaders to draw on the expertise of those around them:

> The starting point is acknowledging that there is, in fact, a problem and then recognising that the church must be part of the solution. A good religious leader will accept that they can't do everything themselves and will seek out the help of others, including laypeople. They must include those who have the skills and knowledge, the personal qualities, to manage these conversations. Let these people have the room to do what they need to do . . . No one person, no one activist, can drive the agenda if you want to create real change. It is a journey that a community – religious or otherwise – must take together.

From my time working with the LGBT Ministry, I have come to appreciate the value of small gestures. In almost all of the stories, the narrators reference moments when they finally felt recognised and valued. Sometimes this occurred in formal settings, such as the ecumenical blessing before Jo'burg Pride, but often it took the form of casual encounters, such as Zee's positive interaction with a member of the Holy Trinity Parish Council.

Structural reform is clearly long overdue, but religious leaders looking to create an affirming environment don't have to start big. As Holy Trinity's experience attests, small acts – for example, a film screening or public lecture – can have an enormous impact.

That being said, religious leaders have a duty to think more deeply about the scriptural imperative for inclusion. While dialogue and sensitisation have their place, these actions are meaningless without a sound theological foundation. It is vital that religious leaders approach topics of inclusion with an open mind, in exactly the same way they would expect their congregants to engage with people from different backgrounds or cultures.

Religious debates on LGBT inclusion have a long history on the African continent, with important theological work coming from all contexts and denominations. Yet theological considerations of sexual and gender rights are too often dismissed as marginal or trivial. If churches are serious about social justice, they must give these issues the attention they deserve.

There is also an urgent need to involve LGBT communities in theological discussions. A plurality of voices and perspectives is paramount to democratising church structures, dismantling oppressive practices and centring a theology of love. No approach to diversity will be successful unless those directly impacted are part of the conversation.

One of the biggest dangers is for theology to become rigid – in other words, for religious leaders to assume that their thinking is flawless. As Fr Russell points out, theology and science need to be in dialogue, for science can help religious communities better appreciate the marvellous complexity intrinsic to humanity. The real danger lies not in the acceptance of diversity, but in the hubris of obstinacy.

Similarly, religious leaders need to be open to revisiting dominant theological positions, in conversation with the communities they serve. Part of this means acknowledging when church teachings have been incomplete and taking responsibility for the hurt and pain caused by specific religious discourses.

Transforming long-held opinions and practices will not happen overnight, nor can it be the responsibility of any one individual. One of the biggest obstacles in bringing about transformation is the deeply homo/transphobic environments in which religious institutions operate. As has been witnessed in many contexts, a political or media backlash can quickly foreclose any attempt at reform, sometimes even preventing a progressive faith leader from continuing their work. But while such factors must be taken into account, they can't be used as an excuse for inaction. There are resources available that outline best practices, as well as networks of African religious communities committed to affirming theological and pastoral engagements.

Writing these reflections, I am reminded of the wide array of experiences shared with me during the project, including the many anecdotes that couldn't be featured in this book. These experiences force us to confront the very real suffering caused by religious-based homo/transphobia, but they also hint at an enormous potential for healing. As Dancio reminds us, 'the winds of change are blowing'.

Not only are LGBT activists mobilising across the continent, but everyday people – including religious communities – are taking action in support of diversity. Their refusal to remain silent in the face of bigotry fills me with hope. My only wish is for society to be more receptive to the stories of LGBT people. If nothing else, communities would benefit from hearing the words of Tino, a gay asylum seeker from Zimbabwe: 'All of us need to work together to create a peaceful society. We must act with love and kindness – just like Jesus.'

Glossary

Amagumagumas Smugglers who transport people illegally across the border from Zimbabwe to South Africa.

Bisexual A person who is sexually, emotionally and romantically attracted to both sexes.

Braai South African word for 'barbecue', originally from the Afrikaans language.

Butch A person who identifies in a masculine way, whether physically, mentally or emotionally. 'Butch' is sometimes used as a derogatory term to refer to lesbian women, but it can also be claimed as a positive and affirmative identity label.

Camp A contested and highly subjective term that can mean different things to different people. In general usage, it describes a man who displays extravagant and/or effeminate mannerisms (i.e. behaviours associated with gay male stereotypes). While the term can be derogatory, especially in historical usages, it is now embraced by many LGBT people and used to signal and celebrate aspects of LGBT culture. The term can also refer to a kitschy design or style aesthetic.

Catechism A summary of doctrine that is used to support formal religious instruction. The Catholic catechism is a summary of the official teachings of Roman Catholicism, including creeds, sacraments, commandments and prayers. In many denominations, young people are required to attend catechism classes before they can undergo confirmation.

Cisgender (or **cis**) A person whose gender identity corresponds to their assigned sex (cf. **transgender**). For example, a person who was designated male at birth and who continues to identify and express as a man would be considered cisgender.

Confirmation A sacrament, ritual or rite of passage practised by several Christian denominations, especially those that perform infant baptisms. Confirmation is the moment when an individual formally affirms their belief in and commitment to Church teachings. In many denominations, it marks the moment when a person is fully admitted as a member of the faith.

Deliverance A deliverance ministry is intended to remove the influence of demonic spirits on an individual. In casting out evil spirits, a deliverance ministry seeks to help the person overcome negative behaviours, feelings and experiences. As well as involving prayer, a deliverance ministry may feature various objects, such as crucifixes, holy water and anointing oils. The concept and practice of deliverance is most commonly associated with Pentecostal and Charismatic churches. In many contexts, LGBT persons are forced to undergo deliverance in order to free them from the 'demonic affliction' causing their sexual orientation or gender identity.

Diocese A district (i.e. group of churches) under the pastoral care of a bishop. A diocese is typically divided into parishes that are overseen by individual priests.

Drag queen A person, usually a man, who dresses in clothing conventionally worn by women and who acts with exaggerated femininity, often theatrically and for entertainment purposes.

Femme A lesbian woman whose appearance and behaviours are seen as traditionally feminine.

Gay A man who is sexually, emotionally and romantically attracted to other men (NB while 'gay' is most commonly associated with men, it is occasionally used in relation to women – that is, a 'gay man' or a 'gay woman').

Gender The roles, activities and attributes that a society considers appropriate for men and for women (i.e. the different qualities associated with being masculine or feminine). Gender is distinguished from 'sex', with the latter referring to biological characteristics associated with men and women (such as sex organs, chromosomes and hormones).

Gender-affirming surgery Any medical procedure(s) by which a transgender person's physical body is altered to align with their gender identity. This may involve top surgery (any procedure involving the top half of the body, such as breast augmentation for trans women or breast removal for trans men) and/or bottom surgery (any procedure involving the bottom half of the body, specifically the genitals). These procedures were previously known 'genital reconstruction surgery', 'sex reassignment' or 'sex change' (such terms are now considered outdated, incorrect and offensive). Gender-affirming surgery is *not* a prerequisite for someone to be considered transgender.

Gender expression How a person expresses their gender identity (for instance, through clothing, behaviours, mannerisms, speech patterns and social activities).

Gender identity An individual's inner sense of being male or female (or both or neither). For some people, their gender identity differs from their physical anatomy or expected social roles (see **transgender**).

Gender-nonconforming A person who either by nature or by choice doesn't adhere to traditional gender norms/roles (i.e. how society expects a man or a woman to look, behave and think). People who identify as gender-nonconforming may vary their gender identity/ expression depending on how they feel (i.e. sometimes identifying as a man and other times identifying as a woman) or may not identify with a binary conceptualisation of gender (i.e. they don't identify as either a man or a woman).

Global protections mechanisms The international bodies, treaties, laws, policies and practices designed to safeguard vulnerable populations. In this context, it refers to systems set up to protect displaced individuals and/or communities (i.e. those who have been forced to leave their countries of birth). Examples of global protections mechanisms include the United Nations High Commissioner for Refugees (UNHCR), third-country resettlement programmes, and regional- or national-level responses to refugees.

Heteronormativity The belief or assumption that heterosexuality is the only natural and normal expression of human desire (in other words, that heterosexuality is the default state of being). A heteronormative society reinforces this belief through practices, systems and institutions that privilege and benefit those who are heterosexual.

Heterosexuality The quality or characteristic of being sexually attracted solely to people of the opposite sex.

Homophobia The fear or hatred of those assumed to be lesbian, gay or bisexual, and of anything connected to these persons and their communities.

Homosexuality The quality or characteristic of being sexually attracted solely to people of one's own sex.

Hormone therapy A treatment process for people seeking to physically change their bodies to align with their gender identity (see **transition**). There are two types of hormone therapy: feminising hormones (oestrogen) and masculinising hormones (testosterone). Hormone therapy is only one way in which a transgender person can medically transition and may or may not be accompanied by surgical procedures. A person *doesn't* need to undertake hormone therapy to be considered transgender.

Inkonkoni A derogatory term for same-sex-attracted people in South Africa. It is derived from the isiZulu word for 'wildebeest', a species known to engage in homosexual behaviours. *Inkonkoni* is also sometimes used to refer to transgender people, but often carries the incorrect and offensive meaning of 'hermaphrodite'. In popular usage, *inkonkoni* has negative and shameful connotations (for example, that the person being referenced is perverse or a 'freak of nature'). However, some LGBT persons see the term as a marker of validation, in that it provides evidence that same-sex sexual practices were known to and described by indigenous cultures.

LGBT An acronym used to refer collectively to lesbian, gay, bisexual and transgender persons.

LGBTQI+ An acronym used to refer collectively to lesbian, gay, bisexual, transgender, queer and intersex persons. The plus symbol is added in recognition of fluid and shifting sexual/gender identities that may not be adequately described by the other terms.

Lobola A Southern African custom by which a groom's family makes a payment in cattle or cash to the bride's family shortly before marriage.

Madrasa A school, college or other educational institution where people learn about the religion of Islam. A madrasa is sometimes attached to a mosque.

Moffie A pejorative term for a gay man. Originally from the Afrikaans language, the word 'moffie' is now used widely across South Africa, especially in reference to an effeminate man. The closest English equivalent is 'faggot'.

Queer In recent decades, 'queer' has been reclaimed as an umbrella term for non-normative identities or expressions (often used interchangeably with the LGBT acronym). However, some people who self-identify as queer see it as carrying an additional political meaning, in that it represents a rejection of cis-heteronormativity as the default and 'natural' expression of human gender/sexuality. It is often associated with a conviction that identity categories are socially constructed, rather than innate qualities, and therefore open to disruption and subversion.

Sexual identity How a person understands themselves in relation to their sexual, emotional and romantic attractions. A person's sexual identity and sexual behaviours are closely related to their sexual orientation, but are distinguished as separate concepts: *identity* refers to an individual's self-perception of their sexuality, *behaviour* refers to their actual sexual practices and *orientation* refers to their overall sexual, emotional and romantic attractions.

Sexual orientation An enduring pattern of sexual, emotional and romantic attraction (i.e. whether a person is primarily attracted to people of the opposite sex, the same sex, both sexes or neither sex).

Shebeen An informal (licensed or unlicensed) drinking establishment, commonly found in townships.

Social apostolate The social apostolate flows from the overall mission of the Society of Jesus: 'to build, by means of every endeavour, a fuller expression of justice and charity into the structures of human life in common'. Members of the order are called to 'carry on research, social education, both doctrinal and practical, and also social action itself in brotherly collaboration with the laity'. While interpreted and actioned in different ways, the social apostolate is best understood as direct social action with the poor and marginalised.

Sodality In the Catholic Church, a sodality is a lay group (i.e. not clergy) that undertakes charitable work as an expression of faith. In general usage, it can refer to a fellowship, association or society.

Spaza A small unofficial shop, usually run from a private house, commonly found in townships.

Stabane A derogatory term for LGBT people in South Africa. Derived from isiZulu, the term is literally translatable as 'hermaphrodite' (i.e.

a person with both male and female genitals), but is commonly used to castigate any person who deviates from cis-heteronormativity. This usage points to widespread misconceptions in South Africa about the difference between sex, gender and sexual orientation.

Straight A person who is sexually, emotionally and romantically attracted to people of the opposite sex.

Transgender (or **trans**) An umbrella term for anyone whose internal experience of gender doesn't match the sex they were assigned at birth (cf. **cisgender**). Transgender people may experience discomfort or distress due to their gender not aligning with their sex and therefore wish to transition to the gender with which they identify.

Transition (also **transitioning, transitioned**) The process of changing one's gender identity and expression. This may take the form of a *social* transition and/or a *medical* transition. A social transition refers to a person's decision to publicly adopt a different gender. This may involve changing their name, pronouns, clothing and modes of address. A medical transition involves physical changes to a person's body so that it aligns with their gender identity. This is a complicated, multi-step process that can take years. A medical transition can also take different forms: some people may choose to take hormones only, while others may also undergo various forms of surgery. A medical transition *isn't* a prerequisite for someone to be considered transgender.

Transphobia The fear or hatred of those seen to transgress or blur social expectations of gender, and of anything connected to these persons and their communities.

Tsotsi A young urban criminal, especially one from a township area.

Ubuntu A term used across Bantu languages that is often translated as 'I am because we are' or 'humanity towards others'. The word signifies the fundamental values of shared humanity (compassion, hospitality, etc.).

Xenophobia The fear or hatred of that which is perceived to be foreign or strange. In South Africa, it is often expressed as anti-migrant sentiments, discrimination and violence, including anti-migrant policies and practices by state officials and agencies.

Notes

FOREWORD

1 Edward Evans-Pritchard, 'Sexual Inversion among the Azande', *American Anthropologist* 72, no. 6 (1970): 1428–1434.

2 Edwin Smith and Andrew Murray Dale, *The Ila-Speaking Peoples of Northern Rhodesia*, vol. 2 (London: Macmillan and Co., 1920).

3 Marc Epprecht, *Hungochani: The History of a Dissident Sexuality in Southern Africa* (Montreal: McGill-Queen's University Press, 2014).

4 Despite acknowledging the existence of *yan daudu* in Nigerian culture history, Kunhiyop opposes homosexuality on evangelical grounds. See Samuel Waje Kunhiyop, *African Christian Ethics* (Grand Rapids, MI: Zondervan, 2008), 301–304.

5 *Catechism of the Catholic Church*, pars. 2357 and 2358, accessed 28 October 2020, https://www.vatican.va/archive/ccc_css/archive/catechism/p3s2c2a6.htm. Despite acknowledging the existence of homosexuality, the catechism advocates involuntary chastity: 'Homosexual persons are called to chastity. By the virtues of self-mastery that teach them inner freedom, at times by the support of disinterested friendship, by prayer and sacramental grace, they can and should gradually and resolutely approach Christian perfection.' This teaching is a clear violation of human rights – chastity cannot be imposed on individuals, as Jesus himself taught (Matthew 19:12; 1 Corinthians 7:32–38).

6 Robert Drinan, *Cry of the Oppressed: History and Hope of the Human Rights Revolution* (San Francisco: Harper & Row, 1987), 191.

7 James Cone, *God of the Oppressed* (Maryknoll, NY: Orbis Books, 2008).

8 Amartya Sen, *The Idea of Justice* (London: Penguin, 2010), 358.

9 Sen, *The Idea of Justice*, 359.

10 Sen, *The Idea of Justice*, 366.

11 Quoted in John de Gruchy, *Cry Justice! Prayers, Meditations and Readings from South Africa* (Maryknoll, NY: Orbis Books, 1986), 113.

INTRODUCTION: REFRAMING SEXUALITY, FAITH AND MIGRATION

1 Moving forward, I use 'LGBT migrants' as an umbrella term for LGBT migrants, refugees and asylum seekers. This is done in recognition that established legal categories do not always align with lived experiences or

reflect individuals' self-identifications. The 'correct' terms will be used when clarification is needed or when referencing specific individuals.

2 Rahul Rao, *Out of Time: The Queer Politics of Postcoloniality* (Oxford: Oxford University Press, 2020).

3 As well as producing a powerful emotive response in readers or listeners, storytelling has a potential to challenge oppressive socio-political hierarchies: '[Storytelling can be used to] reclaim the agencies of people who have been excluded from cultural and political centres and for whom epistemic and political agency remains a struggle . . . Telling their own stories enables [narrators] to claim epistemic authority as well as to counter the objectified, dehumanised representations of them circulated by others.' Shari Stone-Mediatore, *Reading across Borders: Storytelling and Knowledges of Resistance* (New York: Palgrave Macmillan, 2003), 150.

4 Thibaut Raboin, *Discourses on LGBT Asylum in the UK: Constructing a Queer Haven* (Manchester: Manchester University Press, 2017).

5 John Marnell, Elsa Oliveira and Gabriel Hoosain Khan, '"It's About Being Safe and Free to Be Who You Are": Exploring the Lived Experiences of Queer Migrants, Refugees and Asylum Seekers in South Africa', *Sexualities* 24, no. 1/2 (2021): 86–110; David Murray, 'The (Not So) Straight Story: Queering Migration Narratives of Sexual Orientation and Gendered Identity Refugee Claimants', *Sexualities* 17, no. 4 (2014): 451–471.

6 Chimamanda Ngozi Adichie, 'The Danger of a Single Story', TEDGlobal 2009, accessed 5 July 2020, https://www.ted.com/talks/chimamanda_ngozi_ adichie_the_danger_of_a_single_story/transcript?language=en.

7 A focus on Jesus' imperative to love without distinction is a common feature in queer theology and is often contrasted with more literal readings of the Old Testament: 'Those who condemn homosexuality and gender nonconformity tend to attribute their displeasure to the Creator, and those who are more accepting tend to centre their theological understanding on Jesus . . . It would be a mistake to understand this distinction too rigidly, to assume that individual Christians only conceive of God in loving or wrathful terms, or to argue that all anti-LGBT Christians conceive of God as wrathful . . . Yet as [LGBT migrants] seek protection and resettle elsewhere, much of the help they receive is motivated and/or justified by reference to a loving God, and often their own belief in such a God brings them comfort and strength.' Siobhan McGuirk and Max Niedzwiecki, 'Loving God Versus Wrathful God: Religion and LGBT Forced Migration', in *The Refugee Crisis and Religion: Secularism, Security and Hospitality in Question*, ed. Luca Mavelli and Erin K. Wilson (London and New York: Rowman & Littlefield, 2017), 225–226.

CHAPTER 1: BACKGROUND AND METHODOLOGY

1 See Loren Landau, 'Living Within and Beyond Johannesburg: Exclusion, Religion and Emerging Forms of Being', *African Studies* 68, no. 2 (2009): 197–214.

2 B Camminga, *Transgender Refugees and the Imagined South Africa: Bodies over Borders and Borders over Bodies* (Cham: Palgrave Macmillan, 2019).

3 Tonny Onyulo, 'LGBT Refugees Say They Face Hostility, Violence in *Kenyan Camp*', *National Catholic Reporter,* 22 September 2018, accessed 19 October 2020, https://www.ncronline.org/news/people/lgbt-refugees-say-they-face-hostility-violence-kenyan-camp.

4 For a compelling account of the power of storytelling to disrupt hegemonic narratives, see Adriaan van Klinken, 'Autobiographical Storytelling and African Narrative Queer Theology', *Exchange* 47 (2018): 211–229.

5 Beth Ann Williams, 'Mainline Churches: Networks of Belonging in Postindependence Kenya and Tanzania', *Journal of Religion in Africa* 48 (2018): 255–285; Meredith B. McGuire, *Lived Religion: Faith and Practice in Everyday Life* (New York: Oxford University Press, 2008).

6 Ivor Goodson, ed., *The Routledge International Handbook on Narrative and Life History* (Oxon: Routledge, 2017).

7 For an excellent account of life stories in action, see Andrea Cornwall, 'Sangli Stories: Researching Indian Sex Workers' Intimate Lives', in *Researching Sex and Sexualities*, ed. Charlotte Morris et al. (London: Zed Books, 2018), 232–251.

CHAPTER 2: THE POLITICISATION OF FAITH

1 Neville Hoad, *African Intimacies: Race, Homosexuality, and Globalization* (Minneapolis: University of Minnesota Press, 2007).

2 This chapter deals primarily with the major Abrahamic faiths on the continent because these are the religions discussed in the life stories. However, I recognise that other faiths are present and shape community attitudes. I also don't mean to disregard the social role played by indigenous faith practices. Important work has been done on the relationship between African traditional beliefs and sexuality or gender. See, for example, Melanie Judge, 'Navigating Paradox: Towards a Conceptual Framework for Activism at the Intersection of Religion and Sexuality', *HTS Theological Studies* 76, no. 3 (2020), accessed 5 October 2020, doi:10.4102/hts.v76i3.5997; Laura S. Grillo, Adriaan van Klinken and Hassan J. Ndzovu, *Religions in Contemporary Africa: An Introduction* (Oxon: Routledge, 2019).

3 Louise Vincent and Simon Howell, '"Unnatural", "Un-African" and "Ungodly": Homophobic Discourse in Democratic South Africa', *Sexualities*

17, no. 4 (2014): 472–483; Sylvia Tamale, 'Exploring the Contours of African Sexualities: Religion, Law and Power', *African Human Rights Law Journal* 14, no. 1 (2014): 150–177; Thabo Msibi, 'The Lies We Have Been Told: On (Homo) Sexuality in Africa', *Africa Today* 58, no. 1 (2011): 55–77.

4   Senayon Olaoluwa, 'The Human and the Non-Human: African Sexuality Debate and Symbolisms of Transgression', in *Queer in Africa: LGBTQI Identities, Citizenship and Activism*, ed. Zethu Matebeni, Surya Monro and Vasu Reddy (Oxon: Routledge, 2018), 20–40; Hassan J. Ndzovu, '"Un-Natural", "Un-African" and "Un-Islamic": The Three-Pronged Onslaught Undermining Homosexual Freedom in Kenya', in *Public Religion and the Politics of Homosexuality in Africa*, ed. Adriaan van Klinken and Ezra Chitando (London and New York: Routledge, 2016), 78–91.

5   John Marnell, 'Imagined Worlds', *Overland* 216 (2014): 12–18.

6   Adrian Jjuuko and Monica Tabengwa, 'Expanded Criminalisation of Consensual Same-Sex Relations in Africa: Contextualising Recent Developments', in *Envisioning Global LGBT Human Rights: (Neo)colonialism, Neoliberalism, Resistance and Hope*, ed. Nancy Nicol et al. (London: Human Rights Consortium, Institute of Commonwealth Studies, 2018), 63–96.

7   Finn Reygan and Ashley Lynette, 'Heteronormativity, Homophobia and "Culture" Arguments in KwaZulu-Natal, South Africa', *Sexualities* 17, no. 5/6 (2014): 707–723; Henriette Gunkel, *The Cultural Politics of Female Sexuality in South Africa* (Oxon: Routledge, 2010).

8   Savitri Hensman, 'Bishop Okoh's War on Homosexuality', *Mail & Guardian*, 27 July 2010, accessed 1 October 2020, https://mg.co.za/article/2010-07-27-bishop-okohs-war-on-homosexuality/.

9   Francis DeBernardo, 'Cameroon Archbishop Issues Inflammatory Anti-Gay Statement', New Ways Ministry, 20 August 2012, accessed 12 June 2020, https://www.newwaysministry.org/2012/08/20/cameroon-archbishop-issues-inflammatory-anti-gay-statement/.

10 Anne Mireille Nzouankeu, 'In Cameroon, LGBTQ People Struggle to Reconcile Faith and Sexuality', *Religion News Service*, 23 February 2018, accessed 16 May 2020, https://religionnews.com/2018/02/23/in-cameroon-lgbtq-people-struggle-to-reconcile-faith-and-sexuality/.

11 Solace Brothers Foundation, *Human Rights Violations Against Lesbian, Gay, Bisexual, and Transgender (LGBT) People in Ghana*, Shadow report submitted for consideration at the 115th session of the Human Rights Committee, 2015.

12 Anna Pujol-Mazzini, '"Hunted for My Sexuality": How Social Media Is Fuelling Homophobic Attacks in Mali', *The Telegraph*, 22 August 2019, accessed 16 September 2020, https://www.telegraph.co.uk/global-health/

terror-and-security/hunted-sexuality-social-media-fuelling-homophobic-attacks-mali/.

13   Aaron Maasho, 'Gay Gathering Sparks Row in Ethiopia', *Independent Online*, 30 November 2011, accessed 5 October 2020, https://www.iol.co.za/sport/soccer/africa/gay-gathering-sparks-row-in-ethiopia-1188960.

14   While leaders of the major faiths in Egypt have denounced homosexuality in similar ways, Grand Mufti Shawki Allam has cautioned against physically harming LGBT persons. See Melissa Etehad, 'Egypt's Grand Mufti Says Harming Gays Is Unacceptable even as LGBT Crackdown Continues', *Washington Post*, 2 August 2016, accessed 25 July 2020, https://www.washingtonpost.com/news/worldviews/wp/2016/08/02/egypts-grand-mufti-says-harming-gays-is-unacceptable-even-as-lgbt-crackdown-continues/.

15   Human Rights Watch, 'Egypt: Security Forces Abuse, Torture LGBT People – Arbitrary Arrests, Discrimination, Entrapment, Privacy Violations', 1 October 2020, accessed 28 October 2020, https://www.hrw.org/news/2020/10/01/egypt-security-forces-abuse-torture-lgbt-people.

16   'Egyptian Mufti Speaks in Defense of Homosexuals', *Cairo Scene*, 2 August 2016, accessed 24 October 2020, https://cairoscene.com/Buzz/Egyptian-Mufti-Speaks-In-Defense-Of-Homosexuals.

17   'Coptic Church Organizes "Volcano of Homosexuality" Conference', *Egypt Independent*, 28 September 2017, accessed 24 October 2020, https://egyptindependent.com/coptic-church-organizes-volcano-homosexuality-conference/.

18   Sokari Ekine, 'Anti-Gay Rights Crusade in Africa a Distraction', *Pambazuka News*, 26 February 2012, accessed 29 August 2020, https://www.pambazuka.org/governance/anti-gay-rights-crusade-africa-distraction.

19   'Tanzania "Anti-Gay" Force Official Paul Makonda Banned from US', *BBC News*, 1 February 2020, accessed 16 August 2020, https://www.bbc.com/news/world-africa-51339704.

20   Sheila Croucher, 'South Africa: Opportunities Seized in the Post-Apartheid Era', in *The Lesbian and Gay Movement and the State: Comparative Insights into a Transformed Relationship*, ed. Marion Tremblay, David Paternotte and Carol Johnson (Oxon: Routledge, 2016), 153–166.

21   Luiz DeBarros, 'Hate Speech Victory? Cape Town LGBTQ-Hate Pastor Narrowly Avoids Jail', *MambaOnline*, 18 May 2018, accessed 20 July 2020, https://www.mambaonline.com/2018/05/18/hate-speech-victory-ct-lgbtq-hate-pastor-narrowly-avoids-jail/.

22   Vhahangwele Nemakonde, 'Somizi Storms out of Grace Bible Church over Homosexuality Remarks', *The Citizen*, 22 January 2017, accessed 19 August 2020, https://citizen.co.za/lifestyle/1404845/somizi-storms-out-of-grace-bible-church-over-homosexuality-remarks/.

23 Pierre De Vos, 'Cardinal Napier: The Plot Thickens', *Daily Maverick*, 13 April 2013, accessed 3 October 2020, https://www.dailymaverick.co.za/opinionista/2013-04-13-cardinal-napier-the-plot-thickens/.

24 Staff reporter, 'Napier: I Don't Know Any Gays', *Mail & Guardian*, 12 April 2013, accessed 29 August 2020, https://mg.co.za/article/2013-04-12-00-napier-an-explanation-for-everything/.

25 Ashley Currier, *Politicizing Sex in Contemporary Africa: Homophobia in Malawi* (Cambridge: Cambridge University Press, 2019).

26 Tamale, 'Exploring the Contours of African Sexualities'.

27 Asonzeh Ukah, 'Pentecostal Apocalypticism: Hate Speech, Contested Citizenship, and Religious Discourses on Same-Sex Relations in Nigeria', *Citizenship Studies* 22, no. 6 (2018): 633–649; Patrick Awondo, Peter Geschiere and Graeme Reid, 'Homophobic Africa? Toward a More Nuanced View', *African Studies Review* 55, no. 3 (2012): 145–168.

28 Judge, 'Navigating Paradox'; Lere Amusan, Luqman Saka and Muinat O. Adekeye, 'Gay Rights and the Politics of Anti-Homosexual Legislation in Africa: Insights from Uganda and Nigeria', *Journal of African Union Studies* 8, no. 2 (2019): 45–66.

29 Marc Epprecht, 'Religion and Same-Sex Relations in Africa', in *The Wiley-Blackwell Companion to African Religions*, ed. Elias Kifon Bongmba (Malden: Wiley-Blackwell, 2012), 515–528.

30 Kopano Ratele, 'Hegemonic African Masculinities and Men's Heterosexual Lives: Some Uses for Homophobia', *African Studies Review* 57, no. 2 (2014): 115–130; Marc Epprecht, *Sexuality and Social Justice in Africa: Rethinking Homophobia and Forging Resistance* (London: Zed Books, 2013).

31 Patrick R. Ireland, 'A Macro-Level Analysis of the Scope, Causes, and Consequences of Homophobia in Africa', *African Studies Review* 56, no. 2 (2013): 47–66.

32 Adriaan van Klinken and Ezra Chitando, 'Introduction: Public Religion, Homophobia and the Politics of Homosexuality in Africa', in *Public Religion and the Politics of Homosexuality in Africa*, ed. Adriaan van Klinken and Ezra Chitando (London and New York: Routledge, 2016), 1–16.

33 Kapya Kaoma, *Christianity, Globalization, and Protective Homophobia: Democratic Contestation of Sexuality in Sub-Saharan Africa* (Cham: Springer, 2018); Barbara Bompani and Caroline Valois, 'Sexualizing Politics: The Anti-Homosexuality Bill, Party-Politics and the New Political Dispensation in Uganda', *Critical African Studies* 9, no. 1 (2017): 52–70.

34 Ezra Chitando and Pauline Mateveke, 'Africanizing the Discourse on Homosexuality: Challenges and Prospects', *Critical African Studies* 9, no. 1 (2017): 124–140.

35 Epprecht, *Sexuality and Social Justice in Africa*.

36 Jeremy Youde, 'Patriotic History and Anti-LGBT Rhetoric in Zimbabwean Politics', *Canadian Journal of African Studies* 51, no. 1 (2017): 61–79.

37 Adriaan van Klinken and Ezra Chitando, 'Introduction: Christianity and the Politics of Homosexuality in Africa', in *Christianity and Controversies over Homosexuality in Contemporary Africa*, ed. Ezra Chitando and Adriaan van Klinken (Oxon: Routledge, 2016), 1–18.

38 Stephen Bates, 'A Match Made in Heaven', *Guardian*, 22 September 2006, accessed 5 October 2020, https://www.theguardian.com/commentisfree/2006/sep/22/anopportunitymissed.

39 Aislinn Laing, 'Kenyan Politicians Tell Barack Obama to Leave "Gay Rights" Talk at Home', *Telegraph*, 6 July 2015, accessed 12 August 2020, https://www.telegraph.co.uk/news/worldnews/barackobama/11721249/Kenyan-politicians-tell-Barack-Obama-to-leave-gay-rights-talk-at-home.html.

40 Adriaan van Klinken, 'Sexual Citizenship in Postcolonial Zambia: From Zambian Humanism to Christian Nationalism', in *Christian Citizens and the Moral Regeneration of the African State*, ed. Barbara Bompani and Caroline Valois (Oxon: Routledge, 2018), 133–148.

41 Kaleidoscope Trust, *Speaking Out: The Rights of LGBTI Citizens from across the Commonwealth*, 2012, accessed 29 July 2020, https://kaleidoscopetrust.com/usr/library/documents/main/speaking-out-lgbti-rights-in-the-cw.pdf.

42 Kaoma, *Christianity, Globalization, and Protective Homophobia*; María Angélica Peñas Defago, José Manuel Morán Faúndes and Juan Marco Vaggione, *Religious Conservatism on the Global Stage: Threats and Challenges for LGBTI Rights*, Global Philanthropy Project, 2018.

43 Kaoma, *Christianity, Globalization, and Protective Homophobia*.

44 Southern Poverty Law Center, 'Scott Lively', accessed 29 September 2020, https://www.splcenter.org/fighting-hate/extremist-files/individual/scott-lively.

45 Josh Kron, 'In Uganda, Push to Curb Gays Draws U.S. Guest', *New York Times*, 2 May 2010, accessed 1 October 2020, https://www.nytimes.com/2010/05/03/world/africa/03uganda.html.

46 Emily Thomas, '"Eat the Poo-Poo" Anti-Gay Pastor in Hot Water for Ironic Reason', *HuffPost*, 25 April 2014, accessed 15 June 2020, https://www.huffpost.com/entry/uganda-anti-gay-martinssempa_n_5213571.

47 While Ssempa and others admit their international links, they deny being puppets for US Pentecostal movements, instead claiming agency over their anti-LGBT campaigns. See Van Klinken and Chitando, 'Introduction: Christianity and the Politics of Homosexuality in Africa', 9.

48 Edwin Nyirongo, 'Striking Out in South Africa, Anti-Gay American Pastor Steven Anderson Brings His Message to Malawi', *Religion News Service*, 18

December 2016, accessed 16 July 2020, https://religionnews.com/2016/12/18/striking-out-in-south-africa-anti-gay-american-pastor-steven-anderson-brings-his-message-to-malawi/.

49 'Archbishop Tutu "Would Not Worship a Homophobic God"', *BBC News*, 26 July 2013, accessed 27 August 2020, https://www.bbc.com/news/world-africa-23464694.

50 Adriaan van Klinken, 'The Future of Christianity and LGBT Rights in Africa – A Conversation with Rev. Dr Bishop Christopher Senyonjo', *Theology and Sexuality* 26, no. 1 (2020): 7–11.

51 Fredrick Nzwili, 'Faith Leaders React after Kenyan Court Upholds Bans on Gay Intimacy', *SIGHT*, 25 May 2019, accessed 19 March 2020, https://www.sightmagazine.com.au/news/12326-faith-leaders-react-after-kenyan-court-upholds-bans-on-gay-intimacy.

52 Editorial, 'Africa's Anti-Gay Laws', *The Southern Cross*, 29 January 2014, accessed 5 March 2020, https://www.scross.co.za/2014/01/africas-anti-gay-laws/.

53 Human Rights Watch, *More than a Name: State-Sponsored Homophobia and its Consequences in Southern Africa* (New York: Human Rights Watch 2003), 48–49.

54 Rev. Gabriel Tsuaneng, 'On the Recent Judgement on the People of Same-Sex Relationship', The Centre for Popular Education and Human Rights, 19 July 2019, accessed 21 August 2020, https://cepehrg.org/botswana-council-of-churches-statement-on-the-recent-judgement-on-the-people-of-same-sex-relationship/.

55 Michael Adee, 'Because You Are, Therefore I Am', Global Faith and Justice Project, 10 September 2014, accessed 25 June 2020, http://www.lgbtglobalfaith.org/because-you-are-therefore-i-am/.

56 Ryan Richard Thoreson, 'Troubling the Waters of a "Wave of Homophobia": Political Economies of Anti-Queer Animus in Sub-Saharan Africa', *Sexualities* 17, no. 1/2 (2012): 23–42.

57 Kelebogile Resane, 'Theological Dialogue Towards Ethical Restoration in a Homophobia-Riddled Society', *HTS Theological Studies* 76, no. 4 (2020), accessed 5 October 2020, doi:10.4102/hts.v76i4.6030; Hanzline Davids et al., *Stabanisation: A Discussion Paper about Disrupting Backlash by Reclaiming LGBTI Voices in the African Church Landscape* (Johannesburg: The Other Foundation, 2019); Masiiwa Gunda, *Silent No Longer! Narratives of Engagement between LGBTI Groups and the Churches in Southern Africa* (Johannesburg: The Other Foundation, 2017).

58 Van Klinken and Chitando, 'Introduction: Christianity and the Politics of Homosexuality in Africa'.

59 As many scholars note, the Western distinction between the public and private spheres can't be easily transplanted onto African contexts, especially in

reference to the role and purpose of religion. See, for example, Jacob Olupona, *African Religions: A Very Short Introduction* (New York: Oxford University Press, 2014); Stephen Ellis and Gerrie ter Haar, 'Religion and Politics', in *Routledge Handbook of African Politics*, ed. Nic Cheeseman, David M. Anderson and Andrea Scheibler (London: Routledge, 2013), 121–132. That being said, it can still be useful to note that recent crackdowns nominally based on gender and sexuality represent a targeted effort to regulate personal interactions.

CHAPTER 3: A LIFE ON HOLD

1 For an overview of global protections mechanisms and the limitations that often prevent resettlement, see Betsy Fisher, 'Refugee Resettlement: A Protection Tool for LGBTI Refugees', in *LGBTI Asylum Seekers and Refugees from a Legal and Political Perspective: Persecution, Asylum and Integration*, ed. Arzu Güler, Maryna Shevtsova and Denise Venturi (Cham: Springer, 2019), 275–297.

2 Yiftach Millo, *Invisible in the City: Protection Gaps Facing Sexual Minority Refugees and Asylum-Seekers in Urban Ecuador, Ghana, Israel, and Kenya*, Hebrew Immigrant Aid Society, 2013.

3 Hester K.V. Moore, '"The Atmosphere Is Oppressive": Investigating the Intersection of Violence with the Cisgender Lesbian, Bisexual and Queer Women Refugee Community in Nairobi, Kenya', in *LGBTI Asylum Seekers and Refugees from a Legal and Political Perspective: Persecution, Asylum and Integration*, ed. Arzu Güler, Maryna Shevtsova and Denise Venturi (Cham: Springer, 2019), 323–336; Gitta Zomorodi, 'Responding to LGBT Forced Migration in East Africa', *Forced Migration Review* 52 (2016): 91–93.

4 Nicholas Hersh, 'Enhancing UNHCR Protection for LGBTI Asylum-Seekers and Refugees in Morocco: Reflection and Strategies', in *LGBTI Asylum Seekers and Refugees from a Legal and Political Perspective: Persecution, Asylum and Integration*, ed. Arzu Güler, Maryna Shevtsova and Denise Venturi (Cham: Springer, 2019), 299–322.

5 Agathe Menetrier, 'Using Social Networking to Decipher Gender Stereotypes at Refugee Intake Points', *Hermès, La Revue* 83, no. 1 (2019): 177–185; Robbie Corey-Boulet, 'Gambian Gays Flee Persecution in Home Country only to Face Discrimination in Senegal', *New Europe*, 24 October 2013, accessed 14 July 2020, https://www.neweurope.eu/article/gambian-gays-flee-persecution-home-country-only-to-face-discrimination-senegal/.

6 B Camminga, '"Go Fund Me": LGBTI Asylum Seekers in Kakuma Refugee Camp, Kenya', in *Waiting and the Temporalities of Irregular Migration*, ed. Christine M. Jacobsen, Marry-Anne Karlsen and Shahram Khosravi (Oxon: Routledge, 2020), 131–148; Kate Pincock, 'UNHCR and LGBTI Refugees in

Kenya: The Limits of "Protection"', *Disasters* (2020), accessed 29 October 2020, doi:10.1111/disa.12447.

7   A major limitation in this field of research is the lack of data from Global South contexts. Indeed, the vast majority of studies on LGBT migration focus on South–North movement. While much of the research cited here emerged beyond the African continent, it is still useful in highlighting the procedural barriers that obstruct LGBT persons from accessing protection mechanisms.

8   Lyra Jakulevičienė, Laurynas Biekša and Eglė Samuchovaitė, 'Procedural Problems in LGBT Asylum Cases', *Jurisprudence* 19, no. 1 (2012): 195–207.

9   David Murray, 'The (Not So) Straight Story: Queering Migration Narratives of Sexual Orientation and Gendered Identity Refugee Claimants', *Sexualities* 17, no. 4 (2014): 451–471; Notisha Massaquoi, 'No Place Like Home: African Refugees and the Emergence of a New Queer Frame of Reference', in *Sexual Diversity in Africa: Politics, Theory and Citizenship*, ed. S.N. Nyeck and Marc Epprecht (Montreal: McGill-Queen's University Press, 2013), 37–53.

10 Alexander Dhoest, 'Learning to Be Gay: LGBTQ Forced Migrant Identities and Narratives in Belgium', *Journal of Ethnic and Migration Studies* 45, no. 7 (2019): 1075–1089; Calogero Giametta, *The Sexual Politics of Asylum: Sexual Orientation and Gender Identity in the UK Asylum System* (New York: Routledge, 2017).

11 Katherine Fobear, '"I Thought We Had No Rights" – Challenges in Listening, Storytelling, and Representation of LGBT Refugees', *Studies in Social Justice* 9, no. 1 (2015): 102–117; Eric Fassin and Manuela Salcedo, 'Becoming Gay? Immigration Policies and the Truth of Sexual Identity', *Archives of Sexual Behaviour* 44 (2015): 1117–1125.

12 Ariel Shidlo and Joanne Ahola, 'Mental Health Challenges of LGBT Forced Migrants', *Forced Migration Review* 42 (2013): 9–11.

13 Laurie Berg and Jenni Millbank, 'Constructing the Personal Narratives of Lesbian, Gay and Bisexual Asylum Claimants', *Journal of Refugee Studies* 22, no. 2 (2009): 195–223.

14 Deniz Akin, 'Discursive Construction of Genuine LGBT Refugees', *Lambda Nordica* 3–4 (2018): 21–46.

15 For an overview of how resettlement opportunities for refugees from East Africa have decreased in recent years, see Nicholas Crawford and Sorcha O'Callaghan, *The Comprehensive Refugee Response Framework: Responsibility-Sharing and Self-Reliance in East Africa*, Humanitarian Policy Group Working Paper, 2019, accessed 19 August 2020, https://www.odi.org/sites/odi.org.uk/files/resource-documents/12922.pdf.

16 Jennifer Smout, 'LGBTIQ Political Participation in South Africa: The Rights, the Real, and the Representation', in *Routledge Handbook of Queer African Studies*, ed. S.N. Nyeck (Oxon: Routledge, 2020), 63–75.

17 Alex Müller and Talia Meer, *Access to Justice for Lesbian, Gay, Bisexual and Transgender Survivors of Sexual Offences in South Africa: A Research Report* (Cape Town: Gender Health and Justice Research Unit, 2018).

18 Carla Sutherland, *Progressive Prudes: A Survey of Attitudes Towards Homosexuality and Gender Non-conformity in South Africa* (Cape Town: The Other Foundation, 2016).

19 Love Not Hate Campaign, *Hate Crimes against Lesbian, Gay, Bisexual and Transgender (LGBT) People in South Africa*, 2016, accessed 29 July 2020, https://www.out.org.za/index.php/library/reports?download=30:hate-crimes-against-lgbt-people-in-south-africa-2016.

20 LeConté J. Dill et al., 'Son of the Soil . . . Daughters of the Land: Poetry Writing as a Strategy of Citizen-Making for Lesbian, Gay and Bisexual Migrants and Asylum Seekers in Johannesburg', *Agenda: Empowering Women for Gender Equity* 30, no. 1 (2016): 85–95.

21 Elsa Oliveira, Susan Meyers and Jo Vearey, eds., *Queer Crossings: A Participatory Arts-Based Project* (Johannesburg: MoVE and ACMS, 2016).

22 The generally high rejection rate for asylum claims has been noted in many studies. For example, a recent report by Amnesty International found that 'poor decision-making, including mistakes of fact and lack of sound reasoning, has led to a 96 per cent rejection rate, resulting in a massive backlog of appeals and reviews. This has kept some asylum seekers in the asylum system for as long as nineteen years.' Amnesty International, *Living in Limbo: Rights of Asylum Seekers Denied*, 2019, accessed 3 October 2020, https://www.amnesty.org/download/Documents/AFR5309832019ENGLISH.PDF.

23 B Camminga, *Transgender Refugees and the Imagined South Africa: Bodies over Borders and Borders over Bodies* (Cham: Palgrave Macmillan, 2019).

24 John Marnell, Elsa Oliveira and Gabriel Hoosain Khan, '"It's About Being Safe and Free to Be Who You Are": Exploring the Lived Experiences of Queer Migrants, Refugees and Asylum Seekers in South Africa', *Sexualities* 24, no. 1/2 (2021): 86–110.

25 Guillain Koko, Surya Monro and Kate Smith, 'Lesbian, Gay, Bisexual, Transgender, Queer (LGBTQ) Forced Migrants and Asylum Seekers: Multiple Discriminations', in *Queer in Africa: LGBTQI Identities, Citizenship and Activism*, ed. Zethu Matebeni, Surya Monro and Vasu Reddy (Oxon: Routledge, 2018), 158–177; Ingrid Palmary, *Gender, Sexuality and Migration in South Africa: Governing Morality* (Cham: Palgrave Macmillan, 2016); Yellavarne Moodley, *Receiving LGBTI Refugees in South Africa: Towards a Culture of Non-Discrimination and Human Rights*, Working paper series – UCT Refugee Rights Unit, 2012, accessed 1 February 2017, http://www.refugeerights.uct.ac.za/usr/refugee/Working_papers/Working_Paper_5_of_2012.pdf.

26   Mandivavarira Mudarikwa et al., *LGBTI+ Asylum Seekers in South Africa: A Review of Refugee Status Denials Involving Sexual Orientation and Gender Identity* (Cape Town: Legal Resources Centre, 2021).

27   Lawyers for Human Rights, *Costly Protection: Corruption in South Africa's Asylum System*, 2020, accessed 29 January 2021, https://www.lhr.org.za/wp-content/uploads/2020/09/Corruption-Report-V4-Digital.pdf.

28   Similar reports of institutional mistreatment and community violence can be found across the literature. See Ali Bhagat, 'Forced (Queer) Migration and Everyday Violence: The Geographies of Life, Death and Access in Cape Town', *Geoforum* 89 (2018): 155–163; Camminga, *Transgender Refugees and the Imagined South Africa*; Dill et al., 'Son of the Soil . . . Daughters of the Land'.

29   Matthew Beetar, 'Intersectional (Un)belongings: Lived Experiences of Xenophobia and Homophobia', *Agenda: Empowering Women for Gender Equity* 30, no. 1 (2016): 96–103.

30   Marnell, Oliveira and Khan, '"It's About Being Safe and Free to Be Who You Are"'; Bhagat, 'Forced (Queer) Migration and Everyday Violence'; Beetar, 'Intersectional (Un)belongings'.

31   Amnesty International, *Living in Limbo*; Jonathan Crush, Caroline Skinner and Manal Stulgaitis, 'Benign Neglect or Active Destruction? A Critical Analysis of Refugee and Informal Sector Policy and Practice in South Africa', *African Human Mobility Review* 3, no. 2 (2017): 751–782; Roni Amit, *Queue Here for Corruption: Measuring Irregularities in South Africa's Asylum System*, Lawyers for Human Rights and the African Centre for Migration and Society, 2015, accessed 19 June 2020, https://papers.ssrn.com/sol3/papers.cfm?abstract_id=3274014.

CHAPTER 4: PREACHING LOVE

1   Nicoli Nattrass and Seth C. Kalichman, 'The Politics and Psychology of AIDS Denialism', in *HIV/AIDS in South Africa: 25 Years On*, ed. Poul Rohleder et al. (New York: Springer, 2009).

2   Ashwin Desai, 'After the Rainbow: Following the Footprints of the May 2008 Xenophobic Violence in South Africa', *Review of African Political Economy* 37, no. 123 (2010): 99–105.

3   Nonhlanhla Mkhize et al., *The Country We Want to Live in: Hate Crimes and Homophobia in the Lives of Black Lesbian South Africans* (Cape Town: HSRC Press, 2010).

4   Luiz DeBarros, 'Jon Qwelane – Wrong is Wrong', *MambaOnline*, 21 July 2008, accessed 19 August 2020, https://www.mambaonline.com/2008/07/21/wrong-is-wrong/.

5   David Smith, 'South African Minister Describes Lesbian Photos as Immoral', *Guardian*, 2 March 2010, accessed 17 January 2020, https://www.theguardian.com/world/2010/mar/02/south-african-minister-lesbian-exhibition.

6   Louise Vincent and Simon Howell, '"Unnatural", "Un-African" and "Ungodly": Homophobic Discourse in Democratic South Africa', *Sexualities* 17, no. 4 (2014): 478.

7   Angela Quintal, 'Homosexual Activities Are African – Activists', *Independent Online*, 27 October 2006, accessed 17 May 2019, https://www.iol.co.za/news/politics/homosexual-activities-are-african-activists-300415.

8   Wendy Jasson Da Costa, 'ACDP Slams Civil Union Bill', *Independent Online*, 20 September 2006, accessed 23 August 2019, https://www.iol.co.za/news/politics/acdp-slams-civil-union-bill-294452.

9   Names of former LGBT Ministry members have been changed to protect their anonymity and minimise safety risks.

10 The Central Methodist Church, located in downtown Johannesburg, became a haven for migrants fleeing xenophobic violence during the 2000s and 2010s, providing shelter to more than 30 000 people over two decades. It also provides key health and social services for the underprivileged, including those struggling with HIV. For an excellent account of the church's work, see Christa Kuljian, *Sanctuary: How an Inner-City Church Spilled onto a Sidewalk* (Johannesburg: Jacana Media, 2013).

CHAPTER 5: THE STORIES

1   David Kato Kisule was a prominent LGBT rights activist in Uganda. He worked as the advocacy officer for Sexual Minorities Uganda and was one of the first people in the country to publicly acknowledge his sexuality. In 2011, less than a year after Kato's picture was published (alongside those of other gay men) on the front page of the *Rolling Stone* tabloid newspaper under the headline 'Hang Them', he was brutally bludgeoned to death in his home.

Bibliography

Adee, Michael. 'Because You Are, Therefore I Am'. Global Faith and Justice Project, 10 September 2014. Accessed 25 June 2020. http://www.lgbtglobalfaith.org/because-you-are-therefore-i-am/.

Adichie, Chimamanda Ngozi. 'The Danger of a Single Story'. TEDGlobal 2009. Accessed 5 July 2020. https://www.ted.com/talks/chimamanda_ngozi_adichie_the_danger_of_a_single_story/transcript?language=en.

Akin, Deniz. 'Discursive Construction of Genuine LGBT Refugees'. *Lambda Nordica* 3–4 (2018): 21–46.

Amit, Roni. *Queue Here for Corruption: Measuring Irregularities in South Africa's Asylum System*. Lawyers for Human Rights and the African Centre for Migration and Society, 2015. Accessed 19 June 2020. https://papers.ssrn.com/sol3/papers.cfm?abstract_id=3274014.

Amnesty International. *Living in Limbo: Rights of Asylum Seekers Denied*. 2019. Accessed 3 October 2020. https://www.amnesty.org/download/Documents/AFR5309832019ENGLISH.PDF.

Amusan, Lere, Luqman Saka and Muinat O. Adekeye. 'Gay Rights and the Politics of Anti-Homosexual Legislation in Africa: Insights from Uganda and Nigeria'. *Journal of African Union Studies* 8, no. 2 (2019): 45–66.

'Archbishop Tutu "Would Not Worship a Homophobic God"'. *BBC News*, 26 July 2013. Accessed 27 August 2020. https://www.bbc.com/news/world-africa-23464694.

Awondo, Patrick, Peter Geschiere and Graeme Reid. 'Homophobic Africa? Toward a More Nuanced View'. *African Studies Review* 55, no. 3 (2012): 145–168.

Bates, Stephen. 'A Match Made in Heaven'. *Guardian*, 22 September 2006. Accessed 5 October 2020. https://www.theguardian.com/commentisfree/2006/sep/22/anopportunitymissed.

Beetar, Matthew. 'Intersectional (Un)belongings: Lived Experiences of Xenophobia and Homophobia'. *Agenda: Empowering Women for Gender Equity* 30, no. 1 (2016): 96–103.

Berg, Laurie and Jenni Millbank. 'Constructing the Personal Narratives of Lesbian, Gay and Bisexual Asylum Claimants'. *Journal of Refugee Studies* 22, no. 2 (2009): 195–223.

Bhagat, Ali. 'Forced (Queer) Migration and Everyday Violence: The Geographies of Life, Death and Access in Cape Town'. *Geoforum* 89 (2018): 155–163.

Bompani, Barbara and Caroline Valois. 'Sexualizing Politics: The Anti- Homosexuality Bill, Party-Politics and the New Political Dispensation in Uganda'. *Critical African Studies* 9, no. 1 (2017): 52–70.

Camminga, B. '"Go Fund Me": LGBTI Asylum Seekers in Kakuma Refugee Camp, Kenya'. In *Waiting and the Temporalities of Irregular Migration*, edited by Christine M. Jacobsen, Marry-Anne Karlsen and Shahram Khosravi, 131–148. Oxford and New York: Routledge, 2020.

Camminga, B. *Transgender Refugees and the Imagined South Africa: Bodies over Borders and Borders over Bodies*. Cham: Palgrave Macmillan, 2019.

Chitando, Ezra and Pauline Mateveke. 'Africanizing the Discourse on Homosexuality: Challenges and Prospects'. *Critical African Studies* 9, no. 1 (2017): 124–140.

'Coptic Church Organizes "Volcano of Homosexuality" Conference'. *Egypt Independent*, 28 September 2017. Accessed 24 October 2020. https://egyptindependent.com/coptic-church-organizes-volcano-homosexuality-conference/.

Corey-Boulet, Robbie. 'Gambian Gays Flee Persecution in Home Country only to Face Discrimination in Senegal'. *New Europe*, 24 October 2013. Accessed 14 July 2020. https://www.neweurope.eu/article/gambian-gays-flee-persecution-home-country-only-face-discrimination-senegal/.

Cornwall, Andrea. 'Sangli Stories: Researching Indian Sex Workers'
Intimate Lives'. In *Researching Sex and Sexualities*, edited by
Charlotte Morris, Paul Boyce, Andrea Cornwall, Hannah Frith, Laura
Harvey and Yingying Huang, 232–251. London: Zed Books, 2018.

Crawford, Nicholas and Sorcha O'Callaghan. *The Comprehensive
Refugee Response Framework: Responsibility-Sharing and Self-
Reliance in East Africa*. Humanitarian Policy Group Working Paper,
2019. Accessed 19 August 2020. https://www.odi.org/sites/odi.org.uk/
files/resource-documents/12922.pdf.

Croucher, Sheila. 'South Africa: Opportunities Seized in the Post-Apartheid
Era'. In *The Lesbian and Gay Movement and the State: Comparative
Insights into a Transformed Relationship*, edited by Marion Tremblay,
David Paternotte and Carol Johnson, 153–166. Oxon: Routledge, 2016.

Crush, Jonathan, Caroline Skinner and Manal Stulgaitis. 'Benign Neglect
or Active Destruction? A Critical Analysis of Refugee and Informal
Sector Policy and Practice in South Africa'. *African Human Mobility
Review* 3, no. 2 (2017): 751–782.

Currier, Ashley. *Politicizing Sex in Contemporary Africa: Homophobia in
Malawi*. Cambridge: Cambridge University Press, 2019.

Da Costa, Wendy Jasson. 'ACDP Slams Civil Union Bill'. *Independent
Online*, 20 September 2006. Accessed 23 August 2019. https://www.
iol.co.za/news/politics/acdp-slams-civil-union-bill-294452.

Davids, Hanzline, Abongile Matyila, Charlene van der Walt and Sindi
Sithole. *Stabanisation: A Discussion Paper about Disrupting Backlash
by Reclaiming LGBTI Voices in the African Church Landscape*.
Johannesburg: The Other Foundation, 2019.

DeBarros, Luiz. 'Hate Speech Victory? Cape Town LGBTQ-Hate
Pastor Narrowly Avoids Jail'. *MambaOnline*, 18 May 2018.
Accessed 20 July 2020. https://www.mambaonline.com/2018/05/18/
hate-speech-victory-ct-lgbtq-hate-pastor-narrowly-avoids-jail/.

DeBarros, Luiz. 'Jon Qwelane – Wrong is Wrong'. *MambaOnline*, 21
July 2008. Accessed 19 August 2020. https://www.mambaonline.
com/2008/07/21/wrong-is-wrong/.

DeBernardo, Francis. 'Cameroon Archbishop Issues Inflammatory Anti-Gay Statement'. New Ways Ministry, 20 August 2012. Accessed 12 June 2020. https://www.newwaysministry.org/2012/08/20/cameroon-archbishop-issues-inflammatory-anti-gay-statement/.

Defago, María Angélica Peñas, José Manuel Morán Faúndes and Juan Marco Vaggione. *Religious Conservatism on the Global Stage: Threats and Challenges for LGBTI Rights*. Global Philanthropy Project, 2018.

Desai, Ashwin. 'After the Rainbow: Following the Footprints of the May 2008 Xenophobic Violence in South Africa'. *Review of African Political Economy* 37, no. 123 (2010): 99–105.

De Vos, Pierre. 'Cardinal Napier: The Plot Thickens'. *Daily Maverick*, 13 April 2013. Accessed 3 October 2020. https://www.dailymaverick.co.za/opinionista/2013-04-13-cardinal-napier-the-plot-thickens/.

Dhoest, Alexander. 'Learning to Be Gay: LGBTQ Forced Migrant Identities and Narratives in Belgium'. *Journal of Ethnic and Migration Studies* 45, no. 7 (2019): 1075–1089.

Dill, LeConté J., Jo Vearey, Elsa Oliveira and Gabriela Martínez Castillo. 'Son of the Soil . . . Daughters of the Land: Poetry Writing as a Strategy of Citizen-Making for Lesbian, Gay and Bisexual Migrants and Asylum Seekers in Johannesburg'. *Agenda: Empowering Women for Gender Equity* 30, no. 1 (2016): 85–95.

Editorial. 'Africa's Anti-Gay Laws'. *The Southern Cross*, 29 January 2014. Accessed 5 March 2020. https://www.scross.co.za/2014/01/africas-anti-gay-laws/.

'Egyptian Mufti Speaks in Defense of Homosexuals'. *Cairo Scene*, 2 August 2016. Accessed 24 October 2020. https://cairoscene.com/Buzz/Egyptian-Mufti-Speaks-In-Defense-Of-Homosexuals.

Ekine, Sokari. 'Anti-Gay Rights Crusade in Africa a Distraction'. *Pambazuka News*, 26 February 2012. Accessed 29 August 2020. https://www.pambazuka.org/governance/anti-gay-rights-crusade-africa-distraction.

Ellis, Stephen and Gerrie ter Haar. 'Religion and Politics'. In *Routledge Handbook of African Politics*, edited by Nic Cheeseman, David M. Anderson and Andrea Scheibler, 121–132. London: Routledge, 2013.

Epprecht, Marc. 'Religion and Same-Sex Relations in Africa'. In *The Wiley-Blackwell Companion to African Religions*, edited by Elias Kifon Bongmba, 515–528. Malden: Wiley-Blackwell, 2012.

Epprecht, Marc. *Sexuality and Social Justice in Africa: Rethinking Homophobia and Forging Resistance*. London: Zed Books, 2013.

Etehad, Melissa. 'Egypt's Grand Mufti Says Harming Gays Is Unacceptable even as LGBT Crackdown Continues'. *Washington Post*, 2 August 2016. Accessed 25 July 2020. https://www.washingtonpost.com/news/worldviews/wp/2016/08/02/egypts-grand-mufti-says-harming-gays-is-unacceptable-even-as-lgbt-crackdown-continues/.

Fassin, Eric and Manuela Salcedo. 'Becoming Gay? Immigration Policies and the Truth of Sexual Identity'. *Archives of Sexual Behaviour* 44 (2015): 1117–1125.

Fisher, Betsy. 'Refugee Resettlement: A Protection Tool for LGBTI Refugees'. In *LGBTI Asylum Seekers and Refugees from a Legal and Political Perspective: Persecution, Asylum and Integration*, edited by Arzu Güler, Maryna Shevtsova and Denise Venturi, 275–297. Cham: Springer, 2019.

Fobear, Katherine. '"I Thought We Had No Rights" – Challenges in Listening, Storytelling, and Representation of LGBT Refugees'. *Studies in Social Justice* 9, no. 1 (2015): 102–117.

Giametta, Calogero. *The Sexual Politics of Asylum: Sexual Orientation and Gender Identity in the UK Asylum System*. New York: Routledge, 2017.

Goodson, Ivor, ed. *The Routledge International Handbook on Narrative and Life History*. Oxon: Routledge, 2017.

Grillo, Laura S., Adriaan van Klinken and Hassan J. Ndzovu. *Religions in Contemporary Africa: An Introduction*. Oxon: Routledge, 2019.

Gunda, Masiiwa. *Silent No Longer! Narratives of Engagement between LGBTI Groups and the Churches in Southern Africa*. Johannesburg: The Other Foundation, 2017.

Gunkel, Henriette. *The Cultural Politics of Female Sexuality in South Africa*. Oxon: Routledge, 2010.

Hensman, Savitri. 'Bishop Okoh's War on Homosexuality'. *Mail & Guardian*, 27 July 2010. Accessed 1 October 2020. https://mg.co.za/article/2010-07-27-bishop-okohs-war-on-homosexuality/.

Hersh, Nicholas. 'Enhancing UNHCR Protection for LGBTI Asylum-Seekers and Refugees in Morocco: Reflection and Strategies'. In *LGBTI Asylum Seekers and Refugees from a Legal and Political Perspective: Persecution, Asylum and Integration*, edited by Arzu Güler, Maryna Shevtsova and Denise Venturi, 299–322. Cham: Springer, 2019.

Hoad, Neville. *African Intimacies: Race, Homosexuality, and Globalization*. Minneapolis: University of Minnesota Press, 2007.

Human Rights Watch. 'Egypt: Security Forces Abuse, Torture LGBT People – Arbitrary Arrests, Discrimination, Entrapment, Privacy Violations'. 1 October 2020. Accessed 28 October 2020. https://www.hrw.org/news/2020/10/01/egypt-security-forces-abuse-torture-lgbt-people.

Human Rights Watch. *More than a Name: State-Sponsored Homophobia and its Consequences in Southern Africa*. New York: Human Rights Watch, 2003.

Ireland, Patrick R. 'A Macro-Level Analysis of the Scope, Causes, and Consequences of Homophobia in Africa'. *African Studies Review* 56, no. 2 (2013): 47–66.

Jakulevičienė, Lyra, Laurynas Biekša and Eglė Samuchovaitė. 'Procedural Problems in LGBT Asylum Cases'. *Jurisprudence* 19, no. 1 (2012): 195–207.

Jjuuko, Adrian and Monica Tabengwa. 'Expanded Criminalisation of Consensual Same-Sex Relations in Africa: Contextualising Recent Developments'. In *Envisioning Global LGBT Human Rights: (Neo)colonialism, Neoliberalism, Resistance and Hope*, edited by Nancy Nicol, Adrian Jjuuko, Richard Lusimbo, Nick J. Mulé, Susan Ursel, Amar Wahab and Phyllis Waugh, 63–96. London: Human Rights Consortium, Institute of Commonwealth Studies, 2018.

Judge, Melanie. 'Navigating Paradox: Towards a Conceptual Framework for Activism at the Intersection of Religion and Sexuality'. *HTS Theological Studies* 76, no. 3 (2020). Accessed 5 October 2020. doi:10.4102/hts.v76i3.5997.

Kaleidoscope Trust. *Speaking Out: The Rights of LGBTI Citizens from across the Commonwealth*. 2012. Accessed 29 July 2020. https://

kaleidoscopetrust.com/usr/library/documents/main/speaking-out-lgbti-rights-in-the-cw.pdf.

Kaoma, Kapya. *Christianity, Globalization, and Protective Homophobia: Democratic Contestation of Sexuality in Sub-Saharan Africa*. Cham: Springer, 2018.

Koko, Guillain, Surya Monro and Kate Smith. 'Lesbian, Gay, Bisexual, Transgender, Queer (LGBTQ) Forced Migrants and Asylum Seekers: Multiple Discriminations'. In *Queer in Africa: LGBTQI Identities, Citizenship and Activism*, edited by Zethu Matebeni, Surya Monro and Vasu Reddy, 158–177. Oxon: Routledge, 2018.

Kron, Josh. 'In Uganda, Push to Curb Gays Draws U.S. Guest'. *New York Times*, 2 May 2010. Accessed 1 October 2020. https://www.nytimes.com/2010/05/03/world/africa/03uganda.html.

Kuljian, Christa. *Sanctuary: How an Inner-City Church Spilled onto a Sidewalk*. Johannesburg: Jacana Media, 2013.

Laing, Aislinn. 'Kenyan Politicians Tell Barack Obama to Leave "Gay Rights" Talk at Home'. *Telegraph*, 6 July 2015. Accessed 12 August 2020. https://www.telegraph.co.uk/news/worldnews/barackobama/11721249/Kenyan-politicians-tell-Barack-Obama-to-leave-gay-rights-talk-at-home.html.

Landau, Loren. 'Living Within and Beyond Johannesburg: Exclusion, Religion and Emerging Forms of Being'. *African Studies* 68, no. 2 (2009): 197–214.

Lawyers for Human Rights. *Costly Protection: Corruption in South Africa's Asylum System*. 2020. Accessed 29 January 2021. https://www.lhr.org.za/wp-content/uploads/2020/09/Corruption-Report-V4-Digital.pdf.

Love Not Hate Campaign. *Hate Crimes against Lesbian, Gay, Bisexual and Transgender (LGBT) People in South Africa*. 2016. Accessed 29 July 2020. https://www.out.org.za/index.php/library/reports?download=30:hate-crimes-against-lgbt-people-in-south-africa-2016.

Maasho, Aaron. 'Gay Gathering Sparks Row in Ethiopia'. *Independent Online*, 30 November 2011. Accessed 5 October 2020. https://www.iol.co.za/sport/soccer/africa/gay-gathering-sparks-row-in-ethiopia-1188960.

Marnell, John. 'Imagined Worlds'. *Overland* 216 (2014): 12–18.

Marnell, John, Elsa Oliveira and Gabriel Hoosain Khan. '"It's About Being Safe and Free to Be Who You Are": Exploring the Lived Experiences of Queer Migrants, Refugees and Asylum Seekers in South Africa'. *Sexualities* 24, no. 1/2 (2021): 86–110.

Massaquoi, Notisha. 'No Place Like Home: African Refugees and the Emergence of a New Queer Frame of Reference'. In *Sexual Diversity in Africa: Politics, Theory and Citizenship*, edited by S.N. Nyeck and Marc Epprecht, 37–53. Montreal: McGill-Queen's University Press, 2013.

McGuire, Meredith B. *Lived Religion: Faith and Practice in Everyday Life*. New York: Oxford University Press, 2008.

McGuirk, Siobhan and Max Niedzwiecki. 'Loving God Versus Wrathful God: Religion and LGBT Forced Migration'. In *The Refugee Crisis and Religion: Secularism, Security and Hospitality in Question*, edited by Luca Mavelli and Erin K. Wilson, 225–226. London and New York: Rowman & Littlefield, 2017.

Menetrier, Agathe. 'Using Social Networking to Decipher Gender Stereotypes at Refugee Intake Points'. *Hermès, La Revue* 83, no. 1 (2019): 177–185.

Millo, Yiftach. *Invisible in the City: Protection Gaps Facing Sexual Minority Refugees and Asylum-Seekers in Urban Ecuador, Ghana, Israel, and Kenya*. Hebrew Immigrant Aid Society, 2013.

Mkhize, Nonhlanhla, Jane Bennett, Vasu Reddy and Relebohile Moletsane. *The Country We Want to Live in: Hate Crimes and Homophobia in the Lives of Black Lesbian South Africans*. Cape Town: HSRC Press, 2010.

Moodley, Yellavarne. *Receiving LGBTI Refugees in South Africa: Towards a Culture of Non-Discrimination and Human Rights*. Working paper series – UCT Refugee Rights Unit, 2012. Accessed 1 February 2017. http://www.refugeerights.uct.ac.za/usr/refugee/Working_papers/Working_Paper_5_of_2012.pdf.

Moore, Hester K.V. '"The Atmosphere Is Oppressive": Investigating the Intersection of Violence with the Cisgender Lesbian, Bisexual and Queer Women Refugee Community in Nairobi, Kenya'. In *LGBTI*

Asylum Seekers and Refugees from a Legal and Political Perspective: Persecution, Asylum and Integration, edited by Arzu Güler, Maryna Shevtsova and Denise Venturi, 323–336. Cham: Springer, 2019.

Msibi, Thabo. 'The Lies We Have Been Told: On (Homo) Sexuality in Africa'. *Africa Today* 58, no. 1 (2011): 55–77.

Mudarikwa, Mandivavarira, Miriam Gleckman-Krut, Amy-Leigh Payne, B Camminga and John Marnell. *LGBTI+ Asylum Seekers in South Africa: A Review of Refugee Status Denials Involving Sexual Orientation and Gender Identity*. Cape Town: Legal Resources Centre, 2021.

Müller, Alex and Talia Meer. *Access to Justice for Lesbian, Gay, Bisexual and Transgender Survivors of Sexual Offences in South Africa: A Research Report*. Cape Town: Gender Health and Justice Research Unit, 2018.

Murray, David. 'The (Not So) Straight Story: Queering Migration Narratives of Sexual Orientation and Gendered Identity Refugee Claimants'. *Sexualities* 17, no. 4 (2014): 451–471.

Nattrass, Nicoli and Seth C. Kalichman. 'The Politics and Psychology of AIDS Denialism'. In *HIV/AIDS in South Africa: 25 Years On*, edited by Poul Rohleder, Leslie Swartz, Seth Kalichman and Leickness Chisamu Simbayi. New York: Springer, 2009.

Ndzovu, Hassan J. '"Un-Natural," "Un-African" and "Un-Islamic": The Three-Pronged Onslaught Undermining Homosexual Freedom in Kenya'. In *Public Religion and the Politics of Homosexuality in Africa*, edited by Adriaan van Klinken and Ezra Chitando, 78–91. London and New York: Routledge, 2016.

Nemakonde, Vhahangwele. 'Somizi Storms out of Grace Bible Church over Homosexuality Remarks'. *The Citizen*, 22 January 2017. Accessed 19 August 2020. https://citizen.co.za/lifestyle/1404845/somizi-storms-out-of-grace-bible-church-over-homosexuality-remarks/.

Nyirongo, Edwin. 'Striking Out in South Africa, Anti-Gay American Pastor Steven Anderson Brings His Message to Malawi'. *Religion News Service*, 18 December 2016. Accessed 16 July 2020. https://religionnews.com/2016/12/18/striking-out-in-south-africa-anti-gay-american-pastor-steven-anderson-brings-his-message-to-malawi/.

Nzouankeu, Anne Mireille. 'In Cameroon, LGBTQ People Struggle to Reconcile Faith and Sexuality'. *Religion News Service*, 23 February 2018. Accessed 16 May 2020. https://religionnews.com/2018/02/23/in-cameroon-lgbtq-people-struggle-to-reconcile-faith-and-sexuality/.

Nzwili, Fredrick. 'Faith Leaders React after Kenyan Court Upholds Bans on Gay Intimacy'. *SIGHT*, 25 May 2019. Accessed 19 March 2020. https://www.sightmagazine.com.au/news/12326-faith-leaders-react-after-kenyan-court-upholds-bans-on-gay-intimacy.

Olaoluwa, Senayon. 'The Human and the Non-Human: African Sexuality Debate and Symbolisms of Transgression'. In *Queer in Africa: LGBTQI Identities, Citizenship and Activism*, edited by Zethu Matebeni, Surya Monro and Vasu Reddy, 20–40. Oxon: Routledge, 2018.

Oliveira, Elsa, Susan Meyers and Jo Vearey, eds. *Queer Crossings: A Participatory Arts-Based Project*. Johannesburg: MoVE and ACMS, 2016.

Olupona, Jacob. *African Religions: A Very Short Introduction*. New York: Oxford University Press, 2014.

Onyulo, Tonny. 'LGBT Refugees Say They Face Hostility, Violence in Kenyan Camp'. *National Catholic Reporter*, 22 September 2018. Accessed 19 October 2020. https://www.ncronline.org/news/people/lgbt-refugees-say-they-face-hostility-violence-kenyan-camp.

Palmary, Ingrid. *Gender, Sexuality and Migration in South Africa: Governing Morality*. Cham: Palgrave Macmillan, 2016.

Pincock, Kate. 'UNHCR and LGBTI Refugees in Kenya: The Limits of "Protection"'. *Disasters* (2020). Accessed 29 October 2020. doi: 10.1111/disa.12447.

Pujol-Mazzini, Anna. '"Hunted for My Sexuality": How Social Media Is Fuelling Homophobic Attacks in Mali'. *The Telegraph*, 22 August 2019. Accessed 16 September 2020. https://www.telegraph.co.uk/global-health/terror-and-security/hunted-sexuality-social-media-fuelling-homophobic-attacks-mali/.

Quintal, Angela. 'Homosexual Activities Are African – Activists'. *Independent Online*, 27 October 2006. Accessed 17 May 2019. https://www.iol.co.za/news/politics/homosexual-activities-are-african-activists-300415.

Raboin, Thibaut. *Discourses on LGBT Asylum in the UK: Constructing a Queer Haven*. Manchester: Manchester University Press, 2017.

Rao, Rahul. *Out of Time: The Queer Politics of Postcoloniality*. Oxford: Oxford University Press, 2020.

Ratele, Kopano. 'Hegemonic African Masculinities and Men's Heterosexual Lives: Some Uses for Homophobia'. *African Studies Review* 57, no. 2 (2014): 115–130.

Resane, Kelebogile. 'Theological Dialogue Towards Ethical Restoration in a Homophobia-Riddled Society'. *HTS Theological Studies* 76, no. 4 (2020). Accessed 5 October 2020. doi:10.4102/hts.v76i4.6030.

Reygan, Finn and Ashley Lynette. 'Heteronormativity, Homophobia and "Culture" Arguments in KwaZulu-Natal, South Africa'. *Sexualities* 17, no. 5/6 (2014): 707–723.

Shidlo, Ariel and Joanne Ahola. 'Mental Health Challenges of LGBT Forced Migrants'. *Forced Migration Review* 42 (2013): 9–11.

Smith, David. 'South African Minister Describes Lesbian Photos as Immoral'. *Guardian*, 2 March 2010. Accessed 17 January 2020. https://www.theguardian.com/world/2010/mar/02/south-african-minister-lesbian-exhibition.

Smout, Jennifer. 'LGBTIQ Political Participation in South Africa: The Rights, the Real, and the Representation'. In *Routledge Handbook of Queer African Studies*, edited by S.N. Nyeck, 63–75. Oxon: Routledge, 2019.

Solace Brothers Foundation. *Human Rights Violations Against Lesbian, Gay, Bisexual, and Transgender (LGBT) People in Ghana*. Shadow report submitted for consideration at the 115th session of the Human Rights Committee, 2015.

Southern Poverty Law Center. 'Scott Lively'. Accessed 29 September 2020. https://www.splcenter.org/fighting-hate/extremist-files/individual/scott-lively.

Staff reporter. 'Napier: I Don't Know Any Gays'. *Mail & Guardian*, 12 April 2013. Accessed 29 August 2020. https://mg.co.za/article/2013-04-12-00-napier-an-explanation-for-everything/.

Stone-Mediatore, Shari. *Reading across Borders: Storytelling and Knowledges of Resistance*. New York: Palgrave Macmillan, 2003.

Sutherland, Carla. *Progressive Prudes: A Survey of Attitudes Towards Homosexuality and Gender Non-conformity in South Africa*. Cape Town: The Other Foundation, 2016.

Tamale, Sylvia. 'Exploring the Contours of African Sexualities: Religion, Law and Power'. *African Human Rights Law Journal* 14, no. 1 (2014): 150–177.

'Tanzania "Anti-Gay" Force Official Paul Makonda Banned from US'. *BBC News*, 1 February 2020. Accessed 16 August 2020. https://www.bbc.com/news/world-africa-51339704.

Thomas, Emily. '"Eat the Poo-Poo" Anti-Gay Pastor in Hot Water for Ironic Reason'. *HuffPost*, 25 April 2014. Accessed 15 June 2020. https://www.huffpost.com/entry/uganda-anti-gay-martin-ssempa_n_5213571.

Thoreson, Ryan Richard. 'Troubling the Waters of a "Wave of Homophobia": Political Economies of Anti-Queer Animus in Sub-Saharan Africa'. *Sexualities* 17, no. 1/2 (2012): 23–42.

Tsuaneng, Rev. Gabriel. 'On the Recent Judgement on the People of Same-Sex Relationship'. The Centre for Popular Education and Human Rights, 19 July 2019. Accessed 21 August 2020. https://cepehrg.org/botswana-council-of-churches-statement-on-the-recent-judgement-on-the-people-of-same-sex-relationship/.

Ukah, Asonzeh. 'Pentecostal Apocalypticism: Hate Speech, Contested Citizenship, and Religious Discourses on Same-Sex Relations in Nigeria'. *Citizenship Studies* 22, no. 6 (2018): 633–649.

Van Klinken, Adriaan. 'Autobiographical Storytelling and African Narrative Queer Theology'. *Exchange* 47 (2018): 211–229.

Van Klinken, Adriaan. 'The Future of Christianity and LGBT Rights in Africa – A Conversation with Rev. Dr Bishop Christopher Senyonjo'. *Theology and Sexuality* 26, no. 1 (2020): 7–11.

Van Klinken, Adriaan. 'Sexual Citizenship in Postcolonial Zambia: From Zambian Humanism to Christian Nationalism'. In *Christian Citizens and the Moral Regeneration of the African State*, edited by Barbara Bompani and Caroline Valois, 133–148. Oxon: Routledge, 2018.

Van Klinken, Adriaan and Ezra Chitando. 'Introduction: Christianity and the Politics of Homosexuality in Africa'. In *Christianity and Controversies over Homosexuality in Contemporary Africa*, edited by Ezra Chitando and Adriaan van Klinken, 1–18. Oxon: Routledge, 2016.

Van Klinken, Adriaan and Ezra Chitando. 'Introduction: Public Religion, Homophobia and the Politics of Homosexuality in Africa'. In *Public Religion and the Politics of Homosexuality in Africa*, edited by Adriaan van Klinken and Ezra Chitando, 1–16. London and New York: Routledge, 2016.

Vincent, Louise and Simon Howell. '"Unnatural," "Un-African" and "Ungodly": Homophobic Discourse in Democratic South Africa'. *Sexualities* 17, no. 4 (2014): 472–483.

Williams, Beth Ann. 'Mainline Churches: Networks of Belonging in Postindependence Kenya and Tanzania'. *Journal of Religion in Africa* 48 (2018): 255–285.

Youde, Jeremy. 'Patriotic History and Anti-LGBT Rhetoric in Zimbabwean Politics'. *Canadian Journal of African Studies* 51, no. 1 (2017): 61–79.

Zomorodi, Gitta. 'Responding to LGBT Forced Migration in East Africa'. *Forced Migration Review* 52 (2016): 91–93.

Acknowledgements

This project was conceptualised and managed by the GALA Queer Archive, with the generous support of the Other Foundation and the Sigrid Rausing Trust. In line with GALA's mandate to document and promote the history of LGBTQI+ Africans, the interviews on which these stories are based will be preserved in the archival collections and made available to scholars, academics and community members (depending on the access terms granted by individual participants, as some narrators placed embargoes on project materials).

Many people contributed to this project and played a critical role in making *Seeking Sanctuary* possible. I would like to offer my sincere appreciation to Rev. Canon Dr Kapya Kaoma for his thoughtful and moving foreword. Your touching words add so much value to the text. Thank you for being so gracious with your time and for adding an important theological perspective to the book.

I must also thank my colleagues for their support and encouragement, especially for the invaluable feedback on early drafts. In particular, I would like to offer my appreciation to B Camminga, Jo Vearey, Thea de Gruchy, Ntokozo Yingwana, Elsa Oliveira and Kudakwashe Vanyoro at the African Centre for Migration and Society (ACMS) and Keval Harie, Linda Chernis, Karin Tan and Genevieve Louw at GALA. I would also like to thank Jeff Sparrow and Zazi Dlamini, whose expertise and guidance helped me immensely with the writing, as well as the external readers for their constructive comments during the review process.

Most of all, I would like to thank the narrators for sharing their life stories and for putting up with my constant questions. It has been a great privilege to collect these narratives and I remain humbled by your generosity, patience and enthusiasm.

I owe a great debt to Dumisani Dube and Ricus Dullaert for their support and guidance throughout the project. Similarly, I would like to thank Fr Russell Pollitt, Fr Bruce Botha and Fr Graham Pugin for sharing their reflections on the early years of the LGBT Ministry. Your commitment to diversity and social justice serves as an inspiration to us all. I must also express my gratitude to the Holy Trinity Parish Council for giving its blessing to the project.

I would also like to acknowledge the team at Wits University Press for their support, guidance and expertise. In particular, I would like to thank Roshan Cader, Kirsten Perkins, Veronica Klipp and Simon Chislett. I owe a great deal of gratitude to Efemia Chela, whose editorial brilliance helped bring these stories to life. I would have been lost without your support and encouragement.

Finally, I would like to thank my family for their supportive words and endless love. In particular, I would like to mention my father, Kevin, who died before the book was published and who offered so much encouragement in his final days.

Index